ASSESSING DISORGANIZED ATTACHMENT BEHAVIOUR IN CHILDREN

of related interest

Understanding Disorganized Attachment
Theory and Practice for Working
with Children and Adults
David Shemmings and Yvonne Shemmings
ISBN 978 1 84905 044 9
eISBN 978 0 85700 241 9

**Understanding Attachment
and Attachment Disorders**
Theory, Evidence and Practice
Vivien Prior and Danya Glaser
Part of the Child and Adolescent Mental Health series
ISBN 978 1 84310 245 8
eISBN 978 1 84642 546 2

Social Work Reclaimed
Innovative Frameworks for Child
and Family Social Work Practice
Edited by Steve Goodman and Isabelle Trowler
Foreword by Eileen Munro
ISBN 978 1 84905 202 3
eISBN 978 0 85700 461 1

**Empathic Care for Children
with Disorganized Attachments**
A Model for Mentalizing, Attachment
and Trauma Informed Care
Chris Taylor
Foreword by Peter Fonagy
ISBN 978 1 84905 182 8
eISBN 978 0 85700 398 0

**The Social Worker's Guide to Child
and Adolescent Mental Health**
Steven Walker
Foreword by Stephen Briggs
ISBN 978 1 84905 122 4
eISBN 978 0 85700 226 6

ASSESSING DISORGANIZED ATTACHMENT BEHAVIOUR IN CHILDREN

An Evidence-Based Model for Understanding and Supporting Families

Edited by David Shemmings and Yvonne Shemmings

Jessica Kingsley *Publishers*
London and Philadelphia

First published in 2014
by Jessica Kingsley Publishers
73 Collier Street
London N1 9BE, UK
and
400 Market Street, Suite 400
Philadelphia, PA 19106, USA

www.jkp.com

Library of Congress Cataloging in Publication Data
Assessing disorganized attachment behaviour in children : an evidence-based model for understanding
and supporting families / edited by David Shemmings and Yvonne Shemmings.
    pages cm
 Includes bibliographical references and index.
 ISBN 978-1-84905-322-8
 1. Attachment behavior in children. 2. Behavioral assessment of children. 3. Child welfare. 4. Social
work with children. 5. Family social work. 6. Psychiatric social work. I. Shemmings, David. II. Shemmings, Yvonne.
 BF723.A75A84 2014
 155.4'18--dc23
                    2013047573

British Library Cataloguing in Publication Data
A CIP catalogue record for this book is available from the British Library

ISBN 9781849053228
eISBN 9780857006639

Printed and bound in Great Britain

To the memory of Tony Leonard

Acknowledgements

We are very grateful to Yael Schmueli-Goetz from the Anna Freud Centre, London, for her expertise and helpful comments on Chapter 12, and to Michelle Pyle for her contribution to Chapter 16. We also thank Denise Tucker for her skilled job of indexing the book.

Contents

Introduction

David Shemmings and Yvonne Shemmings

Challenges in child welfare and protection work

Across the world, many child protection professionals and the organizations they work in are facing three key challenges. First, they are having to respond to newer forms of abuse, including sexual exploitation, child trafficking and the use of the Internet for grooming purposes (including now by terrorist organizations). Second, in tackling the challenges of the past 20–30 years they are likely to have developed cumbersome, highly bureaucratic, procedurally based systems and practices, which usually involve ever more complex risk assessment processes and paperwork. Third, their efforts over the past five or so years have been impeded by significant reductions in government spending as a result of the financial crisis of 2007–2008 which in turn may have led to double-dip recessions and economic depressions, the result of which has been the imposition of severe austerity measures (which have usually fallen disproportionately on those who can afford it least).

In the UK, there has been a fourth challenge. Referrals to child protection agencies have risen sharply after a number of high-profile child deaths. Coupled with a sometimes unforgiving and punitive stance in some parts of the media, professionals are under a great deal of pressure, caught in the Catch-22 of being 'damned if they do and damned if they don't'. Take a child away from their family by mistake and you are pilloried as a 'nanny-state family wrecker', but fail to remove a child when, often retrospectively, it appears they were at risk, and you will be branded as 'incompetent', 'naive, easily fobbed off', a 'bozo' – to name but a few of the epithets used by the British tabloid press in recent years.[1] Despite these pressures, it is a tribute to the skills of child professionals in the UK that the number of child deaths at the hands of partners/carers remains as low as it has been.[2]

It is an enormously difficult, but certainly not an impossible task, if workers are clear about what they are seeking. They have to be able to 'slice thin' the myriad amount of information they will acquire, first to understand what is going on and then, having made more sense of it, to be able to share these insights openly but sensitively with family members to see how they can be best helped to protect their children. What we have learned is that when professionals are confident, but without ever becoming complacent or arrogant, this leads to safer practice and greater job satisfaction. But to do this they need help to make sense of and face the emotional pressures of child protection work. An examination of these dynamics in practice is the focus of the book.

In this edited volume we have asked some practitioners who have become skilled in the use of a contemporary, evidence-based model to reflect on how they have used it with children and families. The book is written for professionals working with families where there are child protection concerns. It offers practitioners a powerful way of understanding child abuse and neglect, but more importantly it offers hope for families for them to stay together whenever possible.

Background

This book is primarily about the application of the Assessment of Disorganised Attachment and Maltreatment (ADAM) Project to child protection practice. We established the ADAM Project in May 2009 to help professionals investigating allegations of maltreatment and to help families keep children safe, with their parents. At the end of a four-day course spread over four months participants are able to draw upon a number of assessment techniques adapted for use pragmatically by busy child protection practitioners. During the one-month gap between

---

1   See Ian Butler's and Mark Drakeford's 2012 analysis of the media's handling of child abuse and neglect, especially Chapter 7 and their Afterword.

2   Around 50 per year, for example, in England and Wales, for approximately the past 40 years.

sessions, those attending are expected to practise what, for most, are new methods. They are also encouraged to join chat groups and/or email us if they wish to discuss progress or problems when trying out new skills. We have a dedicated website and participants are urged to read all the notes available on each of the techniques.

During the four-day programme we facilitate the responsible use and interpretation of attachment-based techniques that 'pick up' different components of a Pathway Model (described in Chapter 1). This evidence-based and theoretically-informed model identifies 'mechanisms of maltreatment' which current assessment methods are unable to identify (we also examine this claim in Chapter 1). In the programme participants are shown filmed examples of practitioners using the techniques with actual family members. We then analyse in small groups how each technique has been used as well as discuss reliable interpretations of the child's and/or the adult's behaviour, depending on the technique used.

Throughout the entire ADAM programme we emphasise the role of supervisors in determining when individual practitioners should use the techniques. Those practitioners who have completed the four-day programme and who have practised over the four months are encouraged to maintain email contact for at least another year, and longer if required. We are now experimenting with 'direct coaching' methods whereby a practitioner receives 'live' advice using advanced mobile technology to achieve synchronous communication while the practitioner works directly with a parent or child.

We now have a team of very experienced practitioners formally associated with the ADAM Project, some of whom are PhD students with one of us (David), either at the University of Kent or Royal Holloway, University of London. Between them, the different members of the team of the ADAM Project associates have also been trained fully in the attachment-based techniques referred to in the ADAM Project programme. Our associates have also presented the ADAM Project at conferences, seminars and workshops, and many have contributed to this edited volume, which is devoted to experienced practitioners reflecting upon how they routinely use the model in their work with children and families.

Why did we establish the ADAM Project?

Practitioners are desperate for help and guidance when assessing risk in the field of child protection and maltreatment. Attachment theory and research have always been popular with child welfare professionals, especially social workers. The problem is that the level and intensity of training they receive in the subject, either during or post-qualification, is minimal and sometimes superficial. In our travels, we often hear of instances when practitioners use misleading or incorrect assessments around attachment. For example, we read recently, 'The mother doesn't have a secure attachment with her new baby' (the worker is describing a 'bond', not an 'attachment'); or, when describing the behaviour of a 13-year-old moving to his fifth placement in two years, this time in a residential setting, 'He's settled in remarkably well, no problems; just shows how resilient he is'. But such behaviour is more likely to indicate separation anxiety and disrupted attachments. Additionally, practitioners need to be very careful not to use terms such as 'disorganised attachment' to describe his reaction (and they should never use the term 'attachment disorder', as it is a privileged diagnostic category reserved for qualified clinicians and psychiatrists).

Weighed against the relative paucity of reflective and analytical training available, however, there is a tempting smörgåsbord of attachment-based materials, checklists, materials and guides, each one just a click away on the Internet. For example, we found this on one website (we will not say which one, as there are many, and we do not wish to highlight this particular one, as it does much excellent work with and for children):

Disorganised Attachment Signs and Symptoms Checklist

Superficial and charming with strangers

Grandiose acts or extravagant claims/boasts

Restlessness: need for stimulation and activity

Dislike of being touched or held

Lack of affection/bossiness to carers

High levels of resentment

High levels of anger, rage or violence (especially to female carers)

Constant blaming of others

Little eye contact

Poor humour/few smiles

Lack of play

Coercive and demanding

'Crazy', obvious lying in the face of plain facts

Manipulative lying to gain advantage

Early sexual activity

Stealing and conduct disorders

Abnormal eating patterns (e.g. gorging, stealing food, hoarding, refusing to eat)

Poor impulse control

High breakage rate of toys and objects

Poor peer relations

Lack of conscience and moral sensibility

Aggressive toward peers, including sexual abuse of other children

Cruelty toward animals

Preoccupation with fire, blood, gore and weapons (often expressed in violent drawings/play)

Self-neglect/poor personal hygiene

The authors of the website acknowledge that the list is adapted from *Attachment Theory, Child Maltreatment and Family Support* (Howe, Brandon, Hinings and Schofield 1999), but the problem here is that compiling a list in this way leaves it adrift from the explanatory context in which David Howe and his colleagues first described and explained these behaviours. Nevertheless, we argue that even within the context of their book there are too many behaviours here that even securely attached children display at times: without a sound theoretical understanding of attachment, identifying combinations of the above behaviours is likely to lead to net widening (see also Woolgar and Scott 2013, who draw attention to a similar problem with the over-use of 'attachment disorders', especially in assessments of children in the care of the state). Without a deeper knowledge of attachment, the behaviours listed are also likely to be misinterpreted; certainly an alert barrister or defence lawyer would be able to drive a coach and horses through such an argument.

Is the ADAM Project training 'sufficient'?

We agonised over this because we were concerned that participants might end up with a 'little knowledge' which could easily become a 'bad thing'. But we concluded that on balance, and as stated already, because the techniques we cover are freely available in books and on the Internet – for example, *Revealing the Inner Worlds of Young Children* (Emde, Wolf and Oppenheim 2003) contains detailed, helpful examples of practitioners using doll-based story stem work with different children in different circumstances – we should encourage groups of practitioners to join our training sessions to talk, think about and then apply the techniques intelligently. Nevertheless, we always encourage ADAM participants to become fully trained in the techniques referred to in the 4-day programme, typically at the Anna Freud Centre in London, and we know that many do; but we also know that for every practitioner to become fully accredited in each technique would be impractical, both in terms of time and expense.

Equally, other techniques drawn upon in the ADAM Project, for example, the Strange Situation Procedure (SSP), different versions of doll-based story completion, the Adult Attachment Interview and various attachment-based parenting indicators, are also all available online. For the busy, concerned practitioner, anxious to get a report written for court or a child protection conference in a short space of time, such information doubtless feels very reassuring, but it is a chimera and it could include or exclude the wrong children.

So after the exhaustive description and analysis of research we undertook when writing *Understanding Disorganised Attachment* (Shemmings and Shemmings 2011), we decided to offer an in-depth yet wide-ranging programme for practitioners interested in deepening their existing knowledge of attachment concepts and then applying it to their assessments. Our aim was not to attempt to rate behavioural or verbal responses of the different attachment organizations, which requires the full accreditation training, but rather to produce it as 'evidence' for court or child protection conferences. We were content for the ADAM training programme to encourage participants to study the components in the Pathway Model, use the techniques correctly and competently, and then discuss their analyses in a theoretically driven, evidence-based way with colleagues, supervisors, ourselves and other members of the ADAM Project team. But, over and above these aims, the main purpose of the ADAM Project is to *share observations and assessments openly and sensitively with the relevant family members*, so that if abuse or neglect are taking place, attempts are then made to help them to understand, assess and then address the problems. This requires as a prerequisite the (re)discovery of what we have termed 'enhanced relationship skills'. These comprise tried and tested skills, such as active listening and accurate empathy, but we now add three more: 'intelligent kindness', 'unsentimental compassion' and 'non-directive curiosity' (which we discuss more fully in Chapter 2).

Limitations and drawbacks: 'ADAM's Achilles' heel'?

By focusing almost exclusively on relational dynamics between individual family members, the position we have adopted in our work on disorganised attachment behaviour could be criticised for having ignored 'external' factors such as the myriad social injustices that exist in British society, injustices which currently are more marked as a result of many people desperately trying to survive during relatively 'hard times'. The blatant and unfair way in which the excesses of capitalism are once more falling excessively on shoulders already broken by the weight of poverty and inequality is an outrage. But we felt that we had to restrict our focus to what we believe to be our areas of expertise: we are not sociologists or social theorists, so we must leave this aspect of child protection policy to those best able to comment on it. Furthermore, we have an embarrassment of riches in the UK when it comes to articulating new ways of imagining child welfare, protection and the right balance between the two. We need look no further than a UK Higher Education Institute's Joint Social Work Education Conference, entitled *Positive Practice in Hard Times*, at which a number of respected social work academics, in particular, professors Sue White, Brid Featherstone, Harry Ferguson, Tim Kelly and Iain Ferguson, began to articulate an agenda arguing for a re-evaluation of what we mean by 'child protection'. The title of the White *et al.* paper – 'Time to change the conversation on "child protection": towards a new paradigm?' – signals their intention. For them, the balance needs to shift from 'muscular child protection/rescue discourses' and 'an expert screen and intervene model' towards a 'project that celebrates families' strengths as well as their vulnerabilities in the context of considerable adversities and (re)locates workers as agents of hope and support'.

We believe we can support *their* project by offering practitioners an articulation and exposition of what they need to look for to help families directly. We believe that remedial social action is needed urgently to address the attendant curses of our 'advanced' capitalist economy: domestic abuse, sexual exploitation, the commodification and manipulation of organised labour etc. But the causes of child abuse are complex. With the exception of chronic physical neglect which, almost by definition, is more likely to exist among poorer communities, and would be reduced by large injections of cash and/or lasting employment opportunities, other forms of child maltreatment occur in richer communities, too: sexual abuse, emotional abuse and emotional neglect are prevalent within all sectors of society. What is without question, though, is that if you are poor, you are more likely to come to the attention of child protection agencies (which would not necessarily be a bad outcome if they were able to help, but as things are as we write this Introduction, they often are not). This is not a criticism of the many dedicated child protection professionals out there; instead, it is, in part, a condemnation of the defensive, bureaucratised and proceduralised responses that have been created to protect politicians, managers, supervisors and practitioners from, at times, a vicious and predatory section of the media. So, for these reasons, we chose to concentrate on the relationship between parent and child, rather than the pernicious and unequal forces surrounding it.

Structure of the book

We begin with a resume of the ADAM Project and the Pathway Model, and then, in Chapter 2, we outline the relationship skills needed to implement them. In Chapter 3, Yvalia Febrer discusses an example of those skills in practise. In Chapters 4–12, our experienced ADAM Project associates, including Alice Cook, David Wilkins, Lissil Averill, Michelle Thompson, Fran Feeley, David Phillips, Claire Denham and Jo George, outline how they have used the model in their work with families. In Chapter 13, Melanie Hamilton-Perry illustrates why culturally competent practice is needed when using the model by taking as an example the ways in which some of the methods needed to be modified with Traveller families. The authors of Chapter 14 (David Wilkins) and Chapter 15 (Tania Young) describe how they implemented the model across a large section of their organizations (in both cases, London boroughs), and this is followed, in Chapter 16, by an interesting use of the Pathway Model by Henry Smith, in which he shows how it can counter-indicate initial child protection concerns. Our final chapter, the provocative Chapter 17, is led by Sonja Falck. In that chapter she and David Shemmings argue that some family members could be encouraged to *act* differently when their attachment systems are activated, so that they can begin to *think* differently: perhaps it is possible to 'fake it till you make it'. We conclude by outlining how the ADAM Project is likely to develop. (All case examples have been anonymised.)

Chapter 1

The Maltreatment Pathway Model and its Components

David Shemmings and Yvonne Shemmings

It was only three years ago, but it seems longer, that we wrote *Understanding Disorganised Attachment* (Shemmings and Shemmings 2011). This is probably because we have now trained nearly 2500 professionals in the use of the ADAM Pathway Model, and David has addressed over 12000 participants at over 60 conferences. We have travelled the length and breadth of much of the UK as well as Sweden, Germany and Cyprus. What has captured the imagination of these audiences and led to the viral transmission of the model is, as one of them put it recently, 'the refreshingly new way it helps me make sense of what's going on. But it's more than that: it's that I can now see how to help the family, and that is why I went into this job in the first place!'

So what is the Pathway Model? For a fuller description readers can refer to Chapter 2 in *Understanding Disorganised Attachment* (Shemmings and Shemmings 2011) and/or Chapter 10 in *Child Abuse: An Evidence Base for Confident Practice* (Corby, Shemmings and Wilkins 2012), but the gist of it is this: the predictive power of our current, 'best' assessment tools in child protection are very limited because the 'base rate' of the commonly occurring, so-called risk factors is high in the general population. Combined with the fact that serious abuse and maltreatment, i.e. the kind that child protection professionals deal with, are proportionately low; hence, the predictive power of 'risk factor checklists and tools' is not reliable. (Eileen Munro first outlined the application of the 'base rate' problem to the field of child protection in 2002.) So, for example, 'substance misuse' is not much higher in abusing families (around 44%) than it is in non-abusing families (around 34%). A ratio of 1.4:1 is not very informative. Similarly, 'mental health problems' occur in the general population at around 25 per cent (hence, the UK-based mental health charity MIND's powerful message that one in four people will experience a mental health problem at some stage in their lives). Errors in risk analysis and prediction of this magnitude also lead both to the under- or over-estimation of abuse as a result of the inclusion in the child protection system of 'false positives' or overlooking 'false negatives': bringing the wrong families into the system or missing those that need to come to the attention of child protection agencies.

What we are seeing here is the common problem of confusing correlation with causation: many of these 'risk factors' indeed are often present when a child is abused, but they also can be present when children are not abused. The other example we give is that, in the main, girls are more likely to be sexually abused than boys. Furthermore, many professionals have come to believe that being abused as a child is a predictor of abusing one's own children; however, if this were the case, then most child sexual abuse would be perpetrated by women, but still mostly men sexually abuse children, not women (and many of these men will not have been sexually abused as children; see, for example, Testa, Hoffman and Livingston 2011).

The other problem with these 'risk factors' is that they are relatively intractable. Workers cannot easily 'fix' mental health problems, substance misuse, domestic abuse, poverty etc. As we saw in the Introduction, child abuse and neglect are not confined to 'poor families' (and to assume it is can inadvertently lead to unintended discrimination and social injustice). Similarly, when we encounter 'has been abused as a child', 'has been in care as a child', 'learning disability in one or both parents', it is not possible (or even desirable in the last 'risk factor') to do very much, given that these events have already occurred. We can help the parent address the past, but we cannot erase it (and while we are trying to do this, the child is likely to remain at considerable risk).

All of these predisposing features of a family member's current lifestyle and/or childhood need to be understood and addressed, but they are not, in isolation, adequate to explain why a parent abuses their child. Put simply, some mentally ill people are dangerous to their children, but many are not. Unless the professional can pinpoint more precisely how and when the illness *is* dangerous, then all we have is an association between the two. Even floridly paranoid and delusional individuals are not necessarily 'dangerous' to children; or anyone else, for that matter. Any 'risk' depends to a large extent upon where and how the child 'features' in the parent's delusional state of mind. For example, if the parent is defending their child against perceived evil forces, then the child is at less risk of physical harm (because the parent will be defending them). But if the parent thinks the child is a member or part of the 'evil force', then the child might well be at risk. In other words, even using current risk factor analyses, the worker still had to understand the parent's state of mind.

As a consequence, we are focusing on the wrong things in the wrong place. In that sense, it is a tribute to the skill and intuition of our child protection practitioners that they get it right as often as they do. So what are the *right* things in the *right* place? This is where the Pathway Model enters. It was derived from a series of research studies, often involving meta-analysis, i.e. complex procedures combining existing studies to examine the statistical significance and power within the aggregated data. The model suggests the key 'mechanisms of abuse and neglect' and it helps to begin to answer questions such as 'Why do some people who were, for example, abused as children harm their own, whereas others do not; and why do some people who are mentally unwell abuse their own children, whereas clearly others do not (and so on)? The 'right' place is fairly clear now and we have mentioned it already: to find out if a person is a risk to their child, we need to explore with 'intentional' state of mind about their close relationships, hopes and fears, their childhood etc. To appreciate what the 'right things' are we need to examine the Pathway Model (Figure 1.1).

ADAM Pathway Model

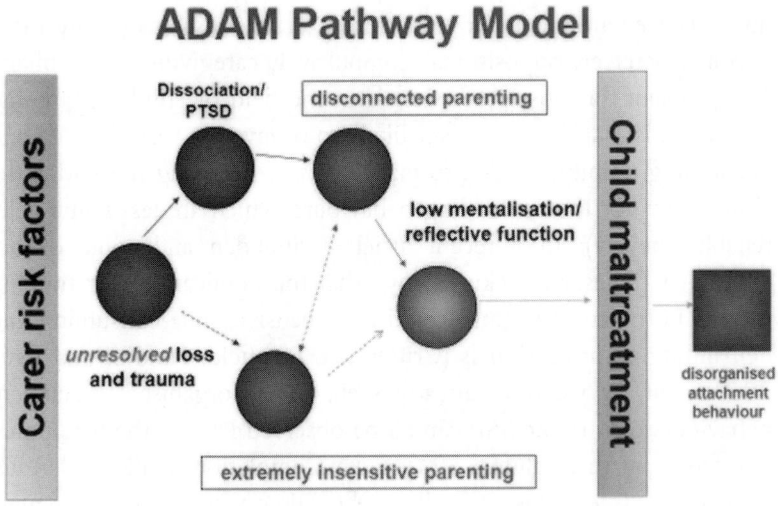

Figure 1.1 The Pathway Model

The Pathway Model identifies one child-related indicator of maltreatment, namely *disorganised attachment behaviour*, alongside three key mechanisms of maltreatment, each centring on parental behaviour. Disorganised attachment behaviour is 'indicative', as distinct from 'predictive', because its presence does not imply that a child will be, or is even likely to be, maltreated in the future; instead, it suggests they may well have been abused already and are still experiencing the consequences of maltreatment, as shown by the way they react and respond to mild activation of their attachment system.

We have decided in this volume to use the term 'disorganised attachment *behaviour*' rather than 'disorganised attachment' because the latter suggests a permanent, fixed way that a child reacts and responds to a caregiver. We were influenced in our decision by the theoretical work of Patricia Crittenden whose Dynamic Maturational Model (DMM) of attachment postulates that child and adult attachment patterns always seek to find a way of organizing themselves, to find a level of security within which to operate on a day-to-day basis. In short, they adapt to survive. It is interesting to note, however, that Bowlby (1988) and Ainsworth *et al.* (1979), and then some years later, Hesse and Main (2000), also noted that the disorganization they observed in infants always resolved quite quickly into one of the other three more organised patterns. Crittenden (2013) proposes that as abused children develop and grow older their behaviour becomes more organised so as to gain more predictability and control over their immediate environment. So consciously or unconsciously they often become coercively oppositional, compulsively caregiving or compliant. The problem for most professionals in the field of child welfare and protection is that they are never likely to receive the very detailed and demanding training needed to make assessments using the DMM (let alone assess for the controlling behaviours, which are less empirically reliable anyway). In a recent article Crittenden and some of her colleagues themselves acknowledge that the implications for training experts in the court setting would be expensive, time-consuming and demanding of professionals (Crittenden, Farnfield, Landini and Grey 2013). But, as we have already seen, the disorganised attachment behaviours seen in the SSP can all be observed later in the techniques referred to in this volume: Story Stem Completion, Child and Adult Attachment Interviews as well as the Disconnected and extremely

Insensitive Parenting (DIP) scale (Out, Bakermans-Kranenburg and Van IJzendoorn 2009). The same fleeting and discontinuous behaviours seen in the toddler resurface later, albeit in different and less obvious ways than in toddlerhood.

We now consider each component of the model briefly.

Disorganised attachment behaviour in the child: a key indicator of maltreatment

The classic experiment designed by John Bowlby and Mary Ainsworth known as the Strange Situation Procedure (SSP) involves short episodes in which a toddler (i.e. a child between one and three and a half years of age) plays with her or his parent, encounters two occasions when a 'stranger' enters and leaves the room, and another two when the parent leaves the child, once on their own and once with the stranger. What the child does when the parent leaves and what they do in the company of the stranger is one of the assessment lenses used by clinicians to determine the presence of an attachment disorder.[1] Bowlby and Ainsworth found that most children displayed one of three *organised* categories, one secure and two insecure, that capture how a child learns to keep their primary caregiver close at hand. But it was in the two reunion episodes that they noticed some children behaved in ways that did not fit into the three organised patterns. They behaved in rather odd ways and noticeably contradictory ways. Although they tended to do what other children did when the carer left the room (i.e. they cried), and pretty much the same when the stranger appeared (i.e. they would not approach or be soothed by them), these children would walk towards the caregiver, but with their head turned away, or walk round and round very slowly as if under water. Some children would fall motionless on the floor for several seconds. Whatever they did at reunion, it seemed to have an eerie, rather peculiar feel to it. But observers need to be alert and attentive because the behaviour only lasts for a short period, often just 10–15 seconds, after which then the child's behaviour tends to 'resolve' into one of the three organised patterns. This seems congruent with Crittenden's argument

---

1   Although there are some overlaps with disorganised attachment behaviour, attachment disorders are different.

(Crittenden *et al.* 2013) that the notion of there being a concept of 'disorganised' attachment, in the sense of a permanent or even semi-permanent state, is a contradiction in terms. We agree, but the fleeting and temporary constellations of disorganised attachment behaviours are most definitely observable and they reflect the child's state of mind. These temporary behaviours are, as we will see, also observed in older children and adults. Child protection professionals learn how to spot these behaviours using the Pathway Model.

It was the way in which such children seemed to become 'stuck' at the reunion that confounded Bowlby and Ainsworth. They did not want their mother to leave, and cried when she did; but then they froze when she came back. Bowlby and Ainsworth were not sure, for example, how they should refer to these behaviours, eventually settling upon what was probably the most accurate term for them at the time: 'unclassified'. Bowlby (1988) discovered later that a large proportion of the children exhibiting these 'unclassified' behaviours had been abused and/or neglected, but it was not until the early 1990s that Main and Solomon began to analyse the behaviour more systematically. It was eventually Mary Main who first coined the powerful phrase 'fear without solution' to capture the central paradox behind 'disorganised' attachment: *understood in its context* it betrays an overwhelming sense of fear that cannot be assuaged in either the short or medium term (see Main and Solomon 1990). We stressed 'understood in its context' because, outside of the SSP, such behaviours can often be observed, for example, when a child is playing make-believe games with friends. Also, children are likely to put their hands up to their face if they are throwing sand at each other, or when playing catch with a parent.

Lyons-Ruth and Jacobvitz (2008) delineated disorganised attachment behaviours in the SSP as follows (note the 'shutting down' quality of each, denoting 'fear without solution'):

> …unclassified infants were observed approaching the parent with head averted; rocking on hands and knees following an abortive approach; or screaming by the door for the parent, then moving away on reunion. What unclassified infants appeared to have in common were contradictory intentions (approaching a parent with head averted), or behaviours that involved apprehension, either directly (fearful facial expressions, oblique approaches), or indirectly e.g.

disoriented behaviours, including dazed or trance-like expressions; or freezing of all movement at the parent's entrance. (p.676)

Main's chilling phrase 'fear without solution' captures very well the dilemma facing the child who is frightened *of* or *for* their carer during the reunion episode: they do not want to be in the room on their own, but also they do not want to go to their parent when the parent comes back, for fear that they might be hurt or frightened by them. The child is terrified by what should be their secure base; simultaneously, their safe haven becomes a source of terror. In such circumstances, their attachment behaviour fails temporarily because they are at the same time frightened by an anxiety-provoking situation *and* the appearance of a caregiver (typically, the return of the parent).

What leads to disorganised attachment behaviour? Is it only abusive parenting?

With regard to the causes of disorganised attachment behaviour, a number of important questions arise:

1. Are children with certain physical or psychological conditions more likely to exhibit disorganised attachment behaviour?

2. Do children exhibit it in the presence of one parent or both (or, indeed, other individuals in general)?

3. Is it related to temperament or genetics?

4. Are children more likely to show the behaviour if their carer is depressed and/or a substance misuser?

5. What about if the parent is depressed and/or is experiencing domestic abuse?

With the benefit of contemporary meta-analytic statistical analyses, we now have some answers to these and other questions. Such analyses have shown that although the prevalence is slightly more elevated, it is still only at moderately low levels of statistical significance (a) with children on the autistic spectrum, with cerebral palsy or Down syndrome, (b) in situations of domestic abuse and (c) with some parents misusing drugs. Nevertheless, compared with maltreated children, levels of disorganised attachment behaviour were lower (Cyr, Euser, Bakermans-Kranenburg and Van Ljendoorn 2010; Van IJzendoorn 1999).

Temperament did not account for differences, either. Instead, 'the findings accrued to date indicate that attachment disorganization emerges *within a particular relationship*; they do not support the notion of attachment disorganization as an individual trait or inborn characteristic of the child' (Lyons-Ruth and Jacobvitz 2008, p.699, emphasis added).

The situation with genetics is not really any different. At first, promising results suggested that a particular dopamine receptor, the DRD4-7+ allele, which affects impulse control and our reward systems, could partially account for higher levels of disorganised attachment behaviour (see Lakatos *et al.* 2002). But two subsequent studies replicated their earlier research and did not find the same connections (Bakermans-Kranenburg and Van IJzendoorn 2004; Spangler and Zimmermann 2007), the Dutch researchers demonstrating that the Hungarian team had not taken sufficient account of 'gene-environment' interactions. For example, a child might inherit a tendency to be overweight, but if there is very little food for them to eat, they will be underweight for their age. Certainly some children appear to be able to 'bounce back' more easily than others, whereas other children are more defenceless in the face of abusive parenting, but their resilience is more likely to be a function of who else they meet later, or who else is around to offer a degree of security, rather than from a purely heritable source.

As a consequence of these findings, researchers concluded that disorganised attachment behaviour is best viewed as a 'relationship-specific phenomenon' (Van IJzendoorn *et al.* 1999, p.235). The implication for child protection professionals is that it is not the characteristics of the parent *per se* – as we saw above, whether they are depressed or were abused as a child, or a single parent etc. – that are most indicative of disorganised attachment behaviour. What these studies show consistently is that these odd and troubling behaviours are related centrally to the *quality of protective behaviour* from carers. The meta-analyses indicate strongly that the maltreatment of a child is far more likely than any other single (or indeed combined) factor to lead to disorganised attachment behaviour. This should not surprise us, because such behaviour is at the root of what maltreatment means: to be frightened of, or for, a person who is meant to love you or who, at the very least, is not supposed to seriously harm you.

Why concentrate so much on disorganised attachment behaviour?

One reason that so much focus is put on disorganised attachment behaviour is that virtually all large-scale studies, worldwide, conclude that around 60 per cent of any representative population is securely attached; hence, around 40 per cent is *insecurely* attached. Therefore, to write in a file that 'the child is insecurely attached to her or his mother or father' unwittingly describes nearly half the world! The main reason, however, that we devote so much time to disorganised attachment behaviour is that, as we have outlined, the developing literature in this field points to a strong connection between disorganised attachment and child maltreatment. Currently, the best estimates conclude that between 48 and 86 per cent of children who are maltreated also show disorganised attachment behaviour. (The lower end of the range may result from the use of one of two coding systems, which is known to underestimate its occurrence; see Van IJzendoorn, Schuengel and Bakermans-Kranenberg 1999, p.228.)

Interestingly, in their most recent meta-analysis, Cyr *et al.* (2010) found that disorganised attachment behaviour was related to maltreatment at a level similar to that of the *combined* effect of five socio-economic status (SES) high-risk factors in a non-maltreated sample. (It is acknowledged by the authors that some of the children living in high-risk SES conditions may also have been abused, i.e. there could have been undetected or unsubstantiated cases.) We agree with these that this finding depends in large part on the definitions of 'maltreatment' given in the studies which tend to equate it with the more 'active' forms of abuse (i.e. physical, sexual and emotional). But when more 'passive' forms of severe emotional neglect are considered, that information may partly explain some aspects of the findings. As the authors state, 'in the absence of direct maltreatment, parental frightening behavior might be proposed to be a key mechanism through which parents at high levels of socioeconomic risk and exposed to more traumatic experiences prompt the development of attachment disorganization' (Cyr *et al.*, p.88).

We include disconnected or very frightening behaviour in the ADAM Pathway Model because we believe it corresponds with 'emotional *neglect*', as distinct from emotional *abuse*, which tends to involve more active kinds of direct parenting behaviours, such as humiliation, belittling, derogation etc., rather than 'disconnected' parenting – what we call 'unpresence' – the appearance of which can have detrimental effects on children: these behaviours may not always be seen as abuse, but they are often, in fact, abusive.

In the UK it is the concept of 'significant harm' that determines whether a child needs a protection plan, and the definition of maltreatment, abuse and neglect includes emotional neglect, not just emotional abuse. Consequently, the appearance of parental frightening behaviour should be considered alongside other factors.

Cyr *et al.* (2010) spell out some of the key implications of their research in relation to high-risk socio-economic factors when studies have assumed that there is no maltreatment (i.e. active forms of abuse) as distinct from emotional *neglect*:

> Without concrete evidence about the higher prevalence of frightening behavior in parents from multiple-risk environments, we would like to suggest two other pathways to attachment disorganization. First, parents' withdrawal from interacting with the child because of overwhelming personal or socioeconomic problems and daily hassles is speculated to lead to a chronic hyperaroused attachment system in the child. Second, domestic violence may more often occur in multiple-risk conditions... Children who witness violence in the family, including partner violence, have been shown to run a greater risk of becoming disorganized... With increasing levels of violent relationships with current partners, mothers were increasingly likely to have infants with disorganized attachments. Zeanah (1996) speculates that witnessing parental violence could elicit fear in a young child about the mother's well-being and her ability to protect herself as well as the child against the violence. Finally, multiple-risk environments lead to parents experiencing more losses and other traumatic events that may remain unresolved and trigger frightening or frightened parenting behavior that has been shown to result in disorganized attachment. (p.103)

The finding from the Cyr *et al.* (2010) meta-analysis is an interesting one which we believe partly vindicates our approach of refocusing professionals' gaze in favour of the more directly observable features of the ADAM Pathway Model, which require a detailed analysis of the *dynamics of the maltreatment itself* rather than a simple linear description of caregiver lifestyles and 'risk factors'. As we have seen, the problem with an over-dependence on so-called risk factors in child maltreatment assessments is that most are highly prevalent in the general population and therefore significantly lose predictive value when applied to a much smaller subsample (i.e. maltreated children). Consequently, we advocate a redirection of professional attention, away from the external to the internal; we need to explore and understand, with intense curiosity, 'states of mind'.

A strong connection between disorganised attachment behaviour and maltreatment, using definitions which include emotional neglect, is one of the most consistent themes in the child attachment literature, along with the likelihood of negative consequences for the child later (although clearly some children are able to bounce back from adverse experiences more easily and quickly than others). Here are two quotes from leading attachment researchers:

> Child maltreatment has a strong impact on attachment. It creates fear without solution for a child because the attachment figure, whom the child would approach for protection in times of stress and anxiety, is at the same time the source of fright, whether this attachment figure is the perpetrator, a potential perpetrator (in cases of sibling abuse), or failing to protect the child against the perpetrator. (Cyr *et al.* 2010, p.100)

> Disorganized behavior is likely [to] occur when an infant is maltreated by the parent, and studies conducted by Carlson, Cicchetti and colleagues (Carlson *et al.* 1989), as well as by Lyons-Ruth (1996), have indicated that almost eighty percent of infants in maltreatment samples are disorganized. (Hesse and Main 2000, p.1105)

Here is David Howe, an author well known to social workers and others involved in working with children and families, writing about the connection between disorganised attachment and maltreatment:

> In…non-clinical samples, around 14 per cent of children might be expected to be classified as disorganized... When children experience abuse, neglect, maltreatment...rates of disorganization rise to 80 or 90 per cent... (Howe 2013, p.153)

The relatively high level of disorganised attachment behaviour in 'non-clinical samples' is thought to be the result of frightening parental behaviours, often a consequence of unresolved loss and/or trauma. The child becomes intensely frightened of, or for, the parent, who feels to the child to be significantly emotionally absent (despite being physically present). While such behaviour is not likely to come to the attention of child protection agencies as an allegation of child 'abuse', the effects on the child are often quite profound and can manifest later as chronically problematic behaviours in nursery, playgroup and school settings. Parents may appreciate the offer of help here.

The number of studies focusing specifically on child maltreatment and attachment disorganization are still quite small; hence, we needed to consider what kinds of parenting behaviours, whether accompanied by high-risk SES factors or not, might lead to 'fear without solution' behaviours in children. Again, drawing upon meta-analyses, three key intervening variables were identified, which we incorporated into the Pathway Model: (a) unresolved loss, (b) disconnected and/or extremely insensitive parenting and (c) low mentalizing capacity. These variables comprise the mechanisms most likely to result in disorganised attachment behaviour in a child and, hence, with care and skill, can be used as part of assessments when allegations of abuse are made. A very brief description is offered of each mechanism, but readers can refer to Chapters 2, 5, 6 and 7 in *Understanding Disorganized Attachment* (Shemmings and Shemmings 2011) for a fuller and more complete explanation.

The three key mechanisms of maltreatment from observing parental behaviour

Unresolved loss and trauma

Unresolved loss and trauma (see Madigan *et al.* 2006) refers to significantly repressed or denied, but re-emerging, interpersonal losses and/or traumas under conditions which remind the parent of their own vulnerability. Caring for infants and toddlers is one such condition. Unresolved loss and trauma may be accompanied by dissociative experiences such as 'blanking out' or becoming what we have termed 'unpresent', i.e. physically but not emotionally present; often a person will also experience post-traumatic stress disorder symptoms. For a child to be with a parent under such conditions is likely to leave a child frightened of, or for, their parent (who is, of course, usually their primary caregiver).

Disconnected and extremely insensitive parenting

Disconnected and extremely insensitive parenting (DIP; Out *et al.* 2009), a consequence of unresolved loss and trauma, is parenting that can include sudden changes in behaviour which are neither accompanied by explanatory gestures or vocalizations, nor by signs of affection or playfulness. Such *disconnected parenting* also includes frightened or frightening behaviour and disruptive emotional communication. *Extremely insensitive parenting* denotes caregiving which is excessively withdrawn and neglectful or, conversely, over-intrusive and very aggressive, typically involving rough handling and/or very hostile language (Lyons-Ruth and Jacobvitz 2008). Because planned or unannounced home visits are somewhat serendipitous and unreliable as conduits for the assessment of parenting capacity, we recommend the use of one or more of the guided parenting tasks (described in more detail in Chapters 6 and 7). Guided parenting tasks involve mild challenges of the kind any parent faces when bringing up a child such as telling a child they cannot have a particular toy just yet, or asking them to clear up when in the middle of playing with a toy they like. Parental *in*sensitivity is a precise term denoting far more than simply being unresponsive to a child's demands. Parental insensitivity on its own, however, is not found to be a significant determinant of disorganised attachment behaviour. Following the recent paper by Dorothée Out and her colleagues (2009), it is now seen as more helpful to refer to '*extremely* insensitive parenting' which includes behaviour such as (taken from DIP): extreme parental withdrawal and neglect; failure to comfort the child when in distress; not intervening in harmful situations; deliberately creating distance from the child; and/or intrusive, negative, aggressive or harsh behaviours (including negative, rejecting or hostile comments about or to the child).

Until relatively recently it was unclear what the exact connections were between extremely insensitive and disconnected parental behaviour, and disorganised attachment. For example, a meta-analysis conducted in 2006 by Sherry Madigan and colleagues (2006) found a link between disconnected and extremely insensitive caregiving as a key determinant of disorganised attachment, but this became more complicated when unresolved loss was included in the equation: in the 12 studies reviewed by Madigan *et al.*, 'less than half of the association between unresolved loss or trauma was explained by mediation of frightening parental behaviour' (Bakermans-Kranenburg and Van IJzendoorn 2007, p.1161). The main point about the behaviours identified in the DIP is that they are evidence-based, unlike many of the interpretations of child and parent interactions seen by professionals during home and contact visits.

The relationship between mediating caregiver variables, i.e. unresolved loss and disconnected or extremely insensitive parenting, and their effect on disorganised attachment is rather confusing. Put simply:

> Some parents who experience unresolved loss and/or trauma may develop dissociative states, some of whom may display insensitive caregiving but which does not necessarily always lead to disorganised attachment behaviour in their children; some parents experiencing dissociative states may unintentionally display disconnected caregiving responses to their children, some of whom will develop disorganised attachment, while others do not (although they will almost always develop an organised insecure attachment pattern and it is never optimal for a child's development to be frightened by a carer's reactions to them). (Shemmings and Shemmings 2011, p.58)

Low parental mentalizing capacity

Fonagy and Target (2005) argue that the 'missing link' to connect these loose threads and distinguish which 'unresolved' parents are more likely to exhibit insensitive and/or frightening behaviour is low mentalizing capacity (see also Allen, Fonagy and Bateman 2008). This is a significantly reduced ability to appreciate that others have different intentions and feelings from one's own. An example of very low mentalizing capacity is the father who, when asked what he thought his six-week-old baby daughter might have said (if she could have spoken) ten minutes earlier, when she vomited on his suit jacket, replied, 'Oh, I know what the little bitch would have said: "I hate you and I'm going to ruin your day by making you late for work. I hate you"'. He was not joking, as this example relates to a serious case of physical injury perpetrated by a middle class, educated and 'successful' individual. Of particular interest is that he did not see that what he said might worry an experienced (and, as it happened, ADAM-trained) professional, as he was not able to mentalise her, either. Parents with low mentalizing capacity often speak about their babies as 'hating them' or they hold wildly inaccurate attributions. Such misattributions or persecutory attributions can be heard regularly among parents who maltreat their children (Allen *et al.* 2008; Crittenden 2008; Slade 2008).

Pathway Model methods and tools

There are five different methods and tools used in the ADAM Project, each of which requires practice to use confidently and effectively. A very brief summary of each is now given, because the following chapters make reference to them frequently, but readers are advised to refer to our *Understanding Disorganised Attachment* (Shemmings and Shemmings 2011) for a more complete profile. As we have seen, ADAM Project participants focus only on the components in the Pathway Model (the details of which are listed in Table 1.1) when using these methods and tools.

The Strange Situation Procedure

As mentioned in the Introduction, the Strange Situation Procedure (SSP) consists of a series of events (see Chapter 7) involving a parent playing with their child, interspersed with two short separation episodes including a 'stranger', who appears twice: once when the parent is present and again when they have left the room. The key opportunity to observe disorganised attachment behaviour is at the two reunions of the child with the parent. The SSP mildly activates the child's attachment system and, hence, provides important information about the physical and emotional availability and receptiveness of the primary caregiver.

The Adult Attachment Interview

The Adult Attachment Interview (AAI; George, Kaplan and Main 1985) is a complex interviewing process using a narrative approach to elicit working models of attachment. Specifically:

> The 60- to 90-minute interview asks interviewees to choose five adjectives to describe their relationship with their mother/father, to supply anecdotes illustrating why these adjectives are appropriate, to speculate about why their parents behaved as they did, and to

> describe changes over time in the quality of their relationships with their parents… (Shaver and Mikulincer 2002, p.136)

At this point, trained AAI raters code the transcript using:

> …five continuous rating scales intended to capture the probable quality of early experiences, separately with mother/father (e.g. loving, rejecting, neglecting), and on 12 scales that describe the individual's current state of mind regarding those experiences (e.g. idealising, continuing anger, derogation of attachment, coherence of the narrative). A primary attachment category is then assigned. (Shaver and Mikulincer 2002, p.136)

After some introductory questions aimed at outlining the composition of the interviewee's family, the 'priming' technique of asking them to choose five words or short phrases to describe their relationships with the parent to whom they feel closest reveals a considerable amount of attachment-related information. Immediately after the five adjectives are identified, the interviewee is asked to try to give an illustrative example, from as far back as they can, to capture the phrase they had chosen to describe their early relational memories. This process has been described as 'surprising the unconscious' (George *et al.* 1985) because, in some ways, this point in the AAI mirrors the stage in the SSP when the carer leaves the infant alone in the room. It is under such circumstances that affect regulatory mechanisms and cognitive processing are uncovered, thus revealing the participant's state of mind with respect to attachment.

Because participants are asked to reflect upon early memories, defences are exposed when focusing upon unwanted thoughts. In most relational situations, individuals can ignore, repress or deny feelings when the attachment system is primed. During the AAI participants are actively ruminating loss, separation, being comforted and their other early memories. The way in which they perform and narrate this task becomes the focus of the subsequent analysis. The AAI includes detailed guidelines about how the interviewer should approach the interview (for example, how to handle silence) because from this point onwards 'the AAI indicates defensive strategies and more emphasis is placed on discourse properties…than on the propositional content of what is said' (Shaver and Mikulincer 2002, p.136).

The Child Attachment Interview

The Child Attachment Interview (CAI), devised in 2003 by Mary Target, Peter Fonagy and Yael Schmueli-Goetz (Target, Fonagy and Schmueli-Goetz 2003), is very similar to the AAI. The questions follow a pattern similar to that of the AAI, except that children are asked to think of three words, instead of five, to describe their relationship with their parent.

Story Stem Completion

There are different variations of Story Stem Completion (SSC) tasks. We summarise them in *Understanding Disorganised Attachment* (Shemmings and Shemmings 2011) as follows:

> Methods include the MacArthur Story Stem Battery (MSSB; Bretherton, Ridgeway and Cassidy 1990); the Story Stem Assessment Profile (SSAP; Hodges *et al.* 2003); and the Manchester Child Attachment Story Task (MCAST; Green *et al.* 2000). The SSAP consists of 13 short 'beginnings' (i.e. stems) of stories which the child is asked to complete with the request 'Can you *Show Me* and *Tell Me* what happens next?' (the use of *both* verbs is important). The stories are 'brought to life' by means of Play People, animals and other 'props' to help make them more concrete, given the age of the child. Each story activates the attachment process for different reasons. The child's responses are gauged in respect of: separation, ability to seek comfort, conflict, external threats, minor accidents and losses, frustration, injury, exclusion and jealousy. So, for example, one of the stories begins with one of two 'adult' Play People saying 'You've lost my keys!' The other 'adult' replies 'I *haven't* lost your keys'. Adult 1 says 'You *always* lose my keys'; Adult 2 replies 'Well, I haven't lost them this time'. It is at this point that the child is asked to show *and* tell what then happens. There are strict 'rules' governing what an interviewer can and cannot say by way of prompts and what many people learning these methods find difficult is that they mustn't praise the child excessively or be too encouraging; they have to remain neutral. (pp.70–71)

The Disconnected and extremely Insensitive Parenting (DIP) scale

The DIP scale (Out *et al.* 2009) builds on work of Mary Main and Erik Hesse who developed the FR (Frightening/Frightened) scale and the AMBIANCE (the Atypical Maternal Behaviour Instrument for Assessment and Classification) by Karlen Lyons-Ruth and colleagues. It distinguishes more clearly, as the name of the full title of the DIP scale indicates, between disconnected parenting and extremely insensitive parenting, partly because insensitive (i.e. significantly misattuned) parenting on its own was not found to be a reliable indicator of either disorganised attachment behaviour or maltreatment.

How are the components of the Pathway Model recognised in practice?

Recognizing the different components of the Pathway Model requires more detail than can be provided here; therefore, readers are advised to study Chapter 3 of *Understanding Disorganised Attachment* (Shemmings and Shemmings 2011). Table 1.1 provides a brief summary to help readers make sense of Chapters 4–13 and 16, which make specific reference to the assessment and understanding of the Pathway Model's components.

Table 1.1 Disorganised attachment behaviour indices and markers

Strange Situation Procedure (see Main and Solomon 1990; see pp.24–25)
Adult Attachment Interview

1. Marked lapses in 'metacognitive monitoring' and logic
2. Mixture of insecure organizations
3. Hostile–helpless (similar to 'good'–'bad' split in children)

Child Attachment Interview

1. Sudden affect switching in response to loss, trauma and/or frightening events
2. Freezing or very long pauses
3. Magic/omnipotence
4. Good–bad split (for example, describing one parent as alternatively 'good' and then 'bad' but without any logical reason, and often accompanied by discontinuous 'switching' in the narrative)
5. Catastrophizing
6. Controlling-caregiving or controlling-punitive responses (including to the interviewer)

Story Stem Completion

1. Catastrophizing responses

2. Good–bad shift

3. Bizarre/atypical responses, for example:
   - impoverished stories or refusal to take part in the story
   - invisible, unknown people controlling events
   - dangerous events left unresolved
   - children sometimes thrown into jail or beaten

What have been some of the difficulties in translating the Pathway Model into practice?

The feedback at the end of training sessions has been consistently and overwhelmingly positive. Participants always comment that they found the insights valuable and relevant. One participant said that it 'revolutionised my practice'. (Many people make this kind of comment anonymously on the end-of-course feedback forms but often also tell us face-to-face and unsolicited during the programme.) To begin with, this enthusiasm resulted in a tendency to 'see disorganised attachment everywhere', so we needed to add a measured and deliberate degree of caution to the sessions, sometimes by drip-feeding access to the materials on the website. (Participants would regularly ask for a complete set of the materials from the website.) Apart from it being a prohibitive task to furnish each of the 20 or more participants with a folder now totalling over 200 pages, we wanted people to read the background material on each of the methods (for example, before trying the AAI we ask them to read two online articles by Mary Main).

We also needed to be careful that participants did not over-interpret the results of their interviews and observations. We stressed that they have to stay firmly within the parameters of a particular method. For example, there is a set number of markers of disorganised attachment behaviour in the SSC tasks – no more, no less – but when we began our work we noticed that some practitioners were not familiar with manualised and standardised assessment procedures and we had to stress the strict requirement not to wander 'off piste'. Furthermore, because so many professionals have been trained and have developed their experience in what one might be forgiven for calling a 'checklist culture' in child protection, some participants wanted to use the indicators as a kind of checklist. For example, they begged us to provide them with a simple summary of each method, together with what to look for during the process. Given their enthusiasm, it was sometimes hard to resist these requests, but it was important that we did so, in order to preserve the integrity of the approach.

Probably the biggest hurdle we encountered was the realization that the success of the methods depended upon, to a great degree, the quality and nature of the relationship the practitioner had developed, or was likely to develop, with family members. It was here that the biggest breakthroughs took place, when those attending could see how much potential there was when using the model, not only to understand but also to help the family, provided they got the relationship right. This is why the next chapter is devoted to exploring this in more detail. There is another reason, however, why that relationship is so crucial: participants are reminded constantly that they cannot stand up in court and say that they 'completed an SSP/SSC/CAI/AAI', because they are not fully qualified and accredited to make such a statement. Neither can they argue, in any setting or meeting connected with decisions about the risk to a child, that 'After using X/Y/Z methods, I found the following indicators of disorganised attachment behaviour (or caregiver indicators), which in turn point to maltreatment'; instead, they have to go back to the family member(s), if they are worried, and explain sensitively and precisely why they have made this assessment. This is probably one of the most difficult conversations to have with a parent because, however it is put, it is hard to say to them, 'I think your child is at risk of harm from either you or someone else'. But if 'evidence' is required, either for the court or a child protection meeting, it must come from an open, honest, but sensitive 'cards on the table' approach by the practitioner, not from the use of a Pathway Model method alone.

The particular method used becomes the conduit for raising concerns with the family, not a forensic 'magic bullet'. In Chapter 11, David Phillips helpfully refers to his experience of triangulating components both within and outside the model so, for example, the practitioner might compare the analyses of an older child doing a CAI with an SSC with a younger child, perhaps alongside an AAI with a parent. Initial impressions would then be compared with information from other workers and child protection agencies. But the essential ingredient that produces fair and balanced assessments is 'an open mind, but not an empty head'. Not doing so can quickly develop into confirmation bias, the process whereby professionals jump to an incorrect conclusion and then only take account of new information that confirms it.

When practitioners use the model correctly, it has a profound impact on their work, and probably the key indicator of success is being able to add at the end, 'I think we can help'. It is the offer of help, support and encouragement that seems to alter the balance, away from, as we are about to see in the next chapter, a somewhat over-proceduralised, sometimes acerbic way of relating that, as Donald Forrester's research shows all too clearly (Forrester *et al.* 2007; Forrester 2012), typifies much of child protection practice in the UK today.

Conclusion

We now have many examples of observing 'fear without solution' in children and young people, of discovering pockets of significantly unresolved loss or trauma in parents, and we have seen many instances of low mentalised, disconnected and extremely insensitive caregiving. But of equal note and importance, practitioners experienced in using the ADAM Pathway Model report times when initial concerns were *not* confirmed, thus enabling them to reassess allegations. (Chapter 16 addresses this specifically and others refer to it *en passant*.) We have also been told of examples when, soon after a child has completed a modified doll-based SSC task, they have asked to speak to the practitioner, with whom they have then disclosed serious abuse. We suspect that this is because the methods used with children involve listening to the child intently for 20–30 minutes or more, which is likely to lead to the kind of trust needed for the child to later talk more about abusive experiences.

We have also learned that some of the techniques need to be reviewed regularly and re-evaluated in the light of contemporary cultural practices. Two examples come to mind. First, during SSC analysis, 'catastrophised' child narratives in which certain dolls end up 'dead' are seen as possible indicators of disorganised attachment behaviour. But many online games played by young children routinely 'kill off' characters in a rather matter-of-fact way. As a consequence, we are learning that more attention needs to be given to the precise circumstances of the 'death': is it violent and unresolved? Is there 'rescue', 'resuscitation' or 'resurrection' (and can the child speak about it coherently, even if somewhat fancifully)? Second, in certainly communities (e.g. in some gypsy and traveller groups), there are no words, for example, for certain concepts in the AAI. (This situation is explained in more detail in Chapter 13.)

Because each of the techniques is predicated on high levels of active and patient listening, attending and empathy, it demonstrates to us the potential for the ADAM Project to help professionals (re)discover the centrality of relationship-based work (see Ruch, Turney and Ward 2010) and thereby prepare them better for a 'post-Munro'[2] world in which procedures, forms and checklists progressively take second place. The next chapter explores this in more detail.

Finally, the question of how long this all takes (i.e. concern about time constraints) has arisen in many of the sessions. We are now able to reassure practitioners that these methods can be used relatively quickly and reveal a lot of important information. For example, guided parenting tasks only take between 10 and 20 minutes, but they help the worker really 'get under the skin' of how the parent responds to their child, as well as identify concerns. Also, the techniques are not used in every case, and our experienced colleagues have become very adept at knowing when to use them. The overriding reason for using the model is because the practitioner is 'looking at the right things in the right place', and this maximises the efficiency of their efforts. It also helps develop the right kind of relationship to help the family later when it becomes more obvious what the dynamics of the situation are.

---

2   In 2011 Professor Eileen Munro from the London School of Economics completed a government-initiated report on the child protection system in the UK. Her extensive, detailed and comprehensive report (see www.education.gov.uk/childrenandyoungpeople/safeguardingchildren/protection/b00219296/munro) has major implications for practitioners.

Chapter 2

The Notion of Enhanced Relationship Skills

David Shemmings and Yvonne Shemmings

Relational skills in the 1970s and 1980s

During the 1970s and 1980s there was an explosion of research into what was loosely termed helping with human relations skills – or 'relationship skills', for short. Robert Carkhuff and his numerous associates (see, for example, Carkhuff 1969) became fascinated by the question of what works best in counselling and therapy, having derived their early work from Carl Rogers, the inspiration, originator and pioneer of modern-day counselling skills (see, for example, Rogers 1951). What took the world of counselling and therapy by storm was that each of their studies arrived at the same conclusion: it was not the helper's technique that led to change; it was whether they could create, demonstrate and sustain certain 'core conditions of a helping relationship', as they called them. These core conditions comprised 'genuineness', 'respect' and the somewhat unwieldy 'unconditional positive regard' ('warmth' is the term used today). Furthermore, these core conditions cannot be taught; they can become 'lost' – and maybe regained – but if an individual does not possess them in the first place, they cannot make a good 'helper', be it as a doctor, psychiatrist, social worker, nurse, teacher, health visitor etc. This idea always possessed a certain validity because how could someone attend a 'warmth' course, for example? We are witnessing exactly the same debate today in the UK as a result of studies, inspections and patient feedback concluding that many nurses have lost their compassion when working with patients.

Carkhuff's work was further developed by Gerard Egan (1986) in his best-selling book *The Skilled Helper* in which he expanded the idea that while the core conditions are, to a greater or lesser degree, innate, a number of other skills essential to any helping enterprise could (and should) be taught. The skills they identified were: accurate empathy, active attending and listening, sensitive challenging, summarizing and the ability to know when and how to encourage another person 'to act differently'. Many such programmes were developed during this period that have stood the test of time, as have Carkhuff and colleagues' original findings (in the field of child protection see Dale 2004; Maiter, Palmer and Manji 2006; Platt 2008; Saint-Jacques *et al.* 2006; Yatchmenoff 2008). The notion of empathy has also seen a sharp rise in relevance and popularity recently – for example, David Howe's *Empathy: What It Is and Why It Matters* (Howe 2013) – partly as a result of claims in the field of neuroscience that it can be 'observed in operation' using functional magnetic resonance imaging.

The contemporary importance of relational skills in child protection

Donald Forrester's elegant studies of how child protection practitioners communicate with family members, using actors as 'parents', are at once revealing and worrying (Forrester *et al.* 2007, 2008). He and his team asked practitioners to respond to a paper-based 'referral' with the actor 'as they normally would'. They found little in terms of empathy, or even basic listening skills, in their analyses. What they did find, on the other hand, were quite acerbic, impatient and hectoring responses; sometimes, the workers used quite threatening phrases.

We have no criticism of child protection practitioners here; no one we have met over the past three years during the ADAM Project training has sought, for example, to defend these examples. Although they were shocked, many practitioners felt they resonated with practice as they saw it. Our position is best expressed, as one of us (David) wrote in *Child Abuse: An Evidence Base for Confident Practice* (Corby, Shemmings and Wilkins 2012):

> …child protection professionals…we believe, do an astonishing job under the most emotionally draining circumstances, and with caseloads that virtually everyone now accepts are far too high. Furthermore, they are constantly being inspected, evaluated and reorganized, and may face dismissal, de-registration and even public humiliation if they are thought to have made a mistake. This is the case across all professions involved in child protection but the most vilified and blamed are social workers. We are concerned that the

system itself, most often devised after knee-jerk reactions to high profile cases, is the primary cause of the defensive practice we are about to describe. The Munro review, on the other hand, has been written more 'in the cold light of day' and we believe it offers a unique opportunity to steer our gigantic procedural supertanker onto a different course before it hits the rocks; and many believe it already has. (pp.212–213)

We are concerned at what seems to have happened as a result of working in 'pre-Munro' organizations. Here is the preamble to an example of 'pre-Munro' practice, from what Forrester and his team uncovered (which has been modified for training purposes):

> You are on duty. A referral is received of a mother who often picks up her eight-year-old child when she seems drunk. You visit and explain the nature of the referral to the mother. The mother says, 'That's not true. I am on anti-depressants and they make me appear drunk' (Forrester et al. 2008, p.8).

The most typical kinds of responses noted in the study were of this nature:

> 'Can I see the bottle of anti-depressants? Where does it say that on the label?' (p.8)

> 'This is contradictory to what the school is saying; the school feels you have presented drunk and this is why we've got the referral and we're concerned. If you're saying it's the anti-depressants, you need to go back to your GP and adjust the dose as it's clearly a problem' (p.8).

The problem with each scenario is that they both assume that the 'mother' is being dishonest or deceptive; of course, she may be, but to start the relationship in such an accusatory way is likely to alienate a parent. An empathic response such as, 'So, for you, you've been accused of something you didn't do?' is more likely to encourage her to open up, possibly by becoming angry or aggressive. She might say, for example, 'Yes and I'm sick of your lot always jumping to conclusions and having a go at me'. Another empathic response along the lines of 'And you're annoyed because you think I'm going to do the same and not listen to you' might well produce a quick and short 'F...ing right, you ____!' but there are very good reasons why empathy is usually the preferred response. One reason is that it is more likely to encourage the person to talk, which is the best way to detect dishonesty, because it is very difficult for a person to maintain a dishonest position when speaking at length. Another reason is that it gives the worker an opportunity to ask the question, 'So what do you make of all this? Can I ask if you know who's worried at the school, and why?' This 'tell me your side of things; tell me what it's like to be *you* at the moment in all this' is a very useful way of equalizing the power dynamic as well as giving the worker the chance to explore the parent's mentalizing capacity, i.e. can they see things from another person's perspective (even if they do not agree with it)?

Empathic responses also make it easier to challenge a parent later, because the worker will have 'earned the right' to do so. We always remember the parent who said to one of us (David) some years ago when she was asked what made a good social worker: 'The ability to say difficult things while cuddling you at the same time, but without the cuddle getting in the way of the difficult thing. Trust is about knowing that they would tell me that they're worried, but in such a way that I'm not made to feel stupid or put down'.

The following is an example of the kind of response, given by a parent to a social worker, found by Forrester and colleagues (2007, 2008). This is not an extreme example by any means, but it becomes clear how this relationship has got off on entirely the wrong foot and a lot of skilled relational repair will now be required for the mother to regain trust to work co-operatively.

Parent: Nobody has worked together with me. Everybody has told me what to do.

SW: I think from the seven referrals, what has happened before, social workers have come out, they have visited you, they have talked to you, you have denied that you have had a drink problem, that you don't need help.

Parent: Yeah.

SW: Those are the opportunities where people have tried to help you and even at the case conference.

Parent: I don't call that help you know, I don't call that help, when somebody comes telling you what everybody is seeing. Nobody is asking me my side, I don't call that help, I call that everybody is telling me what to do and I am beginning to feel you are doing the same thing, you are going by everybody, everybody. I am sitting here and you are telling me what everybody...and this is what's getting to me.

SW: But even when the social workers came out on the other seven incidents they would have asked you your point of view and what happened?

Parent: Were you here? Were you here? You weren't here!

SW: I have reports upstairs.

(Examples given by Donald Forrester in November 2013)

Forrester and colleagues then cite the following two examples, which they titled 'When persuasion fails try raising consequences'. It is possible to have made these responses in a firm but kind way, but now imagine how, if they were said in an acerbic, cajoling or threatening way, they would be experienced by the parent as insensitive practice.

'Well it will be part of the conference protection plan that we want you to access these services and I can't stress how important it is that you actually do do that because if you don't, then that's when we are going to have to really start thinking about how else we can keep Charlie safe'.

' …It's your job, you're the grown-up. I've offered you support services, right. It's up to you to use them. I can't make you go to them. You're his mum, you're the grown-up…and the way I look at it, I consider you have an addiction, an illness, and so your job is to get it treated. If you don't, what could happen, what could happen down the line, is you won't be looking after your boy. I don't want that to happen, I'd much rather he was at home with you: attending school, me not getting reports about you drinking, that he's happy and well and thriving in your care, that's what I want… all right Jeanette?'

Having worked with so many practitioners over the past years, and having seen many examples of excellent communication, we believe that there are three additional components which need to be grafted onto a basic empathic response. We call them 'intelligent kindness', 'unsentimental compassion' and 'non-directive curiosity'. We added each adjective to each noun to stress that they must be 'balanced with an eyes-wide-open, boundaried, authoritative approach aimed at containing anxiety and ensuring that the child's needs and outcomes stay in sharp focus (Fauth *et al.* 2010). Kindness on its own could be dangerous and misguided; it must be tempered with intelligence. As for compassion, if sentimental, it might place a child in danger if the worker over-identifies with a parent.

A lack of 'non-directive curiosity' is perhaps best illustrated with reference to a short exercise we do on day two of the ADAM Project training. We ask the group to reflect on the first three minutes of a three-part BBC Panorama series (which aired January to February 2012) about social work in Bristol called *Protecting Our Children*. Most participants saw it at the time but, to jog their memory, we give the following brief summary (from episode one):

> Suzanne is a newly qualified social worker who is visiting Mike, Tiffany and their three-year-old son, Toby. All we know is that the child has quite a marked speech delay and that there are concerns about cleanliness and tidiness in the home, so the reason for the involvement of child protection agencies concerns possible physical and/or emotional neglect. As the social worker walks down the side of the house, a dog jumps up and barks suddenly from the neighbour's side (which makes most viewers jump). She knocks on the door and goes into the kitchen. The voice-over tells us that the family 'are living in basic accommodation and Toby doesn't yet have a bed to sleep in'. Suzanne asks some introductory questions including 'How's his bed coming on?' to which Tiffany replies, 'It's being delivered later today'. Suzanne asks Mike if he is 'prepared to answer a few questions' and he replies, a little angrily, 'Right, you might be a training social worker but what I'm still fuming about was the way you accused me last Friday'. (We had just been told that bruises had been noticed on Toby.) Suzanne says calmly, 'Well, I'm here to protect children' at which point Mike interrupts and says, insistently but not especially aggressively (although Tiffany asks him to calm down), 'You're out to do one thing Suzanne, and I know you're out to do one thing. You're here to split the family up...and I'll repeat it now with the cameras present: you're out to wreck us'.

We then give each participant a small sticky note and ask them to write down how they are feeling, or what they would be thinking had they seen and heard what Suzanne has seen and heard. They are asked to think of three words or short phrases to capture their thoughts and feelings. (We ask them not to put their name on the note and not to discuss it with the person sitting next to them.)

We have already repeated this exercise with 518 practitioners (and first reported the findings in Corby *et al.* 2012, when we had completed it with 387 participants). The results are interesting but worrying, as they confirm, albeit from a different angle, the findings of Forrester and colleagues (2007, 2008). The three words or phrases fall into three fairly evenly distributed groups. The first group, which we called 'Sympathetic', included: Sad, Frustrated, Powerless, In Need of Help, Unsupported, Neglected, Sympathy, Stressed, Personal Problems, Unloved, Overwhelmed, Desperate, Curious About Why, They Need Help and I Want to Help Them.

The second group we labelled 'Ambiguous', as the direction or 'valence' of each word or phrase could have been either positive or negative (and because the exercise was completed anonymously, we could not check with participants what they meant by what they had written). Examples in the 'Ambiguous' group were: Disturbed, Pity, Emotional Deficit, Damaged, Uncontrolled, Difficult to Empathise With, Angry, Senseless, Unrealistic, Overwhelmed, Shocked, Disturbed, Harsh/Insensitive.

It was the third group (about 30 per cent) which, we must say, shocked us, because the words or phrases included: Appalling, Horrifying, Dislike, Disgusting, Uneducated, Need to Be Held Accountable, Irresponsible, Cruel, Evil, Selfish, Wicked, No Capacity, No Knowledge, Inadequate, Weak , 'What's Wrong with You?', Dangerous, Put Away and Not Let Out, Don't Deserve Children, Should Be Locked Up, Thick. For the sake of immediacy and authenticity, here are the 'judgemental' statements from when we last did the exercise in March 2013 (we have stopped doing it now, as participants are likely to have heard about it!): 'Here we go…', 'They are needy, but the father is an ass', 'Uneducated – déjà vu', 'Hopeless family' (i.e. the parents).

What is worrying about these words is that they were all written by qualified practitioners. (Students and very newly qualified workers were excluded, but we noted that they tended to be in the first group.) What emerges from these data – we discuss the findings with each group to check out our perceptions – is the pernicious 'drip, drip' effects of a system that has become more concerned with forms, procedures, box ticking and self-justification, which unfortunately has become the orthodoxy of pre-Munro child protection work. (Chapter 3 presents two cases where pre- and post-Munro approaches are compared and contrasted.)

What is particularly saddening is that it emerges later in the film that Mick and Tiffany have experienced considerable loss and trauma because they had experienced the death, in total, of seven babies, either *in utero* or very soon after birth. So it is possible to see their behaviour with Toby in terms of the Pathway Model, specifically as a result of the likely effect of these tragedies in the context of probable unresolved loss and trauma. It is noticeable that, for example, Mike becomes very distant and seems to go 'off-line' at numerous points, especially during a contact visit, and it was interesting that the camera crew and editor clearly noticed it too, as so many of these shots were included in the final version.

So what we mean by 'non-directive curiosity' is a deliberate suspension of annoyance and incredulity, and never becoming judgemental, instead replacing such feelings by a more neutral 'I wonder what this is about?' In the example we have just considered, this kind of curiosity might prompt a reaction such as, 'I wonder why Mike and Tiffany can't provide a loving home for their son Toby?' because, given that we later learn of the tragedy of their losses, logically, one might have expected them to wrap him in cotton wool (albeit within their limited finances). One might also wonder why they didn't tidy up, knowing that they were going to be filmed. But in terms of *non-directive* curiosity, these thoughts are only part of the story: the attitude with which they are expressed is crucial. We advocate a tone of quiet and reflective interest in the state of mind that could have produced such perplexing behaviour, but without any judgement to it, and certainly without any hint of impatient incredulity that the parent cannot understand what is wrong and what they need to do to put it right. (Of course, if they could do that, they would not have come to the attention of child protection agencies in the first place!) In fact, we now believe that whenever a professional starts to think, when working with a family member, 'Why can't you see that… ? Why can't you just do…and then it will all be fine?' then the worker should go back to the drawing board and ask themselves, 'Why can't *I* see why they can't… (and why have I lost the interest and compassion to find out why?)'. It helps considerably when professionals can rely on the right kind of supervision to help them to reflect in this way.

Towards enhanced relationship skills

We believe that the Rogerian skills of listening, attending and empathy are necessary, but not sufficient, conditions for child protection professionals (who, at least in the early stages, are *not* acting in the role of counsellor). We argue for an 'empathy+' addition, so that 'intelligent kindness', 'unsentimental compassion' and 'non-directive curiosity' become prominent. We conclude this chapter by offering practitioners some tips for practice, drawing together ideas from *Motivational Interviewing* (Miller and Rollnick 2001). Mixed in is a 'strengths-based'[1] seam (see Gaughan and Kalyniak 2011) along with Andrew Turnell's notion of signs of safety (Turnell 2009). Our aim is to sideline interrogative interviewing methods in favour of more inquisitive and supportive approaches. So, for example, rather than trying to find out *why* someone gambles by asking them directly, the worker gently tries to explore by asking, 'When you do gamble, what does it do for you?' This is not the same question as 'Why do you gamble?' which, in many respects, is a rather pointless question that is likely to lead to a perfunctory attempt at self-analysis (if at all). Instead, the worker becomes interested in the motivational rather than the causal dimension of the question and in so doing switches the direction and balance of the relationship. It surprises the parent, but in a good way. The worker then listens and responds empathically, which encourages the parent to explore the question in more depth.

Tips for practising enhanced relationship skills

We provide the following tips for practising enhanced relationship skills:

1. It is a good idea to be aware of the positive and negative signals one might unconsciously be transmitting to a parent. (Filming oneself is the most unforgiving way of doing this, but self-reflection is quite a good alternative.) Be aware when

---

1   We believe, though, that it is important to stress that a family 'strength' *must* be sufficiently related to the identified 'weaknesses' or problem areas; otherwise, at best it could be a patronizing or even sentimental attempt to say something 'nice' about a parent or carer, and at worst it could be dangerous if it involves overlooking significant risks to a child.

you are not smiling very much (when you could be), and when your intonation too regularly betrays unfriendliness, mirrored by posture and facial expression. Have you forgotten to give supportive comments and appropriate praise (but remember that no one likes being commended for doing something well when they know that it was not)? Maybe in all the rushing around and anxiety of the job, you have forgotten to look towards people, maintain eye contact and show interest by asking their opinion – and then waiting for the answer and checking that you have understood it. Has your communication inadvertently become stale and discordant by becoming inattentive and overly directive or just plain tetchy and intolerant?

2. Oil the wheels if a parent is resistant, but remember that you might resist, too, if someone spoke to you in the ways seen and heard by Donald Forrester and his team. Try using mentalization-based questions such as:

   1. Could you tell me what it is like being a mum at the moment?

   2. If your child could speak, what do you think she would be saying right now?

   3. For the next ten minutes can you 'speak for your child' (and could you give me a running commentary of what is going through *your* mind as well)?

   4. When you look at him or her, what do you see?

   5. What do you enjoy doing together?

   6. Is there anything of which your child is frightened?

   7. What do you do to show them that you love them? What do *they* do to show you that they love *you*?

   8. What worries do you have about your child's development?

   9. How do you feel about the crying (or other reactions) when you discipline the children?

If you can get the timing right, it can be informative to ask the parent, but in a non-directively curious way, '*What do you think I might be making of what you just did/said?*' Always reveal what *you* are thinking, sensitively and openly. Take opportunities to say, 'Actually, you've got a point there!' as this will, again, switch the dynamic. We talk a lot in all our professional groups about challenging power imbalances and empowerment: these are practical examples of how to develop more equality in the relationship without losing the authority sometimes needed in child protection work.

3. You can usually tell when you are getting somewhere if a parent or carer says things such as 'This is serious isn't it?' or when their initial anger or defensiveness turns to 'productive shame', perhaps by them saying, 'Oh God, how could I have let it get like this?' If their reaction is genuine, the way this is responded to is critical as it can become a turning point.

4. During the early stages of a child protection referral there is likely to be resistance. As we have stated, to be perceived as accusing someone of abusing or neglecting their children – which, however you put it, you will be assumed as saying – is one of the most difficult things for a parent to hear. They are likely to argue with you, interrupt or ignore what you say. Try 'going with it' for a while by actively listening and the occasional 'So if I've got it right, you're saying ...?' or 'So the way you see it is something like this... ?'. As long as it does not compromise you or you are not colluding with the parent, you could try what is called 'agreement with a twist': 'Do you know, when you put it like that, I can begin to understand how you see things, and to a point I agree with X/Y/Z...(pause for the reaction, and give an empathic response if appropriate)...but I'm not sure I agree with you when you say P/Q/R'.

5. When it feels right – this is where the value of intuition comes in – you can begin tentatively to move to an action orientation. The techniques of motivational interviewing can prove to be particularly helpful. Here are a few simple examples:

    1. In what ways is this a problem for you? Are there times when it is not a problem. What is the difference?

    2. What reasons do you see for...(specify change)?

3. What makes you think it might be a good idea to...(specify change)?

4. What would be the advantages of...(specify change)?

5. What do you think might happen if you do not change?

6. What can you imagine happening to her or him if this does not change?

Again, if you think you have got a strong enough relationship to say this – you will be surprised by how quickly this can happen if you attend to the basics – you could try something like, 'This might sound a bit odd or even a little rude, but if you did decide to make some changes, what makes you think you could continue with them?' or 'I've noticed that sometimes you seem to be able to stop/start doing something but find it difficult to carry on with it for very long. Do you see what I'm getting at? Can you tell me about this?' Often you will be in a position to challenge more directly, as with 'I guess there might be more of a problem than I first thought. Do you have an idea why I'm saying this?'

When moving to a more action-oriented phase of the work it is important to construct together with family members a plan based on small but sufficiently related steps. In many situations it is wise to devise with a parent what practitioners using cognitive behaviour therapy refer to as 'relapse roadmaps' because if it can go wrong it probably will, and it is always preferable to see it coming in the first place (provided the worker is not a 'wet blanket', i.e. pouring cold water on everything).

Conclusion

In conclusion, from our experience of the ADAM Project, parents respond far more co-operatively if they feel that the practitioner is willing and able to support them to change. Furthermore, working in this way is far more rewarding than ticking boxes endlessly assessing parents and children (participants rarely need persuading of this point!). Donald Forrester also found similar results about the most effective use of child protection practitioners' time and resources in a recent review of the systemic units in Hackney, London, also known by many now as Reclaiming Social Work (see Forrester *et al.* 2013; Rooke *et al.* 2012). Some of our colleagues, now very accomplished in the creative and skilled use of the Pathway Model, demonstrate its use in the following chapters. But before beginning this journey, we offer ten golden rules of the ADAM Project and its associated Pathway Model which we hope will clarify some of its key principles.

Ten golden rules of the ADAM Project and the Pathway Model

1. The main aim of the ADAM Project is to help and support families stay together whenever it is feasible to do so.

2. The components in the Pathway Model are used to understand the mechanisms of maltreatment and are more accurate than external factors such as 'drug misuse' or 'mental health problems'.

3. People can usually change and there is as yet no firm evidence that there are critical periods of child development after which change is impossible (although the longer we leave things, the harder it becomes to overcome abuse and neglect).

4. It is preferable to think of disorganised attachment *behaviour*, not disorganised attachment *per se*. (These behaviours are temporary and fleeting, not an attachment 'style'.) The behaviours are not predictive of maltreatment: they indicate that additional questions need to be posed urgently, as the child already may be experiencing 'fear without solution'.

5. Practitioners need to practise the methods and tools contained within the Pathway Model and then discuss their work with more experienced colleagues.

6. Analyses of Pathway Model components are not sufficient in themselves to produce evidence in court.

7. Practitioners need to make sure that they are not constrained by 'confirmation bias': we have encountered many examples of disconfirmed hypotheses and concerns when the Pathway Model is used with an 'open mind but not an empty head'.

8. Where there are concerns, they must be shared in the family (unless doing so might harm a child).

9. Practitioners need to be 'culturally competent' when using the methods and tools.

10. The Pathway Model is of little use unless accompanied by the enhanced relationship skills of intelligent kindness, unsentimental compassion and non-directive curiosity.

Chapter 3

Using Enhanced Relationship Skills in Practice

Yvalia Febrer

Everyone remembers their teenage years, normally as the time of their life that is at once the most thrilling and the most harrowing. It is the period when one falls in love for the first time, suffers heartbreak, and begins to truly forge one's independence, separating oneself from one's family. For some teenagers that family has been nurturing, for others noxious. Pubescence is a fragile and pivotal time in every child's life, but it is largely accepted that adolescents gravitate to a greater or lesser degree toward risky and dangerous activities during this stage in their development, all the while questioning or possibly rejecting authority. For practitioners, teenagers can be difficult to engage with for precisely these reasons. Teaching from the ADAM Project helps participants understand how children who have been maltreated and display disorganised attachment behaviour can be even more susceptible to becoming drawn into such risky pursuits, and less able to get out of them and stay out of them. The Pathway Model also gives us a framework for understanding their caregivers' behaviour and the interaction between parent and child, which in turn informs a much stronger intervention based on a more accurate assessment of family functioning, need and risk.

For many practitioners working with children and families it comes as a surprise that teenagers are the second most likely age group to be subject to a serious case review. Many practitioners do not know that, after children under 12 months, late adolescents are actually the most vulnerable. It is interesting to note that younger school-age children are significantly less likely to be killed where abuse or neglect is a factor; in fact, for these types of deaths it seems rates are highest in infancy, drop in the preschool years, decline even further when children are in education, and rise again in late adolescence. This has been demonstrated by recent research in the UK, for example, the Department for Education's research report from 2009 to 2011 (Brandon *et al.* 2011). The report found that approximately a quarter of all serious case reviews relate to teenagers as victims and ten per cent of these young people are actually 16 years of age or over, the very age group that is often neglected by child protection services since they are approaching the time when they legally become adults. Despite these findings, people's assumptions can understandably be that teenagers are less at risk by virtue of their size and age. Ironically, it is their age that places them at increased risk rather than acting as a protective factor, as one might initially think. Nonetheless, I have found from my own experience that it is frequently written in assessments concerning domestic violence and physical abuse, for example, that adolescents can 'self-protect' due to their size, age and physical and emotional ability, and that they are therefore perceived to be in less danger, or even not deemed 'at risk of significant harm' at all (The Children Act 1989). While the sentiment is understandable, and common sense might suggest that this age group is less vulnerable, such a generalised assumption fails to take into account the more insidious developmental and environmental risks posed to teenagers, particularly in today's society where gangs and sexual exploitation are increasingly common and in which advances in technology have opened up new avenues for abuse.

One of the inherent and unavoidable dangers for this group is the very fact that teenagers are seemingly predisposed to risk taking; as well as being a fact that is widely accepted in both sociological and evolutionary theory, it has also been demonstrated in recent cognitive neuroscientific research. It is already known among medical researchers that when reality exceeds a person's expectations there is a surge of activity in the brain region called the ventral striatum, but in a study published by Cohen *et al.* (2010) the region's response was shown to be significantly higher in participants between 14 and 19 years of age. Brain activity in the ventral striatum is related to the release of dopamine, a nerve-signalling molecule that helps the brain process rewards; with more dopamine flowing a teenager is likely to feel that a risky behaviour, when it pays off, is so much more gratifying than it might seem to a younger child or adult. This might help explain why teenagers take risks that to adults simply do not seem worth taking. Adriana Galvan, a developmental cognitive neuroscientist at the University of California, says that for teenagers the rewards 'loom so much bigger' than the potential negative consequences, and she goes on to speculate that 'perhaps their willingness to engage in uncertainty is driven by the potential rewards that might result from that uncertainty' (Galvan 2010). This sentiment resonates with the two cases I discuss here from experience gained in my own practice.

One can see how important it is to understand a child's attachment history in order to work with them effectively as a teenager when they reach that pivotal stage in their development, the transition from childhood to adulthood. If we utilise tools such as the Child Attachment Interview in conjunction with the Adult Attachment Interview to assess their parents' reflective function, we can gain an insight into their world and their internal working models of close relationships. This in turn enables us to engage them in a much more effective way.

In addition to giving us this understanding, the ADAM Project training helps reacquaint practitioners with communication and empathic skills that have arguably been sidelined by the bureaucratised focus of British child protection services over the past few decades. This decline in the tools required for direct work, particularly of key interpersonal skills such as listening, attending and empathizing, has been evidenced through Donald Forrester's research into social work practice (Forrester *et al.* 2007, 2008). As well as simply helping us conceptualise some of the more scientific explanations behind adolescent behaviours, the Pathway Model equips us to actually help young people.

Case studies

I discuss below two children that I worked with while practising in a front-line referral and assessment team: one a male gang member, the other a teenage girl who was being sexually exploited.

Case 1: Jake

Jake, a gang member, was a black British child who had grown up in inner-city London with his mother, though for periods of his upbringing he had spent time living with his paternal aunt and occasionally his birth father (who had another family). Jake's parents had separated when he was a young child and he had witnessed domestic violence from his younger brother's father. At the point when Jake was referred to Children's Services and my work with him began, he was already entrenched in gang lifestyle. He carried a knife, was distributing heroin and crack cocaine across greater London and had been involved in stabbings as both victim and perpetrator. Jake was smoking cannabis on a daily basis, was frequently reported missing by his family since he spent periods living with gang members and had been out of education for almost a year. He was well known to the police and already had four convictions for what appeared to be gang-related offences, as well as numerous other arrests and cautions. At that time Jake was only 13 years old.

Jake was first reported missing by his mother at just ten years of age, and by his own account the gang had groomed him from the time he was seven years old. In his words they had 'watched him grow up' and were 'like his family'. From Jake's earliest memories of the 'mandem' (a term used to describe older gang members), it would appear that they approached him when he was in the playground where his aunt lived, that they bought him sweets, gave him cash and as he got older took him for food at a local restaurant. He was bought increasingly expensive gifts and was naturally seduced by the mere fact of being befriended by the older boys on the estate. It is this initial period of building up the child's esteem and trust that forms the basis of the inevitable exploitation that is to follow, in much the same way as those who sexually exploit children operate. By the time Jake came to be referred to Children's Services, he was already well established into the postcode feud between the gang with which he was involved and their rivals. Just prior to my working with him, he had been accosted by rival gang members who held him at gunpoint and took him to an unknown location where they physically abused and pistol-whipped him (beat him around the face and head with the butt of a gun). When he was found dumped in the street unconscious, he was transported to hospital and it was established that he had sustained numerous injuries to his face, head and body, and was suffering a severe concussion.

Before going to visit Jake for the first time, I was already aware that he was not engaging in education, was refusing to attend his Youth Offending Service appointments and was flatly denying any gang involvement. I was also aware that he had been involved with our service two years previously, after his father had physically assaulted him while trying to restrain him from running away, but that the case had been closed immediately after the incident since he had moved to his aunt's care in another local authority and was therefore not deemed 'at risk'. At that time, when he was just 11 years old, there was already information available about his association with boys 18 years of age, and about him frequently going missing and getting into trouble. Jake had actually first shown aggressive behaviour in primary school where he had received fixed-term exclusions and was said to be disrupting other children in class. I was conscious that the professionals who had come across him previously had not succeeded in meaningfully engaging with him and was aware that in a front-line team that is overwhelmed with cases there is little or no scope for taking time to connect with a child. Assessment timescales and the pressure for these to be met coupled with an overload in referrals particularly of very young children following the death of Baby 'P' – young children who by virtue of their age are judged as being more obviously at risk – meant that teenagers could sometimes be very quickly labelled as 'refusing to engage' or 'refusing to accept services' and therefore have their cases closed. Nonetheless, the team manager supported the plan for me to use relationship skills to engage with Jake, shifting the focus away from the bureaucratic aspects of the case towards direct work. This allowed me to spend 80 per cent of my time doing face-to-face work with Jake and only 20 per cent completing paperwork, as opposed to the usual modus operandi of front-line teams that see the reverse.

Prior to beginning my work with Jake, I was also aware from analysing his case history and family relationships that he most likely had a negative internal working model and that his belief about himself and those around him no doubt told him that he was 'unlovable' and that everybody in his life would leave him and let him down. Using my understanding of attachment behaviour learned from the ADAM Project, I concluded that failing to form a relationship with this young person or failing to show that he was not being 'given up on' or 'written off' would only confirm and exacerbate his self-destructive internal working model, thus fuelling his externalizing behaviours and pushing him further into the fringes of society. This would only place Jake at further risk, something that I knew in his case could eventually prove to be fatal. As a result, I decided to employ motivational interviewing techniques (see Chapter 2) in order to try to connect with Jake from the outset, since I was sure that if I took a didactic or prescriptive approach with him, 'telling' him that he was putting himself at risk and that he 'had to stop what he was doing', this would immediately set up a dynamic of attack which he would counter with either defence or attack himself, neither of which would elicit truthful information or meaningful engagement from him. I was conscious that most serious case reviews, from Jasmine Beckford to Baby 'P', highlight the importance of truthful and accurate information when assessing and responding to risk, so I wanted to use an empathic model that would foster truthfulness and disclosure from Jake. I used these techniques on my first meeting with him during a home visit and was surprised, yet pleased, to find that within a very short time he had not only admitted that he was in the gang, but had become tearful about this and disclosed a number of details about his gang involvement without reservation. Despite Jake's initial, momentary reticence and cynicism on being introduced to me, the use of motivational interviewing techniques quickly encouraged him to drop the façade of his gang persona and open up to me as the 13-year-old child that he was. In sharing details of his association with the gang he tearfully recounted many of the initiation rituals he had had to endure, some of which involved elements of 'black magic' and 'voodoo', often used to scare and subdue the initiate into submission. He also admitted to a number of criminal acts he had committed; this was on our very first meeting.

Although Jake had almost entirely eluded all other agencies and professionals, the initial rapport and trust that was established from this very first meeting meant that he visited our offices on almost a daily basis from that point onward. This in itself allowed us to assess and manage the risks he was exposing himself to in a more consistent and effective way. He soon started coming to see me and asking to be taken to his Youth Offending Service appointments, bail bookings and court appearances (appointments that he had previously ignored). I was further able to use this relationship to help Jake to engage in some education and think about a future outside of the gang.

For my part, rather than being constrained by the very rigid boundaries and remit of a child protection practitioner in a referral and assessment team, I was enabled to go beyond simply 'assessing' and referring Jake to other agencies, and was able to actually provide therapeutic support to this boy myself. On one occasion, when Jake had been missing for several days and had not been reachable, he contacted me and asked to be collected from outside a London Underground station. On picking him up I could see that he was physically malnourished and neglected, having lost weight and smelling of cannabis and body odour, and that he had a laceration across his jaw and chin where it transpired a rival member had attempted to stab him in the neck. Moreover, having always been excitable and talkative when we had spent time together, on this occasion he did not speak for the first half hour of our drive, during which he hunched forward with his eyes cast downward. He then, without looking at me, told me he had been living in a crack house, after which he did not speak again. During the remainder of the journey he sang lyrics from one of the gang's rap songs for 45 minutes without respite, slightly rocking back and forth as he did so. In this instance the valuable information about his attachment history and modus operandi within relationships (which I had managed to obtain by engaging him and gaining his trust from the outset) meant that I was able to relate to him in such a way that began the therapeutic process of healing and rehabilitation at that early stage. The time itself and the relationship that we had established also meant that he gave me a wealth of information about his day-to-day living which allowed me to much more accurately and effectively manage the risks posed to him, and indeed to make appropriate and proportionate care plans.

In terms of trying to lure Jake away from the 'mandem', this approach was absolutely key since the relationship itself was the only ammunition I had against such an affluent and well-organised gang. There is a tendency and a temptation to try to compete with the gang by offering young people diversionary activities and material rewards; however, I quickly realised that even in a strong economic climate it would be impossible for a local authority to contend with gangs who are making so much drug and arms money that their YouTube videos show them pouring Cristal champagne down the gutter and driving supercars. Financially, we were unable to compete with this, so the basis of our strategy had to be relational and had to simulate a positive and healthy attachment relationship. Nonetheless, gangs also understand the importance of simulating attachment; the grooming process is integral to their recruitment of new members, in exactly the same way as sexual exploitation begins by mimicking a strong, romantic relationship. This is precisely what took place with the young girl that I had worked with who was sexually exploited by an older man and had to be placed in a secure unit for her own protection, whose case I shall now discuss.

Case 2: Beth

Beth was one of four children living in a middle-class family whose parents were married and whose father was working. The family had never come to the attention of social services before and her school attendance at the local Catholic school was excellent. Beth was subjected to date rape at 13 years of age by a boy whom she knew from the neighbourhood and who was known to her parents. Following this incident, she began to truant from school and then to run away from home. Her parents reported her missing and tried to offer her support, but her absconding became more frequent and she stayed away for longer each time, often coming home very late at night. Just a few months later, she was found in a community centre at night engaging in sexual activity with an 18-year-old male. She then began to steal money from her parents and also make false allegations that they were drug addicts who were physically abusing her, and she was running away for days at a time. It quickly came to light that Beth was associating with a 24-year-old man and that the two were in what she considered to be a romantic relationship. At this time she was still just 13 years of age and had now disengaged from school completely, losing all contact with her friends and peers. Soon Beth was using cannabis on a daily basis, was living in this man's garden shed with no heating or running water and was being prostituted by him in central London. He had made her 'convert' to Islam, something the gang had also attempted with Jake, and had performed a pseudo Islamic marriage such that she believed this man was her husband and she must be obedient to him (as she detailed in her diary). This man had a long criminal history including three previous allegations of rape made against him and one accusation of harbouring a minor.

I was given the case while working in a busy referral and assessment team before I had attended the ADAM Project training, and at that point the serious exploitation had not yet begun. On the way to my first meeting a duty manager had a brief supervisory discussion with me, during which the focus was largely on my 'telling' Beth to curb her behaviours and insist that she stop putting herself at risk, rather than on considering how this might actually be achieved through work using enhanced relationship skills. There was a particular emphasis on telling her to 'stop going missing', 'stop being deceitful with professionals' and 'stop making false allegations against her parents' (all of which she had been doing up until that point). With such a blinkered approach I did not feel enabled to take the time to reflect on what Beth's experiences and point of view were, nor think about what her internal working model might be, particularly following a date rape. Taking such a constrained and constricted approach of simply 'dictating' to a young person what they should do, and informing them that they 'must' change (often with inherent threats if those changes are not made) can be an easy default position to fall into in a front-line team that is both overwhelmed with referrals and pressurised by deadlines. It is this kind of acerbic approach that was evidenced in Donald Forrester's research into social work practice (Forrester *et al.* 2007, 2008).

In setting up this dynamic of power imbalance, condescension and accusation, I immediately failed to engage Beth, which in this case was all the more catastrophic since her exploiter had already coached her in how to evade and manipulate professionals. Because Beth saw this man not only as the love of her life but also as her husband, failing to empathise with her and truly envisage the situation from her point of view meant that not only did I not connect with her, but also that I lacked a comprehensive risk assessment since she gave me no information or disclosure. Once Beth had been found and placed in a secure unit on welfare grounds, it was discovered that this man had been anally raping her, bringing other young girls to his flat to have sex with them in her presence, prostituting her, denying her food, providing her with drugs and forcing her to clean his house, effectively treating her as a slave. Her mental health was seriously compromised and her arms and wrists showed evidence of self-harming behaviour. If Beth had opened up to me at the point when I first met her, she might have given me key information that could have been used to prevent such a rapid escalation of the abuse.

Failing to incorporate an understanding of Beth's internal working model and her self-belief after the date rape, and neglecting to empathise with her and appreciate that from her perspective this man loved her, I was instead taking an authoritarian stance that immediately put her off. This kind of didactic approach is one that I have found few teenagers respond positively to, since adolescents naturally reject authority as part of their development and independence building. Because I 'told' her that this man was a risk, was dangerous and was not to be trusted, and I did not use any approaches using enhanced relationship skills or similar techniques to engage her, I did not get any of the detailed information about her day-to-day living like that Jake had given me, nor did she visit my office or attend any appointments during the time I held the case. In fact, the next time I saw her following our first meeting was when police found her after she had been missing for over a month and we had placed her in a secure unit. At that point she was severely malnourished, traumatised and had been routinely sexually abused by this man in such a way that he had caused her physical injury. Once she was in the unit and began to disclose what had been happening to her, we also discovered that she had twice taken an overdose of paracetemol in an attempt to take her life. One can see from this how crucial it is to establish a relationship that fosters dialogue with a young person, particularly when that dialogue is one's primary source of information. Overall my approach with Beth stood in stark contrast to the model I employed with Jake, and as such the intervention was not just unsuccessful but was effectively non-existent, since I had failed to engage her from our very first meeting.

Conclusion

In conclusion, it is easy to see not only how important an appreciation of attachment and enhanced relationship skills is in understanding how teenagers operate and indeed in working with them, but also how vital a direct-work approach is when trying to reduce risk. These two cases from my own practice demonstrate the way in which one's initial meeting with a young person can decide the nature of one's whole involvement with them, and in turn the degree of success of one's help and support. The stories of Jake and Beth also show us as practitioners how the risks they face as teenagers can easily lead not only to significant harm but also to possible fatality, despite their appearing old enough to protect themselves from certain harm. For Jake just one stabbing could have ended his life, and for Beth a successful suicide attempt was probably only months away. Both cases illustrate the very serious risks that teenagers can be exposed to, particularly in today's society, and they equally demonstrate how the adolescent stage in itself has much to do with this; for Beth it was the lure of what appeared to be a first love and the transition from girlhood to womanhood, and for Jake it was a time to forge his independence away from his family, assert his identity and court popularity and fame in the process. These are common pursuits to almost all teenagers, but for some it can lead down a path from which it is difficult to find a way back. For those young people who have trouble relating to others, including children who have experienced prolonged maltreatment, the way back can be ever more challenging, and the practitioner's task requires even greater knowledge and skill. With the offer of a new era in British child protection practice following the publication of Professor Eileen Munro's Review of Child Protection (Munro 2011), practitioners working with teenagers must have a command of the enhanced relationship skills required for effective direct work with this age group. In essence, it represents a return to the kind of work that most practitioners joined the profession to do and, for me, a renaissance of true social work.

Chapter 4

Exploring Mechanisms of Maltreatment in a Family

Alice Cook

In my work with parents I have focused on the three key elements of the model that can be better understood to predict maltreatment on the part of the caregiver: unresolved loss and trauma, disconnected and extremely insensitive parenting and low mentalization. I have explored these explanatory mechanisms through observations and working closely and often intensely with parents. Focusing on such elements has allowed me to piece together not only what that child is experiencing, but what has led up to this point.

The Pathway Model offers a framework to use in order to try to understand the reasons behind the maltreatment. It is this understanding which evokes the necessary empathy, attitude and approach in order to work with parents effectively. It is also incredibly hard to assess whether change for a family is possible without knowing some of their difficulties and the complex way in which this is affecting their parenting capacity. In addition, a greater understanding of why a parent is behaving in the way that they are enables a practitioner to decide on the most effective intervention in order to make a clear assessment on the potential for change and the best outcome for the child. In this chapter I describe one family with which I worked and the way in which the Pathway Model shaped this work.

Case study

Case: Family A

The family comprised Mr and Mrs A and their daughter Sarah, three years of age. (The local authority's concerns had arisen before her birth.) Mrs A had two boys removed previously by the local authority and Mr A had one younger child with whom he had no contact. The local authority had sought the removal of Sarah at birth due to historic concerns of neglect and emotional harm, but they were not granted an Interim Care Order. The local authority remained involved with the family for the following three years and concerns continued to mount. This became a classic neglect case, whereby they were challenged to prove 'imminent risk of harm', and therefore practitioners had great difficulty in moving forward. Mr and Mrs A did not drink or abuse drugs, they were not overly aggressive towards professionals, there was no domestic abuse and neither of them had an enduring mental health problem. These are all elements of a case that can cause it to drift. It required intensive work with Mr and Mrs A and Sarah in order to provide a clear picture of what life was like for this child and her experiences whilst in their care, as well as exploration of why they were struggling, the likelihood of change and, most importantly, the impact of all of this on Sarah and her future development.

At the start of my work I tend to use the Strange Situation Procedure in order to gain insight into the attachment relationship. It is normally used with children between 18 and 36 months of age. Although Sarah was showing developmental delay and functioning at a much younger age, it was nevertheless deemed appropriate.

I explained to Mr and Mrs A what I would ask one of them to do. Mr A's response was to tell me that Sarah would not care if she was left alone or with a stranger. If this was seen to be true, then it could have indicated the possibility of an attachment disorder, but such a 'diagnosis', which can only be assessed by a qualified clinician, is now thought to be used too liberally (see Woolgar and Scott 2013).

To gain clearer insight into Mr and Mrs A's relationship with Sarah, I asked them to give me five words to describe her. They were able to give me two words: 'stubborn' and 'outgoing'. I then asked them why they had chosen these words and asked for examples of her behaviours that explained why they had chosen them. This question is of a similar nature to the beginning questions of the Adult Attachment Interview. Asking the parent to give examples as to why they have chosen particular descriptive words provides additional insight into their knowledge and feelings about their child.

One of the phrases that Mrs A used to describe Sarah was, 'She knows what she wants and she does what she wants'. I asked her to elaborate on this. She said she felt that Sarah would rather play by herself and that she would not want them to play with her. Mrs A said that Sarah would tell her to go away and leave her alone. I asked Mrs A if Sarah would actually say those words to her and she said, 'She would just turn away from me'; thus, Mrs A believed that in Sarah's mind she did not want her to be part of her play and was rejecting her. Regardless of whether Sarah would actually behave in the way Mrs A described (e.g. turning away from her), Mrs A may still feel rejected by her. This thought process may have contributed to Mrs A failing to offer Sarah the level of engagement and stimulation that she needed. This can become a self-fulfilling prophecy which begins in infancy as the parent feels the child does not like them or is rejecting them, and therefore there is limited positive interaction and the child starts to view their parent as unavailable. As a consequence, the infant may start to demonstrate behaviours such as turning away and avoiding eye contact, which in turn reinforces the parent's thoughts of rejection.

In order for me to gauge Mrs A's mentalizing ability and her subsequent attachment relationship with Sarah, I asked her a series of questions:

- What are your child's likes and dislikes?
- What do you enjoy doing together?
- Is there anything of which your child is frightened?
- What do you do to show her that you love her?
- What does she do to show you that she loves you?
- Can you tell me what it is like being a mum?

It is important to ask these questions in a considerate and non-intrusive manner. They need to be discussed at the beginning of the work, as later observations combined with getting to know the child can confirm or deny initial hypotheses about the situation. Mr and Mrs A's answers painted a picture of low mentalizing capacity, as shown in the following example:

1. What are your child's likes and dislikes?

> *Mr A*: Um…she likes everything really…um (shrugs shoulders)… yeah…

> *Mrs A*: Yeah…she doesn't like having her hair brushed…she won't stand still.

Mr A chose to give a general answer which lacked any specifics, possibly because he could not think of anything his child liked. In some cases it may be appropriate to prompt parents by providing categories such as favourite foods, toys etc. Mrs A also had difficulty identifying what her daughter liked. When this is the case, we need to understand why this is and what it means for the child. Is the child showing little or no enjoyment, preference or pleasure in anything? Were Mr and Mrs A unable to interpret her cues and therefore unable to understand what she likes?

Mrs A did manage to come up with a dislike, but exploration would be needed as to why this was the case. Is Mrs A too rough with her when she brushes her hair? Does she talk to her and reassure her when she does it?

2. What does your child do to show you that she loves you?

> *Mr A*: Sarah says, 'I love you so much daddy'. She tells me all the time.

I knew from the brief time that I had spent with Sarah that she was unable to put this many words together and she lacked the cognitive ability to understand the meaning of these words. I had also not observed her calling Mr A 'daddy', or in fact use any name for him at all. This was of concern and could have been a result of neglect, or she may have been fearful of him.

3. Can you tell me what it is like being a mum?

> *Mrs A*: Once they are here you can't return them. When they are born they are the ones in charge, then things change and they hate it. Sarah was in charge when she was six months old, but at 12 months things changed. 'If you scream you just won't be fed'. Sarah likes to think she is in charge now but that's not true.

This response is reason for concern, as it is negative and focused on the control that she perceives the child has over her, and it is as if she feels this is deliberately and consciously used against her. This indicates an impaired capacity to understand what is actually occurring in the mind of an infant; it is also indicative of her holding persecutory attributions.

At the beginning of my work with Mr and Mrs A I carried out a number of observation sessions. Observation is a powerful tool and can often be overlooked. This may be the result of time limitations or the need to discuss a number of concerns with families on visits, rather than just sitting back and observing. Additionally, some practitioners may struggle with what it is they are specifically seeking. The Pathway Model provides markers and indicators to help practitioners make informed decisions about what it is they have actually seen.

Child maltreatment does not occur only between the hours of nine and five; therefore, I carried out observations that enabled me to see breakfast time, lunch and dinner time, bath time, bedtime and what was happening in between. To make sound judgements we need to know what the child is experiencing last thing at night and first thing in the morning. When conducting this many observations, a parent may struggle to be able to sustain care that is beyond what they normally deliver; therefore, these observations can inform decisions and, in the majority of cases, inform the court of what life is really like for a child.

During my observations I began to understand Mr and Mrs A's difficulty mentalizing and witnessed some insensitive parenting. Here is an example:

> Mr A had given Sarah a bowl of spaghetti hoops for dinner. He had not encouraged her to sit at the table and gave it to her whilst she sat on the floor. Consequently she dropped a large amount on the carpet. She then started to play with the hoops and move them across the carpet. Mr A was extremely cross about this and he told her to pick them all up. When she did not do this, he bent down beside her and said in an aggressive tone, 'You're gross you are'.

Mr A had expected Sarah to eat her dinner whilst seated on the floor. Given her age, there was a high chance that Sarah would spill some of it. Yet he was angered when this happened and verbally insulted her for doing so. Despite Sarah's lack of understanding of words such as 'gross', she was still regularly exposed to negative and aggressive tones directed at her from both Mr and Mrs A. This, of course, will have begun to impact on her levels of self-esteem and self-worth, the root cause of which being an unfavourable mix of her parents' limited child development knowledge and mentalization difficulties.

Supporting parents needs to focus on improving mentalization abilities as well as their knowledge of child development. A parent will struggle to see something from a child's perspective when their expectations of their child are beyond or below that of which they are developmentally capable. Here are another two observation examples:

> During one of my visits it was a cold evening and Sarah was wearing just a nappy, yet Mrs A was wearing a jumper and jogging bottoms. She herself felt warm and therefore struggled to think that Sarah would be experiencing things differently. I informed Mrs A that Sarah's nappy appeared heavy and in need of changing. This was a regular occurrence during my visits, and although Mrs A would notice that Sarah's nappy needed changing, she would often not change it. Mrs A was unable to think about Sarah's experience of being in a dirty nappy and, most importantly, the physical discomfort Sarah would be feeling.

> During another visit, Sarah had been undressed whilst Mr A was running the bath. She was wandering around the flat naked. At this time Mr and Mrs A had made no attempts to potty-train her, but would sometimes say, 'She knows where the toilet is'. Before being placed in the bath, Sarah had urinated on the carpet. When Mrs A discovered this she became angry and shouted, 'That's horrible!' She then took Sarah's arm and led her over to the wet patch on the carpet, and made sure Sarah was facing it. She bent down next to Sarah and said in an aggressive and increasingly loud tone, 'Look at this! Are you sorry…are you?' Sarah did not respond and looked down. Mrs A then said, 'You're horrible. You're a horrible child'. Mrs A believed that Sarah had done this deliberately and thus felt the need for her to be punished.

Perhaps one of the most worrying things about this observation is the fact that this occurred whilst in my presence. I was therefore concerned about what went on when this family was alone. Practitioners need to be careful about saying this in court, as defence lawyers will point out that 'the witness is not required to be clairvoyant!' Nevertheless, it is important to be aware that a parent who struggles to mentalise their child will also struggle to mentalise the practitioner as they do not appreciate what is problematic about what they have said or done.

After completing my observations, which were conducted both in the family home and also in the community, I used the assessment tools within the ADAM framework to further add to my analysis of their parenting capacity.

I used a guided parenting task (see Chapter 6) with both parents and witnessed intrusive and insensitive behaviours, such as not letting Sarah use the felt-tip colour that she wanted, simply because Mrs A was using it. When Sarah was not looking at Mr A, he would remove the toy with which she was playing and as she reached for it back he would begin to give it to her and then take it away. In his mind this was a game, whilst Sarah was becoming increasingly upset and confused. The 'don't touch' task with both parents resulted in Sarah throwing herself on the floor in frustration. Neither parent communicated with Sarah; therefore, she was not distracted by anything else but wanted to play with a Barbie doll. Mr A repeated in a loud voice, 'Don't… don't…don't' whenever Sarah reached for it. The reading task was equally distressing to watch as Sarah was pinned down in between Mr A's legs whilst he tried to get her to look at the book. Sarah became increasingly distressed but Mr A failed to recognise her level of distress and the fact that he was causing this.

Alongside my written observations I used the Disconnected and extremely Insensitive Parenting (DIP) scale to explore more deeply what they were struggling with. Ordinarily I would have also used the Adult Attachment Interview with both parents; however this had already been completed as part of the assessment in the court proceedings. I read through the interview and was not surprised to read that both parents had experienced significant childhood maltreatment and neglect, which appeared to be unresolved. The Pathway Model provided a framework to use in terms of piecing together what I knew about the parents' attachment experiences, how this may have contributed to their parental behaviours and the impact of this on their attachment relationship with Sarah.

I felt fairly certain that before I began my intervention work with the family, there was a very small chance of improving their parenting capacity, owing to their low levels of mentalizing capacity and consequent insensitive behaviour. Regardless of this, due to the fact that the case was in court proceedings, if I was going to be stating that these parents lacked the capacity for change, then I needed to evidence all attempts at working with them.

I provided Mr and Mrs A with feedback from my observations and the guided parenting task, and highlighted the concerning behaviours that I had witnessed from them. This was done with each parent separately in order to ensure a more structured session and limit feelings of animosity between the two of them. When I recalled the incidences of insensitivity towards Sarah, both parents said that they could not remember saying or doing those things. If this was the case, despite the difficulty in recalling those events, one would hope a parent would be shocked at what they had done or at least acknowledge that it was inappropriate; however, at the core of such emotions is the ability to mentalise and therefore understand what might be occurring in Sarah's mind during those times of insensitivity and aggression.

I asked both parents questions in order to get their perspectives on the events I had observed, and I encouraged them to think about what Sarah may have been thinking and feeling: 'What do you think Sarah might have been thinking at this point, and what makes you think this? How do you think Sarah may have felt, and why?' I then explained to the parents what I thought Sarah may have been thinking and feeling and what it was about her presentation or communication that was telling me this. This is where I began to use child development knowledge regarding children's emotional needs and its importance. If deemed appropriate, and certainly if it is not possible to conduct an Adult Attachment Interview, a session could be scheduled in which the parent is asked to reflect back on their own parenting experiences and the impact they think this may or may not have had on them. They can be asked whether there are things they would do the same along with what they might do differently.

I structured the majority of my support work around play sessions with both parents. This gave me the opportunity to encourage the parents to have positive one-to-one time with Sarah and for me to model the tone of voice, communication and actions. In my experience, even if a family has a negative attitude towards me at the beginning, once they see me sitting on the floor, making play dough shapes or playing a game, and they see their child smiling and enjoying positive interaction with me, they begin to feel less threatened. In the most optimistic situations they are left feeling eager to achieve this level of positive interaction themselves and this can help to bring down their defensive barrier when it comes to listening to advice.

For many parents the prospect of getting down on their knees and playing with their child is daunting, due to its unfamiliarity, and they may feel embarrassed. It is encouraged, however, because apart from benefiting the child, it provides practitioners with an important opportunity to help a parent see things from their child's perspective. Examples of questions to ask parents during the play session include:

1. What do you think your child is thinking and what are they doing or saying to make you believe this?

2. Do you feel they are giving you any signs that they want you to join? If so, what are they? If not, what are they doing to make you feel that way?

3. When you do join, how do you think your child feels about this and what do they do to show you they are feeling this way?

In these sessions using the method of 'speaking for the child' can prove to be effective. If a parent struggles with cues, the child is 'given a voice' (by the practitioner) in order to help them understand what is occurring in their child's mind. For example, with Sarah, when Mrs A would not let her use the felt-tip colour she wanted, I might say, 'I would really like to draw with that one mummy; mummy, can I have that one?' In another example, if I were to observe a child resting their hand on a parent's lap, I could give the child's response as, 'It's nice to feel you next to me; it makes me feel close to you'.

In the case of Mr and Mrs A, they did engage in a handful of play sessions, but they failed to prioritise sessions and frequently had visitors over during the times we had agreed. On occasions they would say there were other things they had to do, or there were places they needed to be. There were times when they would be angered or irritated by something and would tell me that they were not in the mood for our session. Sarah, however, was always in the mood and this highlighted their difficulty acknowledging her enjoyment and prioritizing this over their own needs.

The Pathway Model helped me to structure my work from the first few visits through to writing my assessment at the end. The assessment tools supplied me with information at the beginning that was far more informative than simply meeting with a family and having a discussion. The observations were perhaps the most powerful part of the work that I did, as they provided important evidence of the parent's restricted ability to mentalise and the damaging effect this was having on all areas of Sarah's development and emotional well-being. The model also enabled me to offer the parents support that had a precise focus. They lived a very chaotic lifestyle, and for their benefit, as well as mine, I needed to be clear about exactly what it was I wanted them to improve. This also enabled me to assess whether any improvements already had been made.

Conclusion

In conclusion, this case had not been addressed properly for three years, with negative implications for Sarah and her development. Professionals were all in agreement that her situation was not 'good enough' but struggled to articulate the ways in which this had manifested. The Pathway Model played an important part in providing the analysis needed to achieve the best outcome for Sarah.

Chapter 5

Identifying Low Mentalizing Capacity Using the Adult Attachment Interview

David Wilkins

I applied the Pathway Model using the Adult Attachment Interview (AAI) with three of the parents from the two families I discuss in this chapter. I also used the framework and ideas contained within the model as a way of organizing and understanding the other information I gathered from other methods.

By using the AAI, I was hoping to find out more about the mentalizing abilities of the parents. As I explain in the following sections, in the two families I worked with I felt there was a need to understand how far the parents were able to appreciate the intentions and feelings of their children and, in the first family (Family A), each other as parents. Although parents can simply be asked whether they understand the minds of their children, it is a difficult concept to assess without a formal assessment tool such as the AAI. In what might be described as typical 'question-and-answer' sessions, we may notice that the parent speaks somewhat unsympathetically about their child, that they seem to struggle to articulate the child's needs and desires, but without the kind of framework provided by the Pathway Model, it is not always possible to explain the potential importance of this and how it might affect the child in question. By using the AAI, I was able to gain more insight into the minds of the parents being assessed but to also place the information I gathered from other sources into a more coherent framework for understanding their parenting capacity.

Case studies

At the time of the work, there were concerns about the children, albeit in quite different ways, in both families discussed below.

Case 1: Family A

Family A comprised Mr A, Mrs A and their two children, Roger and Naomi. Roger was known to the local authority because he was a 'child in need' due to his diagnosis of Down syndrome. At the time of the intervention, Roger was eight years of age and his sister, Naomi, was 16 years of age. Mr and Mrs A had separated acrimoniously some years prior to the period presented, and since that time, Mr A lived in Germany whilst Mrs A and the children moved to the UK. After several years in the UK, Naomi disclosed to a teacher that her mother regularly hit and beat Roger, including with implements such as belts and shoes. The local authority applied for an emergency protection order and subsequently an interim care order. For a brief period, the children were placed with foster carers; however, when Mr A heard about what was happening, he moved to the UK and sought an interim residence order for both children, which was duly granted by the court.

There followed a series of court hearings regarding final residence and contact, with the court eventually finding that Naomi's disclosures were probably true, and that the children should remain with their father. A contact order was put in place restricting the amount of time Mrs A could spend with Roger and initially requiring all such contact to be supervised. Naomi declined to have any contact with her mother, who maintained throughout that Naomi's disclosures were fabricated. Given her age and understanding, Naomi was not made the subject of a contact order. Contact between Roger and Mrs A took place at least weekly, but the organization of it and the relationship between Mrs A and Mr A remained very acrimonious. Mrs A regularly criticised Mr A, reporting relatively minor concerns, such as scuff marks on Roger's trainers or paint on his jumper, to his social worker. Mrs A would also make more significant allegations, suggesting that Mr A was not medicating Roger properly or that he was giving false or misleading information to professionals. Given the volume of these allegations, it became very difficult to know whether Mrs A was genuinely concerned about Roger or whether she was seeking to undermine Mr A's parenting, with the hope that the children, or at least Roger, might be returned to her care.

The situation remained as described for around 18 months before concerns began to increase regarding Mr A's care of the children. On several occasions, care staff visiting the home to support Roger noted that the house had mould on the walls, that he did not seem to have his own place to sleep and that Naomi was frequently asked to care for him. The situation culminated in the discovery that Mr A had left the country during a school holiday, leaving Roger and Naomi home alone. This came to the local authority's attention when, a few days after her father left, Naomi contacted her mother to say she needed help as she had no food in the house and could not take Roger out on her own. This led to Roger and Naomi being made the subject of child protection plans, with the concerns centring on: (a) Mr A's ability to understand his children's needs, particularly Roger's needs, alongside his impaired capacity to meet them, and (b) Mr and Mrs A's ability to understand the impact on the children of their continued animosity and their inability to work together as co-parents.

In typical interviews with Mr A and Mrs A, they both reported that whilst they *were* able to place the children's needs first and did understand the impact of the difficult family situation on them both, it was the other parent who did not and therefore was to blame. Due to Roger's learning disability, it was difficult to understand from him directly how he experienced daily life and significant events such as contact. In order to make more sense of what was going on, I interviewed Mr A and Mrs A separately using the AAI. Neither parent displayed any significant signs of dissociation or unresolved loss or trauma, although Mrs A did display low-level indications of both; however, what struck me from both interviews were the significantly low levels of mentalizing capacity demonstrated by both parents. The interview with Mrs A was especially interesting, as it revealed her own parents' history of separation and divorce and how these events had influenced what she believed post-separation parenting 'should' be like. The fact of Mrs A's own parents having separated when she was a young child was unknown, despite several social workers having taken apparently detailed family and social histories.

The use of the Pathway Model and the AAI in particular helped with Family A by making it easier to understand particularly Mrs A's behaviour with regards to contact arrangements and the difficulties that she and Mr A had in understanding Roger's needs. Mrs A recounted how her parents had separated and divorced when she was about five or six years old. Mrs A gave a series of very 'rose-tinted' examples of what life was like for the family afterwards. From Mrs A's recollection, it would appear that family life continued much as before, with her father an ever-present – a *physically* ever-present – person in her life, with the relationship between Mrs A's parents, if anything, improved by their separation and no sense of family discord whatsoever, even when Mrs A's parents started relationships with new partners. From Mrs A's descriptions, these new partners were quickly integrated into family life, along with their own children, and the family simply grew in size and happiness. Whilst such a scenario is not impossible to imagine, it was via the AAI's approach of seeking examples and probing 'feeling' states as well as memory states that enabled me to conclude that life had not been as resoundingly positive for Mrs A as she was describing. Indeed, based on ideas taken from the coding of the AAI, it became possible to understand that a realistic account of early memories should include a balance of positive and negative recollections, whereas Mrs A could not recall a single negative thing about her father. The most negative thing that Mrs A could tell me about him was that he was such a good artist that at times he would be so absorbed in his work and might not notice that a young Mrs A was watching him work; however, Mrs A ended this story by telling me how her life-long love of art was due to the influence of her father, so, in her view, even this potential flaw should really be understood as a positive.

The richness of this information and Mrs A's views on what separated parenting 'should' be like had not been obtained before, despite the local authority having worked with the family for over two years. It also helped me understand Mrs A's deep sense of loss regarding her family. I say this not because a sense of loss was inappropriate on Mrs A's part; clearly, she had lost the care of her children in difficult circumstances and her life changed substantially in a very short period of time. Nevertheless, there always appeared to be something going on 'under the surface' regarding her subsequent behaviour. After conducting the AAI, I was able to have a subsequent discussion with Mrs A about how she had hoped the relationship between Mr A, the children and her would develop post-separation and, as anticipated, Mrs A had very high expectations for how close they would be and how much time they would spend together as a group.

It also became somewhat easier for professionals to work with Mrs A, having been given a plausible explanatory framework for her behaviour and the number of allegations she made against Mr A. Although these allegations continued, albeit at a reduced level, professionals were often more able to engage Mrs A in a discussion about the reasons for the allegations, reminding her that post-separated parenting can be very difficult at times and that her expectations of Mr A and how he 'should' be treating her were not necessarily realistic. Although the more serious allegations she made could not, of course, be ignored, it was often possible to prompt Mrs A to show an increased level of insight into the more important aspects of Roger's care, such as managing his medical needs, on which they did need to agree, and that some instances, such as relatively minor scuffs or stains on his clothing, could be overlooked. The second way in which the use of the AAI helped with Family A was in providing an insight into Mr and Mrs A's understanding of Roger's needs. Recall that at this time Roger was the subject of a child protection plan and the trigger for this plan was that Mr A left Roger at home with only his older sister to care for him. Using the AAI with both Mr A and Mrs A, it became clear that both of them had relatively low mentalizing capacity. Both of them struggled to articulate how other people experienced a separate internal world from their own. Mrs A had a tendency to project onto other people her own feelings and assume that other people felt the same as she did. An example of this can be seen in this extract from Mrs A's interview:

> *DW*: How do you feel now when you are separated from your children?
>
> *Mrs A*: How do I feel, David? How can you ask me this, when you know how I feel? I feel like I have died a little inside. Like a part of me is missing, yes? This is how everyone feels when they are apart from the ones they love, from their little ones. And Naomi feels this too, even though she does not want you to know it because she is clever; she can hide how she feels from people like you, but from her own mother? No. She feels the same as me because she is the same as me and we are going through the same thing, the same things... So that is that...Roger, you cannot say because he is special. But he misses mommy, this is obvious. Obvious to you, to you, to you...even to the father. We feel...apart. Do you have another question?

This provided a framework for interpreting how she spoke about Roger, as she often appeared to assume that if she felt upset with Mr A, Roger must feel the same thing. The interview with Mr A was equally insightful, although for him, other people's internal worlds were apparently mysterious and unknowable; he often seemed confused about what other people might be feeling, and rather than attribute his own feelings to them, he would often 'give up' and acknowledge that he simply did not know what was occurring in other people's minds. An example of this can be seen in this extract from Mr A's interview:

DW: I wonder if you can tell me whether, as a child, you felt closer to one parent in particular?

Mr A: You mean now, who I am close to now? My mother.

DW: No…that's fine, yes, but as a child, do you remember feeling closer to one of your parents than the other?

Mr A: Oh, yes. Yes, well the same anyway. It's my mother. My mother was closest to us.

DW: Could you tell me a bit about why you say your mother, why you felt closer with your mother as a child?

Mr A: She was always there. She was there with us as children and, I just…I think she was the one who looked after us and did all the… you know, the things kids need like the cooking, the cleaning, the clothes. That kind of thing.

DW: And can you say why you did not feel as close with your father?

Mr A: My dad…my dad had to work. He worked all hours God sent and then some more. He was so dedicated to us. He loved us so much that he just could not stop working. He started with just a bag and he collected…I remember this bag actually; sometimes I used to get in it…or no, not me…I mean, it was my kid brother…he used to get in this bag and hide and dad would play this game, like uh-oh, where's my son, my baby son? But that's…anyway, you didn't think about the bag, did you? Dad, he just started with collecting and washing clothes and he was good, you know, he was good at it. So it went like that. But you asked about my mother, actually, so let me tell you about her. She worked hard. She worked so hard for us. She…I mean, it was obvious she loved us but…I mean. There was different…I can't say the words exactly, but I said I had lots of brothers and sisters, right? I said that. And she was closer to some than others, but I think she liked me the best so I liked her the best, you know…isn't that how kids think sometimes? I think so anyway. So she would do things for me, different things. Sometimes I don't know what she was going to do, but she would surprise me. So I felt close to her because kids like to get things like that...treats...and to feel...you know, to feel...think they are special.

DW: Do you know why she treated you differently? More special?

Mr A: No, you need to go and ask her that question. That question is not for me, you know. I can't ask you, oh why, why does your wife do this and do that? You'd tell me to go and ask her. You ask my mother. Why people do things? You're the social worker, not me!

This passage and others like it were useful in understanding two things about Mr A: that he would naturally struggle to understand why Mrs A acted the way she did regarding contact and other issues, but also that especially with a child such as Roger, who was primarily non-verbal in his communication, from Mr A's point of view this would make Roger almost opaque in terms of understanding his internal world. As Mr A said, his way of understanding why people behave as they behave is to 'go and ask (them)'. With Roger and Mrs A, for different reasons, Mr A could not ask them, and therefore, their motivations, their internal worlds, were a source of great mystery for him. This explained, but did not excuse, why Mr A had felt he could leave Roger for what he thought would be a short time in the care of Naomi. He had asked Naomi how she felt about this, and Naomi had reassured him that she would cope, and from Mr A's perspective, that was as much as he could hope to find out.

In conclusion, the above information informed the report provided to the court by the local authority regarding contact arrangements and also the progress of the child protection plan. We were able to take account of the need to allow for Mr and Mrs A's restricted understanding of each other's motivations and difficulty in interpreting the behaviour of other people based on underlying 'feeling' states. We did this, for example, by working with both parents on thinking about – together and separately – what the other parent might want to achieve from contact. Initially, both parents tended to say they did not know, but with prompting and support, they started to consider things such as the break from caring that Mr A would gain from contact and the feeling of being a mother that Mrs A would derive. As we were able to discuss these motivations openly, it was instructive to see the trust that Mr A and Mrs A had for one another increase.

Case 2: Family B

Family B comprised Mrs B, Mr B and their two children, Ben (two years of age) and Abigail (four years of age). Abigail was referred to the local authority by her nursery due to poor attendance, concerns about Mrs B appearing to be under the influence of alcohol when she collected her and reports from the police of incidents of violent domestic abuse between Mrs B and Mr B. These concerns led to both children being made subject to child protection plans. The assessment work up to that point indicated that Mr B was known to police as a possible drug dealer, that Mrs B was most likely a user of alcohol, cannabis and cocaine, and that Mrs B and Mr B's relationship was characterised by verbal and physical abuse.

We also received several reports from neighbours that they regularly heard shouting and screaming from inside the home, including what sounded like an adult female shouting that she would 'throw you down the stairs if you don't shut up'. Ben was found to be losing weight and missed several medical appointments. Abigail stopped attending nursery and, very quickly, Mrs B and Mr B began avoiding professionals. The local authority initiated legal proceedings and applied for an interim care order. The start of legal proceedings did, for a time, prompt the parents to re-engage with professionals and a parenting capacity assessment was completed for Mrs B and Mr B together. The results were not positive, and the plan for both children was to seek a final care order and place them with alternative carers; however, prior to the final court hearing, Mr B separated from Mrs B and took both children into his care and away from her. Mr B said that Mrs B would drink alcohol and take drugs every day, and that she would shout at him and the children. Mr B admitted he had been violent towards Mrs B, and that he had also taken drugs. Mr B told the court and the local authority that he would engage with any support programme they deemed necessary, and that he was determined to care for his children properly and safely.

The court asked the local authority to assess Mr B as a single carer and determine whether he had the potential to change and improve his parenting quickly enough to meet the needs of the children. It was as part of this assessment that I undertook an AAI with Mr B. At this point in the proceedings, Mrs B had again withdrawn from professional contact, so I was not able to use the same method with her. As noted above, there were significant concerns about Mr B's parenting and the situation the children had been in when living at home with Mr B and Mrs B.

The aim of completing an AAI with Mr B was to establish, as quickly as possible, how likely it was that he would be able to make the necessary changes in order to care safely for the children. What I wanted to know in particular was whether Mr B was able to understand the impact on the children of all the difficulties there had been in the family. Given what we knew about Mr B – that he was most likely a drug dealer, that he could be violent and that he took drugs himself – my expectation was that his ability to do this would be very low. It was something of a surprise, therefore, when Mr B was able to evidence a very high degree of mentalizing capacity, providing an insightful account of how his childhood had impacted on him as an adult and how things needed to change very quickly for his children in order that their life prospects could be improved. For example, Mr B spoke about the death of his sister when he was around eight years old. At the time, his sister was 16 years old, and Mr B described how she was having difficulties with depression, alcohol misuse and a violent ex-partner, and how she had one day walked in front of a bus and was killed. From Mr B's recollection – he was not sure at the time, and remained so now, whether she had done so on purpose or by accident – her death was unexpected and traumatic. Mr B gave a very insightful account of how this affected him and how it made him 'grow up very fast' and try to act how 'he thought a man should', which in his terms meant being tough and, where 'necessary', violent. Without seeking to excuse his own behaviour, Mr B's interview evidenced very strongly that he understood the links between the trauma he had experienced as a child and his own subsequent drug misuse as well as his difficulties with anger and violence towards others. Mr B also gave a very eloquent account of how Abigail could be affected by living with parents who are unpredictable, who shout at the children for no apparent reason and who make threats to each other and the children.

The outcome of this assessment work was that the local authority recommended to the court that the children be placed with their father, following a period in foster care to enable Mr B to engage in an anger management programme and get treatment for his drug use. Mr B completed both of these programmes very successfully, and within 12 months, the children were living with him and his new partner, attending school regularly. Ben had gained sufficient weight and was thriving, and the local authority was able to close the case. Having worked with what appeared to be very similar families on many occasions previously, it had been my expectation that the children would end up in permanent alternative care, with neither Mr B nor

Mrs B capable of making the necessary changes. By using the AAI and gaining detailed information on Mr B's surprisingly high abilities of mentalization, we were able to reassure the court that allowing the hearing to continue for another three to six months was reasonable and would likely be sufficient time for Mr B to demonstrate that he could make permanent changes.

Conclusion

I found the contrast between these two families to be very interesting. In Family A, I was able to use the model and the approach behind it to improve the levels of trust between the two parents. Although there were worries about the children in Family A, determining the level of concern about them was not the primary purpose of using the model in this case. In Family B, there were more significant reasons to be concerned about the children and, in this case, I applied the model to help determine whether the children would be safe enough with their father. As described above, it was interesting to find out that although there were lots of reasons to think Mr B would not prove capable of being a 'good enough' father, it was the use of the model that gave us sufficient reason to continue supporting him because he had the potential to improve. In other words, although the children in Family B were at risk as a result of alcohol consumption, drug misuse and the presence of domestic violence, and whilst these factors were clearly important in their own right, they were neither particularly helpful in assessing the risk to the children nor in planning how best to help and support the family, and then re-assess the risk subsequently; however, by obtaining a better understanding of Mr B's mentalizing capacity, it became easier to understand how the risk to the children could be managed and how his potential for change could be developed and ultimately lead to better outcomes for the children.

Chapter 6

Using a Guided Parenting Task

Lissil Averill

This chapter considers how the guided parenting task can be used to assess a child's risk of maltreatment from their carer/parent, within the framework of the Disconnected and extremely Insensitive Parenting (DIP) scale (Out *et al.* 2009). When used in conjunction with an Adult Attachment Interview, assessments are enriched by an insight into the emotional foundation from which the carer is parenting.

Guided parenting tasks may be used with any child who is still interested in playing with their parent. This chapter describes the process through the observation and analysis phases, and considers its value in the context of a statutory assessment.

Direct observation is useful for exploring the impact of a child's early relationships on their internal working model of attachment (McMahon and Farnfield 2004). The guided parenting task formulates a more structured, directive observation; the worker requests the parent to undertake four discrete activities with their child as follows:

- Ask the parent to be with their child whilst they play, but not to join in.

- Ask the parent to play with their child.

- Ask the parent, with the child, to tidy away all of the toys.

- Ask the parent to read a story book with their child.

It is also advisable sometimes to use a 'don't touch' task for the second task, whereby the parent is asked to introduce an attractive but unfamiliar toy...but the child cannot play with it yet. (They are, of course, given the toy after a minute or two!) The 'don't touch' task is something that all children and parents find difficult because it includes a level of 'challenge' for the parent. In terms of the Pathway Model it accelerates the speed with which the practitioner is able to assess the risk, by observing parenting under mild pressure. The purpose of doing this, however, is to be able to work out with them what help and support would be best. In total, these observations can be done in around 30 minutes, which would mean each step taking around five to ten minutes.

We know intuitively that the presence of an onlooker alters the natural order of a relationship. When this onlooker is a child protection professional, it follows that the parent may act more sensitively – or less harshly – than usual; however, if their parent is acting differently to how they are accustomed, the child would seem surprised or confused and, for this reason, the method requires close attention to the child's responses. The ADAM Project advises that, whilst video recording the session is preferable, it is possible to analyse the behaviour 'from memory' later.

Observation of the parent's sensitivity and responsiveness to their child informs an assessment of disconnected and extremely insensitive parenting, a building block of the Pathway Model. Mindful of this underpinning research, during the guided parenting task the worker should pay attention to the nature of the communication between parent and child (e.g. their facial expressions). Does the parent seem interested and engaged? Does the child seek the parent's interaction or help during the first task? What constitutes the verbal communication; is the child allowed to speak? We are looking for indicators such as eye contact, signs of openness and engagement. When joining in the play in the second task, is the parent being led by the child, or taking over? Is the parent critical of the child's attempts to play, or even attributing negative interpretations to the child's actions? Are they smiling at one another, enjoying their time together? When tidying away, we are looking at whether the parent imposes or negotiates this boundary and how they involve the child in the task, through verbal and non-verbal communication. Throughout all of the tasks, the parent's facial expressions are crucial: Do they display any of the frightening behaviours that are indicative of low mentalizing capacity, such as scary facial expressions, assuming an attack pose or freezing (Hesse and Main 2006)? This may link to the risk factors for disorganised attachment identified by Out *et al.* (2009). When used in conjunction with an Adult Attachment Interview (AAI), the guided parenting task becomes particularly informative of the parent's experience, and provides an opportunity to explore whether they are parenting in the context of unresolved loss or trauma.

Shemmings and Shemmings (2011) describe how unresolved loss and trauma can result in disconnected, insensitive parenting. In the Pathway Model they illustrate how, when this results in low mentalizing capacity, there is a heightened risk of child maltreatment. Out *et al.* (2009) surmise that a parent's disconnected behaviours may be reduced by redirecting their attention to the child, thus preventing absorption and the intrusion of unresolved memories and affects. Video recording the guided parenting task provides an opportunity to reflect with the parent on how they are interacting with their child, to point out to the parent times when the child responds positively to their interaction, and thus reinforce this positive behaviour by giving the parent more confidence and greater insight into the child's experience.

Case studies

In order to illustrate the application of the guided parenting task, I will discuss two parent-child dyads with whom I worked in a statutory referral and assessment team.

Case 1: Danny and Nicky

Danny had just turned four years old when his mother Nicky was anonymously reported to the duty social work team on two occasions, approximately eight weeks apart. The referrer said Nicky was frequently heard to shout at Danny at home, and he had been seen walking behind her 'crying his eyes out' on a local pavement the previous day. The referrer reported seeing Nicky shouting to an adult male outside the house that she 'didn't want the child anyway'. Nicky, now 24 years old, was previously known to children's services, having entered the young people's homeless pathway as a teenager, following difficulties with her relationship with her parents. Her relationship with Danny's father had been characterised by domestic abuse and she had proactively ended the relationship; legal orders were obtained and there was no current contact with him. She was now a relatively young single parent and, while her relationship with her own parents was now improved, this had been a stressor in the past.

When the first referral was received, a duty social worker had attended the family home unannounced to ascertain whether there were signs of neglect of Danny and discuss the referral with Nicky. A full assessment was not undertaken as there were no concerns from the professional network or from this initial contact with the family and the referral was concluded as likely to have been malicious. The assessment of the subsequent referral, therefore, needed to be more robust and enquiring. Children's services needed to be satisfied that Danny was not experiencing emotional or physical harm. Also, social work resources needed to be used effectively to avoid every anonymous referral resulting in the deployment of social workers to check on the child's welfare on an ad hoc basis. I felt that only a live observation of Danny and Nicky's relationship would adequately inform such an assessment.

Nicky's reaction to the referrals was rather defensive. She was quite fixed on figuring out the identity of the referrers, and in gaining acknowledgement from the social worker that it is not 'illegal' to shout at children. I gave Nicky the opportunity to release her frustration about the consecutive referrals and describe the relational system, within her family and community, in which she is parenting. Rooke (2012) describes how facilitating families to 're-story' their lives with the social worker is enabling and empowering, refocusing the family narrative from problem-saturated stories to one that recognises the system in which the family lives. The therapeutic value of being listened to was immediately gratifying for both Nicky and myself, and set a positive starting point for the guided parenting task.

For Nicky, the proposal to use the method was met with apprehension. She articulated nervousness about being 'judged', about feeling awkward playing with Danny in front of a stranger, and even suggested that Danny would feel awkward for the same reason. In line with anti-oppressive practice, I was mindful of the power dynamic for Nicky of having a social worker in her home, investigating her relationship with her child and proposing that the way they interact on this visit would be indicative of her parenting style. I offered the parallel scenario that, were she to watch me at my keyboard, I would likely make many typing errors but my ability to spell would still be clear, trying to acknowledge to her that feeling scrutinised is universally uncomfortable but the essential quality of what is observed will remain evident. Of course, alongside and as part of assessment, the practitioner is exploring how best to help the family and the parenting by observing interactions.

To begin, I asked Nicky to watch Danny play for five minutes without participating, and Nicky described this to Danny quite clearly. For the first few minutes, Nicky interspersed appropriate comments and encouragement of Danny's play with nervous laughter and declarations of embarrassment to me. Although the worker should remain quiet and uninvolved, I could not desist from assuring her that this was fine and that I was not laughing at her interactions. Danny, meanwhile, appeared pleased to have his mother's full attention and keen to involve her in his play. As the tasks moved on, it seemed clear that Danny was used to playing with Nicky and the themes he was introducing in his play were following those of previous play sessions – names and games which meant nothing to me were introduced and implicitly understood by both Danny and his mother. At no point did Danny appear taken aback at this focused engagement with his mother. When it came to the tidy-up task, Danny asked whether it was time to go to bed 'even though she's [me] here', and Nicky informed me that their normal routine is to play after dinner, before Danny goes to bed. When Nicky told Danny they would read a story next, he went without hesitation to retrieve a selection of books. Nicky reasoned with him that some were unsuitable (not enough words, too long) and he did not argue. He settled next to her with a particular cuddly toy and was immediately quiet. He assumed a natural posture and it appeared quite clear that this was not an unusual activity for him.

Nicky, meanwhile, was energetic and appeared able to relate to Danny's play. She reinforced his positive play, and discouraged the more aggressive pathways he was taking. (It was in this that I felt my presence was most keenly felt!) She took Danny's lead in the narrative he was creating in his play, they shared physical space with ease and shared eye contact when interacting verbally. When Danny's inspiration faltered in his game, Nicky gently suggested other things to do with the characters. When Danny was reluctantly tidying up, Nicky appeared patient, repeating the same consistent instruction to him. He responded, albeit testing her resolve by doing it slowly, and was able to suggest to his mother a 'compromise' of keeping one toy during the reading. Nicky remained engaged with Danny throughout all of the tasks, and when reading the story, she encouraged regular eye contact at points where, for example, the story was gaining pace, using intonation to which Danny responded by making animated faces back to her.

I arranged an additional visit with Nicky, during school time, to do the AAI. Nicky was able to discuss her own childhood in clear terms, identifying patterns and reasonable explanations for her experiences. For example, when talking about her teenage years, she reflected on her parents' responses to her in terms of their cultural backgrounds, her position as their only child and her own boundary testing, and she related these themes to her own position as a mother. The AAI includes three questions for indicating low mentalizing capacity, including asking the interviewee: (a) to think about how their childhood has affected their adulthood, (b) to think about causes and reasons for their own parents' behaviour towards them as children and (c) to reflect upon whether overall their mother/father loved them as a child. The indicators for unresolved loss and trauma – inconsistencies and lapses in discourse – were absent from Nicky's narrative; instead, she coherently related her present to her past, and her parents' behaviours and relationships to her own. Thus, the AAI complemented the guided parenting task and confirmed my assessment that Danny is unlikely to be subject to ongoing maltreatment.

Case 2: Joey and Louise

The second child with whom a guided parenting task was used, Joey (age three years), lived with his mother, Louise (age 35 years), and his brother, Conor (age seven years). The family had already had a succession of social work assessments related to serious domestic abuse. Conor had no contact with his father, the perpetrator of the domestic abuse, and described Joey's father, Dan, as being his own father. Dan was currently in prison for violent crime. Louise's eldest child, Becky (age 14 years), lived apart from the family with her father (for reasons which were unclear).

This assessment followed Louise's contact with the mental health team after self-reporting that she was having a breakdown, and that she required support from family services because she was unable to cope with being a full-time parent alone. My initial visit piqued my concern about what life was like for Conor and Joey, particularly due to Conor's descriptions of Louise's problems (e.g. 'mum's family is being mean to her' and 'mum had to hit and kick Becky because she was naughty') and the home environment – clean and tidy in the communal areas, but when I asked to see where Louise and Joey sleep, Louise said I could not. Once I persuaded Louise to let me see it, I found it to be extremely cluttered, dark and oppressive. Additionally, Conor tried to hug me on a number of occasions and tried to sit on my lap and give me his mobile phone number, while Louise laughed and called him a flirt. In subsequent contacts with Conor, I was able to establish his wishes and feelings using other direct work methods; however, given Joey's stage of development, his experience was better understood through the guided parenting task, as shown below.

Louise is, in the main, an antagonistic user of social work services. Her attitude to social work and public services generally was ambivalent: she simultaneously pleaded for help from services while describing in clear terms the antipathy and contempt she felt for the social care system and all those working within it. Therefore, her children were at risk of being shunted away behind the shield of aggression and derision she was erecting. I was effectively being worn down, and it was indeed effective. However, Shemmings and Shemmings (2011) anticipate such responses from families, aware that this is the reality of all too many of the interventions required of social workers; thus, they recommend that the worker try to engage the parent in reciprocated mentalizing, whereby both the professional and the parent are geared away from confrontation and towards thinking about how the other experiences things. Demonstrating empathy, or even just a willingness to try to empathise, 'makes the other person feel valued, enabling them to feel their thoughts and feelings have been heard, acknowledged and respected' (Baron-Cohen 2011, p.13).

Establishing a workable, trusting relationship with Louise was time-consuming but, without this groundwork, the guided parenting task would have been impossible. When the time came to attempt the task, Louise's anxiety manifested in loud comments deriding social work practice, at which both children looked at me with eyes widened. My insistence that this was a fairer and more transparent method to assess the children's welfare was on thin ice, but we got started nevertheless.

Louise did not describe to Joey or Conor what we were going to do. Joey had been banging Lego pieces together for some time, and Louise sat down with arms folded next to him. Where the parent sits in relation to the child – enabling eye contact or not – can be informative about how accustomed they are to playing with their child (Shemmings and Shemmings 2011). Joey continued banging, and Louise commented how aggressive he is, how he is 'a devil child' while Conor is soft 'like a poofter'. Joey did not initially acknowledge Louise's presence, and she did not engage with him during this task, only rolling her eyes at having to do the task. My own discomfort caused me to shorten the allotted time for this task, and I asked Louise to join his play after less than five minutes. Joey had begun to move around the room by now (and Conor had not responded to the direction to go to his room and play on his own during this time) so Louise caught his attention, shouting 'Oi' and throwing a brick gently towards his feet. He guffawed, picked the brick up and ran towards Louise with the brick in his hand as though to hit her shoulder with it. Louise turned to me and said, 'See? He's always hitting me, the devil' and, to Joey, she said, 'You should cherish your mother, like I cherish you', while holding his wrist. He continued chortling. Conor then attempted to get Joey to play with him, next to Louise. Louise remained with the boys as they played – Conor making a wall out of the Lego and Joey, still laughing unrestrainedly, driving a car into it. Louise was not joining in the Lego game, and talked about how many toys the children have, and how 'spoiled' they are. To refocus her on the task, I suggested she try to play with Joey and the cars. She took Joey's car from him and 'drove it' gently along his back before rolling the wheels along her own hand. He was still laughing, running in circles and over to the window. Conor continued building his Lego wall, asking me to comment on it, watching his mother and smiling (weakly, I felt) at her. Again, I accelerated the task time and asked Louise to request Joey to tidy. Joey was unperturbed about the toys being put away – he was no longer playing with them – but would not help in tidying. After a few demands that he tidy (Conor had started to do this), Louise stood up and left the room, walked into the kitchen and came back again saying, 'I don't care anymore'. I cajoled her into continuing with the task (without tidying up) to read a book with Joey. She said this was a waste of time and that she needs to concentrate on herself, that she is always thinking of the kids and that the only reason I was there was because she had requested support.

Clearly, this guided parenting task was technically quite unsuccessful in terms of Louise demonstrating her parenting and engagement with her children. In fact, I felt stressed by the observation and was keen to leave the house as soon as possible! However, it was also a microcosm of the general engagement between Louise and Joey – and illustrative of Conor's role in the family. I could not see Louise deriving any pleasure in engaging with her sons; she quickly described Joey in highly negative terms. Bakermans-Kranenburg and Van IJzendoorn (2007) found that attributing negative intentionality to a child is a feature of maltreating parents. It also indicates low mentalizing capacity (Shemmings and Shemmings 2011).

Louise also demonstrated intrusiveness when grabbing Joey's car from him. She was disconnected, literally, from the children's play, but also demonstrated 'disconnectedness' in the DIP's use of the term, i.e. showing a sudden, unpredictable change in behaviour by abruptly leaving, and saying frightening things in the children's presence (e.g. 'I don't care anymore'). She exhibited no affection towards the children during this session, nor at any other time that I had contact with the family.

My task of then sitting with Louise and reflecting together on the positive aspects of the interaction felt difficult; however, I pointed out the value for the children in knowing that she was sitting with them while they played. Louise counteracted each positive with a negative attribute both to herself and the children and concluded the conversation by saying that the setting was artificial and that my presence made the children uneasy because they know I want to take them away from her. I needed to spend a lot more time in the 'reciprocal-mentalization' phase with Louise before this intervention would sink in enough to benefit Joey and Conor.

Following this, I felt apprehensive about continuing my assessment with the AAI. After some false starts, Louise engaged with the AAI and appeared to find it cathartic, at least, to reflect on her own experiences of being parented; however, quite quickly, some of Hesse and Main's (2006) indicators emerged in her narrative. Her reflections on her life experiences – encompassing sexual abuse, domestic violence and a murder – were peppered with inordinate attention to minor details, and some contradictory descriptions of her own primary attachments. As Crittenden (2008) succinctly puts it, 'what s/he can't say coherently suggests what s/he doesn't understand'. As this method was described more fully in Chapter 5, suffice it to summarise that Louise's discourse and presentation indicated that she may be parenting in the context of unresolved loss and trauma.

Case comparisons

For Danny and Nicky, my stated goals for this intervention rang true at the conclusion of the assessment. I was able to gain an insight into Danny's experience of being parented that went beyond loose observations of his home environment or general interactions in a possibly staged domestic situation, and instead the parent and child had an opportunity to engage positively with one another and for this to be considered in terms of sensitivity and responsiveness. Nicky was able to understand the assessment process and felt empowered; her confidence was boosted by its outcome. The social work department was reassured by this assessment and felt it was sufficiently robust to counter the anonymous referrals and conclude that no ongoing social work involvement would be necessary. Personally, I feel the absence of subsequent referrals for this family may be due to the positive reinforcement that Nicky derived from the process; perhaps her interactions with Danny have been tempered now, focusing more on the positive methods she employs and weeding out her less sensitive parenting behaviours. This, of course, is unmeasurable and merely my own, possibly over-optimistic, hypothesis.

For Joey and Louise, the outcome was less encouraging. The interaction observed during the guided parenting task was in itself cause for concern. Louise matched up to the descriptors of 'extreme insensitivity' (Shemmings and Shemmings 2011, p.167): failing to initiate responsive behaviour to Joey when he was playing, being physically intrusive towards him – grabbing his toy, later his arm – handling him roughly, and acting and speaking negatively about both children. Observing disconnected behaviours is the point at which video recording is especially useful, as these can be subtle and more difficult to articulate. Louise's behaviour during the guided parenting task indicated a degree of disconnectedness (e.g. unpredictably leaving the room and her trance-like rolling of the toy despite all the action around her). This, coupled with the extreme insensitivity observed and assessed in light of her Adult Attachment Interview, corroborated strongly with the associated risk factors for child maltreatment. Joey was observed to have unregulated emotional reactions to Louise, never calming down or having any meaningful interaction with her for the duration of the activity. Conor, meanwhile, four years Joey's senior, was watchful and pensive, trying to help Louise in a way which I construed as 'parentified' and indicative of a very insecure attachment, characterised by fear of unpredictable outbursts and the consistent threat of a loss of control. Mapping these indicators onto the maltreatment pathway model, I felt confident concluding that Louise's children were at risk of maltreatment on the basis that she exhibited extremely insensitive and disconnected parenting. Coupled with her likely unresolved loss and trauma, these characteristics were liable to combine their effects along with low mentalizing capacity.

Perhaps the most challenging task for a child protection professional is that of confirming an antagonistic parent's worst fears. While this intervention attracted a reasonable amount of hostility and aggression, in itself the approach can be quite therapeutic. For Louise, she was given an opportunity to be heard, to present her own life history and create her own narrative for the assessment. She also understood how the assessment would be undertaken, by way of the guided parenting task, rather than experiencing what must be an uneasy ambiguity – a practitioner in her home looking, asking and talking, then returning some weeks later with a written account of her family, in possibly unintelligible jargon, based on glimpses of the interactions during that visit and derived from seemingly untailored conversation. With the guided parenting task, the assessment process was identifiable. It was also grounded in a clear research base through which I could approach an understanding of the children's attachment patterns and identify a clear risk of maltreatment for Conor and Joey. While held in the duty team, there was no presenting evidence of actual maltreatment; however, the 'gut feeling' of anxiety that the family evoked in me was bolstered by the evidence base and the children were made subject to child protection plans, with a view to supporting Louise to develop her parenting, with a specific emphasis on developing mentalizing capacity and reducing frightening behaviours.

Conclusion

In conclusion, the value of using the Pathway Model in these cases was twofold. As a child protection practitioner, assessments are made using evidence-based, theoretically sound practice. The confidence derived from using clearly defined assessment methods, and a deepened understanding of the layers of attachment behaviours for both caregivers and children, is immediately evident in social work assessments. My new-found understanding of the impact of low mentalization, for example with Louise, turned an 'uneasy feeling' into a clear analysis of the emotional basis from which she was parenting and the evidence-based likelihood that Conor and Joey were at risk of maltreatment.

The model was also valuable for the parents involved. They were able to identify the manner of the assessment process and therefore understand the conclusion of that assessment and how it was reached. Beyond this, it provides caregivers with the opportunity to illustrate their parenting techniques directly, which for Nicky was especially useful to counteract the third-party claims bringing her parenting into question. The guided parenting task also caters for a 'positive feedback loop', where the worker is able to identify positive elements of the parenting with the parent. This bolsters the caregivers' confidence and, perhaps, gratification in their work as parents, thereby reinforcing the positive caregiving behaviours.

Chapter 7

Using a Strange Situation Procedure and Guided Parenting Tasks

Yvonne Shemmings and Michelle Thompson

In this chapter we explore in more detail the use of some of the features of the Pathway Model with a young, single mother, Leah, and her two-and-a-half-year-old son, Riley, who does not yet use language. At the time of our involvement, Leah lived with Riley in a flat where she was helped to move after a series of domestic abuse events perpetrated by her partner, the father of Riley, who was known to the police as a user of cocaine and someone with problematic alcohol use. The relationship had been marked by violence, but nevertheless Leah continued to see him after the move, despite the fact that she was regularly rejected and humiliated by him, as well as experiencing sexual and financial abuse. He showed little interest in his son, calling both him and Leah derogatory names.

The family had come to the attention of the social services department after concerns were expressed by Riley's health visitor about his development and Leah's demeanour, and as a result of an assessment Riley became subject to a child protection plan (CPP) initially under the category of 'emotional harm' and subsequently under the category of 'neglect'. Riley's father did not co-operate with the CPP, but under the auspices of the plan a support worker was allocated to Leah as she received statutory visits from the local authority social worker. She went to parenting groups but rarely stayed for the whole session. They yielded no discernible change.

Riley's development and behaviour continued to be of concern. The professionals involved with him noticed that he rocked back and forth during home visits, and would focus on looking at his fingers and thumbs, rather than seeking to explore. He had not started to speak, despite there being no organic or physiological reason for the delay. He was left for long periods in his cot or chair and as a consequence had not crawled. Riley did not learn to walk until he was 17 months old, but when he did start he frequently had bumps and bruises, thought to be a result of being left alone and unsupervised while Leah slept.

It emerged during assessment that Leah had experienced a troubled childhood, including sexual abuse from her violent stepfather, and she described the relationship with her mother as lacking in warmth and protection, leaving Leah, in effect, to raise herself. She spent much of her time alone in her room, with only the television for company. Leah had experienced suicidal ideation and had been assessed as suffering with depression.

Offers of help had not been successful, but due to Riley's age and the continuing concerns about his developmental delay, combined with the evident difficulties that Leah was experiencing, it was thought that alternative methods of intervention should be explored to attempt to increase her sensitivity responsiveness towards Riley (we discuss this in Chapter 8). It was considered important to try to see how, and in what ways, Leah's own experiences were specifically impacting on the way she was parenting Riley. Using traditional observation and interview techniques alone were not making an impact on Riley's experience of being parented. Parenting classes had not produced the changes that had been desired. Family support visits had not made progress in helping Leah become more sensitive to Riley, nor had there been an increase in the bonding and attachment relationship between them. As mentioned above, there had been reported instances of Riley rocking and head banging, as well as some indications that he sought comfort from relative strangers while in the presence of his mother. It was becoming apparent that alternative methods might help accelerate some understanding of the situation.

Disconnected and extremely insensitive parenting is thought to be associated with, among other things, unresolved trauma and loss. Although it was known that Leah had been abused as a teenager, and that she had experienced a separation from her mother (and stepfather) for three years when she was sent to live with relatives, it was not clear whether she was left with unresolved loss or trauma, and as a result whether she might display 'dissociative' behaviour when in the presence of her son. To explore this, we conducted an Adult Attachment Interview with her, not to establish specifically what attachment 'style' she had, but to get an indication as to whether she showed signs of unresolved loss or trauma. Leah found the prompts about connections between the way she was brought up as a child and the way she was bringing up Riley very difficult; indeed, she saw none. Although the interview did not indicate specific *unresolved* loss or trauma, she did describe a childhood in which her mother largely ignored her and during which she spent much of her time alone in her room. In adolescence she was sexually abused by her mother's new partner, and she was sent to live with relatives. When talking further about her experiences and her family background, she found it difficult to empathise with a family member who had become severely disabled, comparing her coping ability unfavourably to others in the same situation. Her demeanour was flat and lacked emotional openness during the interview.

Strange Situation Procedure

Because of the behaviours that Riley was exhibiting, we wanted to see, using the Strange Situation Procedure (SSP), if he showed signs of disorganised attachment. There are variations of the SSP, but we used the following steps:

1. The parent sits and plays with the child or quietly observes their child while she or he plays.

2. A stranger enters unannounced, chats with the parent and then approaches the child with a toy.

3. The parent leaves quietly. The stranger leaves the child to play with the toy unless he or she stops, and then the stranger tries to interest the child in them.

4. The parent returns and waits for the child to respond. The stranger leaves quietly.

5. Once the child is settled, the parent leaves again.

6. The stranger re-enters and tries to interest the child with another toy.

7. The parent comes back, waits for the child to respond. The stranger leaves inconspicuously.

Riley settled quickly to playing with the toys in the unfamiliar room, confidently walking around the room exploring what was there. Leah sat immediately adjacent to the door. He played with the beads on the baby bouncer chair, which contained a doll. When Leah moved a toy with wheels Riley went to see it, looked at her and took it. He then went to the door and banged it with his hand and she directed him away. He went to a table and found a toy and began to play. He had his back to Leah, with the door on his left. Leah looked over to where he was with one hand raised to her mouth and the other hand across her body. The stranger entered the room and Riley briefly glanced up at her as she entered and went past him to sit opposite Leah. He did not look at Leah. The stranger sat down. After one minute, Riley glanced at the stranger and then looked at Leah and went to the door, banged it and smiled at Leah, who impassively looked at him, remaining in the same position with her hand to her mouth and the other hand across her body. Riley looked over to the stranger and smiled while moving to a different part of the room. When Leah left the room for the first separation, he quickly noticed, and despite the stranger encouraging him to play, he tried to run out after her. When Leah came back into the room she did not speak to him, but he quickly settled to play with the same toy on the table. The stranger left the room and then Leah left the room. During the second separation, he took three seconds to notice that Leah had left (because he was engrossed in the toy), although she was about a metre away from him. He looked around and went to the door. He then vocalised with a short tonal screech of protest and tried to open the door. He went across the room to the sofa where the stranger had been sitting and returned to the door and started to 'cry hard'.

The stranger re-entered the room and attempted to comfort him with words, and leaned down towards him and showed him a toy, but he continued to cry loudly, attempting to leave the room. Leah returned to the room and he looked up at her as she came through the door. She put her hands on his shoulders and turned him towards the room. He made a couple of vocalizations, went over briefly to the sofa and turned to look at Leah. She said, 'Don't stress yourself' and he went over to the door (next to which Leah was sitting), looked at her and smiled and banged the door with his hand. Leah looked at him, which he returned, and then she smiled at him and gently wiped away a tear with her hand. Riley went and took a trundle car to Leah and she set it up on its wheels for him, sounded the hooter and tapped the seat, inviting him to sit on it. He touched his head and vocalised (made a sound), then laughed and tried to sit on it back to front. Leah helped him sit down, and he also sounded the hooter, got off and wheeled it back and forth. Very few words were offered by Leah, other than 'here' and 'car'. Riley got off the car and pushed it back and forth. Leah took the toy phone and tapped it. Riley went and took it and held the receiver to his ear and Leah said, 'Hello, hello'.

The important thing to note is that most children protest when their mother leaves the room, and it is typical for children not to be comforted by the stranger. Because Riley is a mobile child, he was well able to try to open the door to attempt to follow Leah. It had been noted on previous occasions that he had refused food from his mother, but took it willingly from the family support worker with whom he had developed a relationship. He also climbed on my lap during a visit, despite the fact that I (Yvonne) was not particularly familiar to him. It had been this behaviour that had prompted us to consider using the SSP. We wanted to see if he showed signs of disorganised attachment behaviour (which might be indicative of maltreatment).

In the SSP, when his mother left, Riley could not be comforted by the stranger, nor did he give her any attention – as is typical of most children his age, whether securely or insecurely attached; instead, he devoted all his energy to getting his mother back in the room (and was not interested in the toys when left alone). When Leah returned, Riley vocalised his protest to her, despite not yet having language, and he was soon content to continue playing, including playfully hitting the door and looking at her teasingly. This indicated that he was not afraid of her, and certainly not faced with an unresolvable dilemma when she entered the room; in other words, we did not see 'fear without solution'. This does not, however, mean that there were no problems with his care or in his relationship with Leah. It may suggest that he was not being physically abused by her, although he evidently was developmentally delayed in his speech, and was displaying some externalised behaviours in respect of her. For example, he angrily hit her and 'shouted' at her when she interfered with his play on another occasion (see the guided parenting tasks on the next page). The emotional coldness being experienced by him, possibly as a result of her apparent low mentalizing capacity and to some degree disinterested – but not disconnected – parenting may have contributed to his seeking affection elsewhere whenever possible.

During a brief conversation with the 'stranger' during the SSP, Leah was asked how she was getting on with Riley. She immediately supplied a list of the things that he does wrong, saying, 'He's stressful, he has temper tantrums all the time; he doesn't do what he's told; he does things…like, he knows it's wrong but he does it anyway…and he just does very naughty things'. These comments were replicated when she was asked to talk about Riley for two minutes during the home visit when I conducted the guided parenting tasks. At that time, Leah started by saying that he was 'sociable', but then she said how difficult, naughty and disobedient he was. This suggested low mentalizing capacity.

Guided parenting tasks

It is generally the case that when visiting service users practitioners rely on interview and formulaic questionnaires to determine whether a child is 'at risk' in the family. They ask questions, seek clarification and form 'written agreements', usually based on what the parent 'must do' before the worker's next visit. Much of their assessment and knowledge relies on self-reports from parents. They may see them interacting with their children, but this may be an artificial situation which does not 'test' parenting. It relies on the worker serendipitously seeing something which just happens to take place, but which cannot be guaranteed as representative of their parenting at other times.

The ADAM Project aims to give practitioners a set of skills and techniques to use pragmatically, in everyday practice, rather than being specifically trained in all the technical aspects, although it is recommended that some staff do undertake formal training in such aspects so that qualified practitioners can be used as consultants. The guided parenting tasks are based on the Video Intervention to Promote Positive Parenting and Sensitive Discipline programme developed at the University of Leiden in Holland by Juffer, Bakermans-Kranenburg and Van IJzendoorn (2008).

As we saw in Chapter 6, the tasks involve asking the parent to undertake some activities which provide a level of 'challenge' to both parent and child. First, the parent watches their child play for a few minutes without becoming involved (but shows interest in what the child is doing). For the next task, they are asked to play with their child for three minutes with some toys provided by the social worker. After two or three minutes, they are asked to get the child to clear the toys away. This is usually quite difficult for a child while they are engrossed in the new toys. Many parents would find this difficult, as it does test their negotiation and distraction skills! Observing how the parent handles this tricky situation gives the worker an insight into how difficult situations are managed and how sensitively they react to the child's (potential) distress. The practitioner notes whether the parent actually ignores the instruction, letting the child continue regardless. They observe whether they take over for the child and clear the things away themselves, or whether they encourage the child and divert them by saying they can then do something else together. Similarly, asking the parent to show the child some new toys, but not allowing them to touch them for two minutes, demonstrates how they accomplish this. Some parents do this by clamping the child between their legs and holding their hands, while others gently tell the child what they are going to do, and gradually introduce the toys, placing them on the floor whilst gently reminding the child not to touch them yet. (If the child is older, more time is introduced.) Other activities include: showing the child a book, preparing and having a snack with the child, doing a jigsaw puzzle and building a tower with stacking pots. Parents are asked to play a game or sing songs with their child. Parents are sometimes worried that their child will not co-operate. They are told that they can just do what they would normally do in those circumstances.

The first three tasks which were undertaken with Leah and Riley are described in detail below.

Disconnected parenting (identified by Out *et al.* 2009, adapted from Main and Hesse 1998) and extremely insensitive parenting (a concept adapted from Bronfman, Parsons and Lyons-Ruth 1993) were observed and measured on a scale of one to ten against the behaviours given in the Disconnected and extremely Insensitive Parenting (DIP) scale.[1]

To undertake the work outlined in Chapter 8, six sessions were filmed with Leah and Riley. It is usual to undertake the tasks in the home, but due to fears about an abusive partner possibly being present,

---

1   For the full paper (which includes the complete list of behaviours as an appendix) see: www.marinusvanijzendoorn.nl/wp-content/uploads/2012/07/OutBakermans-KranenburgVanIJzendoorn2009AHDDIPdisorganizedattachment.pdf

it was recommended that the first visit take place at a family centre. We now provide a description of what took place.

The first session began with Leah being with Riley while he played. Riley moved around the room, turning chairs over, trying to leave the room and investigating the bathroom. This was a new environment for Riley, and Leah had some difficulty retrieving him from outside the room, dragging him by the arm up the stairs. When they had settled, she was asked to be with him while he played. Riley chose a toy which played a tune with rotating discs. He placed small cars on them and watched them whiz around, moving them occasionally. Leah sat on the furthest end of a sofa leaning slightly forward with her arms folded, looking at Riley play. She sat motionless, but after 45 seconds she looked out of the window and bit her lip, looking anxious. Riley continued to play with the game. She then resumed her previous position, continuing to bite her lip and 'hug' herself. After one minute, she leaned over and looked towards the floor for half a minute, and then looked back towards Riley. He did not look up during this time. What was most noticeable was the silence in the room, except for the toy's music. It felt uncomfortable and rather 'unnatural', given that he was in an unfamiliar place, with a stranger holding a video camera. While Leah's demeanour looked somewhat 'dissociated', it is not rated as 'disconnected' in terms of the DIP because at the time she was not parenting Riley.

The second activity involved asking Leah to join Riley in play, and I provided a bag of toys he had not seen before. Leah sat on the floor and tipped the toys out and started to sort them out, and then said 'Riley' without looking up. Riley went over to Leah and stood looking for a couple of seconds. She did not say anything.

Riley returned to his toy, while Leah continued to sort 'her' toys. She glanced up briefly and after four seconds said 'Riley'. He continued playing for three seconds and then walked over, looked at the toys and took a car back to 'his' game. Leah continued to sort the toys and then I stopped filming and said she could now join him to play together. She leaned forward and arranged the cars, pushing the button to make them spin. Riley screeched in an irritated way and pushed her hand away. Leah did this twice, and each time Riley screeched louder in protest and pushed her hand away, on the last occasion pushing both hands against her legs. She stood up and smiled and then leaned forward again and pushed the button. Riley responded by screeching in a rhythmic way three times. This was repeated once more and then Leah stood up and he pushed her towards the sofa where she sat down on the edge, smiling and looking down to the floor, seemingly hunched before she looked at him and leaned down to the toys and said, 'Come and have a look'. He turned briefly to look at Leah and picked up a toy. Riley then turned and started playing with the car machine again. Leah yawned and picked up a car from the floor and asked him to see the car. Riley went towards her and she put the car down. He was about to return to his game when she picked up two bricks and banged them together. He screeched and knocked them out of her hands. She picked them up again and gave a little smile, but Riley picked up a car and returned to his game. Leah called his name and moved up closer on the sofa. She pushed the button twice, and again Riley said something like 'no, no' and pushed her hand away. She did this twice more, and each time he screeched. Riley played for a few moments, and Leah again quickly pushed the button. This resulted in Riley going over to her, pushing her hard and screeching again. Riley went back to his game, but she repeated the button pushing. He became very frustrated and screeched loudly. Leah smiled and sat with her hands between her knees. Riley threw a car off and carried on playing. Riley seemed to smile a little while he played, and then he took a car and sat on the floor with the other toys, with his back to Leah. She moved to sit down on the floor behind him and picked up a booklet and looked at it. Riley played quietly with a truck with his back to her.

The third task I asked Leah to undertake was to show Riley a book. It is good to give the parent a book which has interesting tabs and pictures, not just a story book. Leah sat with Riley on the sofa with her arm around him and the book on her lap. She said the title, 'Tractors', and Riley rolled away and she pulled him back by his arm. He protested initially and then went quiet. Leah gave a little smile, opened the book and looked at the page. Riley protested again, and she turned the page and began to read, lifting the book a little. Riley cried. She pulled the flaps and Riley began to touch the book. She pulled his hand away roughly and then silently opened some flaps. Riley fussed again, pushed the book and wriggled. Leah struggled with him and pulled him back up. He resisted and climbed off the sofa. Leah read a bit of the story and Riley briefly looked at the book on her lap, went away and then turned back, and Leah tapped the sofa and said, 'Riley, come'. He turned away and she looked away with a slight smile. She said 'Come' again, and he went to the sofa and pushed the book. Leah leaned back and tapped the seat saying, 'Sit down'. Riley walked away and touched a plug switch. Leah called out 'No', and then he looked at me and touched the switch again. Leah stood up and pulled him away, lifting him by one arm and pulling him, and he struggled and cried on the sofa.

Leah opened the book but Riley broke free from her, struggled off the sofa and went over to a small table and moved it before going to the plug socket again. Leah called his name, and he looked over his shoulder to me, then over to Leah, who was looking at the book. He walked away to a pile of toys and picked out a digger and held it up looking at Leah. She did not respond. He then held it up towards me. Leah called his name and he looked towards her and then put the digger down. Leah looked down at the book. Riley pushed the toy back and forth on the floor, looked up at me and gave a big smile. He then glanced at Leah and sat down with the digger and turned around towards me and made another big smile towards the camera.

The other tasks involved doing a jigsaw puzzle, the 'don't touch the toys' activity, preparing and having a snack and building a tower with the child. Some tasks are repeated during each session, and it was evident that Leah's sensitivity towards Riley did improve during that time (which is described more fully in Chapter 8) and she was able to join in his play more constructively. For example, she took some cars and followed the ones he was pushing along. On another occasion at the third visit, Riley enjoyed banging his own bricks together in rhythm with hers, and changed them over, taking hers and exchanging them with his. He now seemed more able to tolerate being physically close to her. He sat next to her playing with the bricks, smiling and looking at her, and he joined her on the sofa to do a jigsaw puzzle. He allowed Leah to assist him in fitting a piece in correctly, and Leah said 'Hooray!' when he did it. During one of the early tasks Leah had not been able to enjoy imaginative play with Riley, and when faced with a range of toys, including a toy tea set, she said she did not know what to do; however, after talking about it during the next session, she tried it, and by the fourth session she was pretending to have food and drink with Riley, which they both enjoyed.

Using the DIP measure as our guide, Leah did not show frightening or threatening behaviours, but she did show some evidence of 'frightened parental behaviour', as seen when she retreated from Riley when he was aggressive towards her. This was seen as a 'low' score. Although Leah seemed rather 'absent' at times, she did not meet the criteria for 'dissociative' behaviour. She also scored low on the scale under 'deferential behaviour', as she did not 'fail to stop the child from parent-directed aggression'. Leah did not show any 'disoriented behaviours'. Under the 'extreme insensitivity' category, under the heading of 'failure to initiate responsive behaviour to the child', she scored 'very high' for the item 'the parent does not respond to the child's repeated vocalizations and cues'. There was no evidence that she 'actively created physical distance from the child', but she did show a level of 'intrusive, negative, aggressive or otherwise harsh parental behaviours'. For example, she teased him for a protracted period when she was pressing the buttons on his toy, despite his protests. Leah also handled him roughly on one occasion, pulling him by the arm and dragging him. This was rated as 'low'.

Conclusion

What we have attempted to demonstrate in this chapter is how the use of Pathway Model methods gives practitioners the opportunity to explore, examine and then analyse indicators of attachment (dis) organization during controlled reunion episodes, as well as identify some of the 'mechanisms of maltreatment', specifically, in our example, insensitive caregiving.

Chapter 8

Working with Disconnected or Insensitive Parents by Increasing Mentalizing Capacity

Yvonne Shemmings

In this chapter I focus on what happened next with Leah and Riley. In Chapter 7, the guided parenting tasks undertaken with Leah with her son were as follows:

- Be with your child while she or he plays (but do not join in the play).

- Play with your child.

- Show your child a book.

- Do a jigsaw puzzle with your child.

- Sing a song or read a poem with your child.

- Prepare a snack and have it with your child.

- Show your child how to build a tower with pots.

Having completed the tasks, I played each session back to Leah on each subsequent visit, with the aim of increasing her sensitivity towards Riley and helping her become more sensitively attuned to his signals. Leah was both inconsistent and insensitive in her approach to discipline, and by age two years Riley had learned to 'turn up' his negative behaviour to gain some attention. Leah rarely spoke to him other than to reprimand or instruct him. A script was prepared following each visit and included messages about praising him when he was good and ignoring his behaviour when he was not (unless dangerous or destructive). Combined with giving him compliments when he was playing and encouraging him to comply by giving him alternatives, the work was aimed at creating a warmer relationship with Riley. It is important that the feedback focus on positive interactions – even if they are fleeting – recognizing moments when the mother picked up on her child's signals, when they have eye contact and noting smiles and 'warm' moments. (Chapter 9 provides more details of the formal approach to the Video Intervention to Promote Positive Parenting and Sensitive Discipline; Shemmings and Shemmings 2011.)

In the first session, as we saw in Chapter 7, Leah was asked to watch her son play, show an interest, but not becoming involved. She seemed rather 'switched off' during this time, and I asked her what she thought he might be thinking in this unfamiliar environment. She said she did not know, but that he was 'alright'. She said very little to him and I wondered if this was usual for her. She said she did not know what to say to him, so I asked her to show him what was outside the window. There was a busy high street scene, but she said there was nothing to show him. Thinking she might find it easier to talk to Riley if there was a 'purpose' to it (as she would see it), I showed her some children's songs she could try, as well as suggested that she could take him to the park before the next session, and that she could name all the playground toys for him, such as swings and slide as he went on them. I gave her a DVD called 'Chatter Matters'[1] and some attractive cards giving snippets of information about child development for children of Riley's age.

Riley was already engrossed in play when I asked her to join his game. Leah got some toys out, but he was not attracted to them at that time. She passively called his name, and he did respond to her by looking and then walking over to her, but his interest was not sustained by her attention. I commented by 'talking for the child', saying, 'Children of my age aren't always ready to change games, as this one is such fun and I'm making it better by adding cars – I'll take this one that you've got and try it on my turntable'. I added, 'Children like their mum to watch them play and sometimes to join in their fun'. As we saw, Leah went to his toy and pushed the buttons repeatedly, despite him giving clear signals that he did not like her doing so. He screeched loudly each

---

1   See www.ican.org.uk

time she pushed the button. Leah persisted, to his growing irritation, culminating in him pushing her onto the sofa. Again, talking for the child, I said, 'Mummy, I have made my own game and I would love it if you will watch me, but for me, I am feeling frustrated that you are making it a different game. I love it that you want to join in, but I like it when you play beside me, too'. I continued, 'Children like to have their mum watch them play, and enjoy it with them. They love it when you smile and comment on what they are doing'. It was important that I remain 'kindly disposed' to Leah and that I 'voice' Riley likewise.

Encouraging parents to recognise moments when their child connects with them helps develop a warmer relationship and sensitises them to their child's signals. If the session is not filmed, it is easy to miss these sometimes fleeting moments of closeness, but when they are seen, these things can be commented on promptly. I said, 'What a clever boy; he really is good at concentrating on his game! Is this something he is good at when at home?' Showing warmth about the child indicates that he is likeable. This friendly approach helps the mother feel she is not being criticised and demonstrates empathy for both mother and child. Any 'learning points' are delivered through 'inductive statements' or 'corrective messages' which are given after positive comments have been given to the mother. So when Leah was reading with Riley, it was important to recognise that she was having trouble getting him to sit with her, saying something like, 'It's difficult for Riley to make the change from playing his game to sitting still. He doesn't know yet that this is going to be a good book to look at! Children of his age like to have a bit of warning that something else is going to happen soon.' When Leah pushed his hand away I could show empathy with Riley by saying, 'This is a fun book, mummy, because I can pull the flaps and see what's underneath'. Similarly, I could speak for Riley and say to Leah, 'I can see you are moving the flaps, mummy, and I would like to try for myself so that I can see underneath, too'. This could be followed with, 'Sometimes children of this age can be a bit heavy-handed and maybe you were predicting he might tear the page and you were worried about this?'

In Chapter 7, we described how Riley went to the toy box and found a digger. He had climbed down from the sofa while Leah was showing him the book, at which she continued to look. Riley looked over to her and lifted the toy. This signal was not recognised by Leah, so, speaking for the child, I said, 'Look mummy, I've got a toy nearly like the picture in the book – you see, I *was* listening to what you were saying!' I then said, 'What a good memory he has; what a clever boy!' Helping Leah see these signals helped her recognise that she is important to him. By only remarking on the positive interaction, the fact that Leah had not responded to his signal was ignored. It was not necessary to point out to her that he turned towards the camera, held up the toy and gave a big smile, as it would probably have been quite hurtful for her to have seen this. (It might also be the case that he does not want to smile at her; or that he does, but she ignores it or, more worryingly, does not understand, i.e. mentalise, what it means.)

During the previous session, Riley had moved a table to find a plug point and had switched it on and off. The first time he did this Leah told him 'No', and when he did not move, she went and pulled him away roughly by the arm. He went back and looked towards her, and she said 'No' again but did not move to take him away. He turned and looked at me for a few seconds and then moved away. This type of behaviour was described by Leah as 'defiant' and 'naughty'. This was a good opportunity for me to contextualise his behaviour, saying, 'Two-year-olds are very curious and like to explore. At this age they are still checking the rules. For us, it can sometimes seem that they are being defiant when they repeat something they've been told not to do. But often they are just checking the rule – "If I do this again, do I get the same response, and do I get the same response from someone else?" Being consistent helps children feel secure as well as know why they may not do something.' So in these circumstances, Leah can be encouraged to begin to view her child in a different light: he is not doing it to annoy her, but is learning why he must not do something which is potentially dangerous (in the case of the electric plug). She was also encouraged to use distraction, rather than harsh discipline. For example, she could tell him in advance that they would soon put the toys away, but that they would then play something else together. Building empathy for Riley (as well as Leah) helps her see things from Riley's point of view and appreciate *his* subjective experience. For example, one of the tasks is to show the child how to build a tower with interlocking pots. This is a challenge for a child of Riley's age and developmental stage. The aim is to see how Leah responds to Riley when he tries to build the tower. Gaining his attention was difficult and Leah began building the tower, which Riley immediately knocked down. He took the pots and rolled them around. Seeing how parents undertake the task can be illuminating. Some parents ignore the request if the child does not co-operate, others hold the child firmly while attempting to do the task and others try hard to engage their children, making the game fun and interesting, or use distraction techniques to help guide their child back to a task.

By 'speaking for the child' I again acknowledged the difficulty of the task for Riley and set the comments in the context of his development. 'Children of this age love to explore. He is seeing for himself what he can do with the different sizes'. Empathizing with Leah, I said, 'It is sometimes hard to watch children find out for themselves. We *know* how the pots stack, but that is not important to him right now, he is just happy to roll them around and see what they do.' Similarly, with the 'show your child the book' task, Riley wanted to pull the flaps and go randomly through the pages. So I said, 'Young children do not yet know that a story goes from front to back; they just see the pictures and want to flip around, to explore all the pages, go back and forth. That can be frustrating for us adults because we know already that the story flows one way. So showing the child the book does not have to mean that we control how they can see it, and it does not mean they do not get pleasure out of the experience.'

In undertaking the guided parenting tasks, it is possible to determine how consistent and how sensitively the parent handles discipline. Leah tended to pull Riley around when he did not comply, and when he ran to different rooms she was not consistent in her response over the same situation. For example, sometimes she would shout at him without moving from her position, but at other times she would go and get him, dragging him back and pulling him onto a chair with her, gripping him hard. Leah found talking to Riley very difficult and did not give explanations about why he should not do things, nor did she use diversionary techniques to distract him. As a consequence, he was exposed to very little language other than the occasional use of 'Riley, no!', and 'Riley – here!' Leah was not comfortable talking to Riley, so using the book to help her find some words to say directly to him was a start. Similarly, showing him how to do a jigsaw puzzle gave her an opportunity to speak to him.

Naming children's emotions for them is also important as they develop. Helping Leah to develop a less negative discourse about Riley was an important first step, and using the guided parenting tasks provided the scaffolding for this. Sensitive responsiveness seems to be dependent on a capacity to 'mentalise', that is, to be able to understand Riley's mind: What might it contain? What might he be thinking? What are his intentions? In short, 'What is it most probably like to be him right now'?

Continuing to 'speak for the chid' was helpful in offering an alternative explanation to his behaviour. Leah believed Riley was deliberately behaving badly to annoy her, to give her a 'hard time'. She was in turn both punitive and passive when dealing with him, which was confusing for him and reinforced his strategy for getting a response and gaining attention.

Riley had already learned to behave in extreme ways to gain the attention of his mother, even if it was negative attention that was elicited. He had already abandoned any nuanced ways of attracting her attention when he needed something. For example, as an infant he would have started by giving low-level distress signals but, if he did not receive an appropriate response, he would have learned from experience that this was an ineffective strategy.

Using the tasks was also a good platform for discovering Leah's parenting style, as they provide a challenge both to the child *and* the parent: it is hard for a child to put toys away that they are interested in playing with, and it can be hard for a parent to prevent a child from touching toys which are new to them. The tasks demonstrate how the parent handles this tricky situation and gives an opportunity to explore some ideas to encourage sensitive discipline.

Leah was asked to play alongside Riley, the aim being to encourage her to 'follow' him. The toy bag contained a small tea set (among other things). At first Leah passively sorted them out, slowly putting them straight, in silence. There was a strong sense of isolation while she was doing this, and Riley soon became restless and started throwing bricks around the room. Leah often described Riley as a naughty and disobedient child and it was therefore important to try to re-frame his behaviour (as well as help her find ways to cope with it). By Leah ignoring his signals, he had learned that he needed quickly to escalate his behaviour to gain her attention once more. In speaking for him, we helped Leah find words for his feelings such as 'I'm feeling a bit confused about what I can do with these toys – they are new to me and mummy is playing on her own and I don't know that she is watching out for me'. Leah said she did not know what to do now that she had got them out. I sat on the floor with them and offered her a cup and saucer and poured 'pretend' tea into the cup, asking her if she wanted milk and sugar. Riley immediately took up the game and pretended to eat from a plate with a fork. I made lots of eating noises in response, and Riley offered 'food' to Leah, who said, 'Yum'. I did not play directly with Riley because during these sessions my relationship is primarily with the parent. When these toys were taken to the home on the third visit, this game was replayed spontaneously with a good deal of smiling and enjoyment from both Leah and Riley, who repeated something he did during the first time: he had put his hand inside the tea pot and Leah had pulled it out for him. He had remembered this as something to which she had responded, and it was good to see that this was repeated. Talking for the child, I said, 'Look mummy, I have a very good memory. This was a game we played before, and I've remembered it was fun'. I reinforced this to Leah, saying, 'What a clever boy he is; it is so sweet to see that he has remembered that moment with you'. (He also banged the bricks together, as his mother had done with him in a previous session.)

Conclusion

In conclusion, some progress was seen over the course of six one-hour sessions. Initially Leah had found it very difficult to be with Riley, to understand how he might feel and join in his play constructively without being intrusive. Most notably, Riley played in a solitary way and seemed to have no expectation that his mother might be someone with whom to have fun. He physically pushed and hit her when she tried to join his play, and strongly resisted her attempts to have him sit with her while she showed him a book. When he did show an interest by exploring the flaps on the page, she slapped his hand away; however, by the third session, when Leah called him to come to her, Riley voluntarily went to the sofa where she was sitting and climbed up to her. He sat with his foot on her leg and Leah put the jigsaw puzzle on his lap, tapping a piece of the puzzle. He looked at her and smiled, and she picked up the signal and smiled back, tapping the piece near the appropriate slot. He took it and she guided his hand a little before he slid it into place. He looked up at her and Leah said, 'Hooray!' Leah joined in his play when he was banging two bricks together, doing the same as him, which he clearly enjoyed. When Riley played with his cars, she followed his play, pushing 'her' cars around, and showed him how to fix two magnetic cars together when they broke away from each other.

These small but significant events indicated that Leah was beginning to 'see' her child as an individual with thoughts and intentions of his own. She had begun to have more face-to-face contact with him and could follow him in his play. Riley loved this and rewarded her with smiles directed at her, and he had begun to copy sounds and words she made for him. He began to tolerate close proximity to her and became more compliant when she spoke to him.

Chapter 9

Using Modified Story Stems

David Wilkins

With the two children discussed in this chapter, I applied the Pathway Model using story stems. The primary reason for this was to establish whether either of the children I worked with was exhibiting signs of disorganised attachment behaviour. I focused on this aspect of the model because with the first child, we needed to determine whether he was being sexually abused at home, and with the second child, we needed to evidence how the neglect he was experiencing was affecting him. The purpose of using the story stems in this second case was not necessarily to gather evidence of neglect but to better understand the harm being caused and for use as a 'baseline' comparison between the nature of the stories he told when he was living at home and the nature of the stories he told after being placed with alternative carers.

Case studies

I discuss below two cases, the second in more depth and detail than the first.

Case I: Aboyomi

Aboyomi was an eight-year-old boy living with his mother and father, Mr and Mrs D, and his four-year-old sister, Aba. Aboyomi was referred to the local authority by his school shortly after transferring from another out-of-borough school. The school found Aboyomi's behaviour very challenging to manage and he was swiftly excluded. The school referred to social services because of the nature of his behaviour, which they felt was indicative of sexual abuse in the home. They described how Aboyomi had masturbated in class, how he had touched female teachers' breasts and asked male teachers to hit him on the bottom. Aboyomi's parents angrily denied that there was anything untoward occurring at home and believed that Aboyomi's behaviour was explicable because of the intense peer abuse (bullying) that he had suffered at his previous school, abuse which included being forced to show his penis in class, being physically assaulted and having his head forced down the toilets. On one occasion, the physical assault he suffered was so severe that a passer-by had called the police. Nevertheless, his current school did not believe this was a sufficient explanation for his behaviour and asked the local authority to undertake an assessment of the home circumstances. Following a typical child protection assessment, interviews were undertaken with both parents, individually and together, and checks were made with previous and current schools. We also spoke with Aboyomi alone and asked him about his wishes and feelings, his home life, what things made him happy and what things made him worried, and if he was being abused (using as 'child friendly' language as possible). Nothing of any concern arose from this, although his mother did say she was considering leaving the family home as she considered her relationship with Aboyomi's father to be over. She did not give any reasons for this decision other than saying she was no longer happy; however, despite this potentially significant issue, about which we had very limited information, there was nothing to suggest that Aboyomi was being sexually abused but, equally, no firm evidence that he was not and no explanation for his behaviour at school. The use of story stems with Aboyomi was an attempt to obtain a better degree of insight into his experience of family life, and to try to understand whether he viewed adult carers as generally available, helpful and caring, or as unpredictable, threatening and a source of fear. If Aboyomi was being sexually abused at home, it seemed a reasonable conclusion that he would view adult carers as typically the latter rather than the former.

Case 2: Jimmy

Jimmy was seven years old and lived at home with his parents, Mr and Mrs Y. Jimmy came to the attention of the local authority because of his parents' learning difficulties and concerns about how they were coping. Jimmy would often arrive at school in dirty or unkempt clothing and his language development was noticeably behind that of his peers. Jimmy also had difficulties with his behaviour in class, often isolating himself from his friends by spitting at them or saying insulting things, and this often resulted in his having no one with whom to play at break time.

Following assessments of the home, it was discovered that it was in a poor state of repair, with water marks on many of the walls, clumps of dust on the floors and no clear area for Jimmy to sleep, eat or play. Jimmy also had very dry skin, several rotting teeth and was often being fed with leftover food that his parents found in the local communal refuse-bin area; however, although there was quite clear evidence of physical neglect, it is difficult, in my experience, to initiate court proceedings based 'only' on neglect, as courts will often want to know why an application is being made *at this point in time* and whether, with more time and support, things might improve for the child – a good example of how the 'rule of optimism' can operate in practice (Dingwall, Eekalaar and Murray 1983); however, by this point in time, the local authority had been supporting Jimmy and his parents for many years through the provision of home care and a package of short-break support for Jimmy outside of the home, in addition to various parenting classes and other forms of parenting support for Mr and Mrs Y. Despite these efforts, however, there was no evidence of any sustained change for Jimmy. It was also evident that Jimmy's parents struggled to understand things from his point of view (in the language of the Pathway Model, they had low mentalizing capacity) and they also treated Jimmy with quite marked and extreme insensitivity. On one occasion, witnessed by the social worker at the time, Jimmy was sent home from school with a very high temperature and his mother was advised to take him to see his doctor. Jimmy was the subject of a child protection plan at the time and one of the aims of the plan was for Jimmy to attend school more regularly so that he could spend more time in his 'nurture group' and hopefully improve some of his social skills. Perhaps because of a misunderstanding of this part of the plan, Mrs Y was very angry with Jimmy and told him off for being at home, saying that he would get her in trouble. From the social worker's observations, it was clear that Jimmy was frightened of his mother when she shouted at him, but when discussing this with the social worker, Mrs Y showed no insight into how this must have felt for Jimmy, especially considering he was unwell and may have been hoping for some extra-sensitive love and care from his mother at that point (or perhaps not, given his past experiences).

Discussion

For both children, the use of story stems was instructive, and for Aboyomi, story stems had a material impact on the decision-making process. For Jimmy, although the long-term outcome of the case was probably settled before the use of the story stems (namely, that the local authority would seek a care order with the plan for him to live with alternative carers), the use of this particular method changed the care plan for him in more minor ways but, from his point of view, in significant ways. It also allowed us to compare his internal world and understanding from living at home with his parents to that nine months after he had been placed with alternative carers.

First, with Aboyomi, I used the story stem approach in order to help decide whether it was more or less likely that he was being sexually abused at home. His parents were cautious about agreeing to him being filmed but were more than happy for individual work to be completed with him. They presented as worried parents, keen to know what was occurring with their son. As Aboyomi did not have a school place at the time of the work, I completed the story stems at his home. This seemed to have the effect of reassuring his parents to some degree, and they did agree to my filming the work. Aboyomi did not present with any markers of disorganised attachment behaviour, although he certainly told some wonderful, albeit often unfocused and meandering, stories, as can be seen from the following extract:

> *DW*: So, in this story, we need mummy and daddy and both of the children. Do you remember what we called the children?
>
> *Aboyomi*: Jamie and, and…Jason!
>
> *DW*: That's right, Jamie and Jason. And in this story, they are all in the kitchen. Can you see me putting them in the kitchen? Yes, good. And here they are sitting down to have a drink. I don't think they will fit on the chairs actually so let's pretend and I'll just put them on the floor, okay?
>
> *Aboyomi*: I sometimes sit on the floor to drink.
>
> *DW*: So the family are having a drink and then, look can you see what I am doing, Jason is getting up and he is not really looking where he is going and…oh no! He's spilled the juice all on the floor. Can you show me and tell me what happens next?
>
> *Aboyomi*: Well, so he spilled the juice. So what is going to happen now?
>
> *DW*: It's your story now, can you show me and tell me?
>
> *Aboyomi*: Okay. So, well…he's spilled the juice and his father says…he says, 'You naughty boy. I was going to drink that'. And…and…Jamie cries because she doesn't…um…she wanted the juice as well, see?
>
> *DW*: Okay, and then what happens?
>
> *Aboyomi*: Well, so daddy is angry with, with, with…
>
> *DW*: With Jason?

> *Aboyomi*: With Jason. So he says…he says, 'You clear that up right now and go to bed'. So Jason gets a cloth and he wipes it, yes, and he says, 'It's done now, daddy'.
>
> *DW*: Okay, and so does anything else happen? Does mummy do anything in this story?
>
> *Aboyomi*: Mummy…mummy…mummy. Mummy says that she can fix the jug because she's got glue, okay, but she's left the glue at the neighbour's house and so she says, 'I need the glue, the glue' and daddy says, 'No that's not…I mean, we're going out, okay? So we can get the glue later'.

The story continues like this for quite a while. The family does go out, but it is not clear from what Aboyomi says if they are looking for glue, or whether Jason is with them, and there is no real end to the story. One of the difficulties with Aboyomi was in ending the stories and moving to the next stem, but in terms of actual markers of disorganised attachment behaviour, there were none evident. Clearly, these kinds of tentative hypotheses need to be reviewed regularly; they are not definitive and must be updated in the light of new information.

What else proved useful about the stories, as I also found through the use of the Adult Attachment Interview (see Chapter 5), is that as well as providing evidence (or not) for particular markers for disorganised attachment behaviour with children, or the carer characteristics for parents, these methods also provide a rich source of information about a range of areas. For Aboyomi, his absolute and desperate need for friends his own age was very evident from the stories; on many occasions, he talked about the character of Jason looking for friends, feeling lonely and being unable to talk to anyone about how he really felt. Although it is important in any projective method not to over-interpret what is being said and demonstrated, it did not feel unreasonable to draw the conclusion that something had happened to Aboyomi at his previous school in terms of peer abuse, and that this had a significant impact in terms of how he saw himself and what he understood about how to make friends. Seemingly, Aboyomi had learned that the best way to gain acceptance within a peer group was to be prepared to be the 'clown' of the group, and perform a series of 'dares' at the request of the children with whom he hoped to make friends.

By using this particular method with Aboyomi, in conjunction with other sources of evidence, we were able to reassure ourselves that it was less likely that Aboyomi was being abused at home, but he was, clearly, a deeply unhappy boy and desperately needed help and support in order to make friends.

With Jimmy, the aim of using story stems was not to establish whether he was being neglected, as the procedure was not developed with that mind; rather, it was to explore the emotional consequences for him of having been neglected. We also wanted to gain a more objective way of comparing Jimmy's presentation when living with his parents with his situation after a length of time placed with alternative carers; therefore, and in contrast with Aboyomi, the information obtained from the story stems with Jimmy did not impact on the outcome of the case *per se*, although it did provide useful information with which we were able to tailor his care plan, making it more 'child focused' than might otherwise have been the case. I first used the story stem method with Jimmy whilst he was living at home and, later, after he had been living with his aunt and uncle for six months. Although it is difficult to be specific about how quickly children of different ages will be able to change and adapt their internal working model of attachment to a different and more sensitive caregiving environment, there was a noticeable difference between the sets of stories that Jimmy told on the two occasions. With the first set of stories, Jimmy showed distinct markers of disorganised attachment behaviour. His stories often included examples of 'good/bad splits' in adults, catastrophic resolutions and bizarre or atypical content. An example of this can be seen in the following extract:

> *DW*: So, in this story, the whole family are in the kitchen. Can you see them? Yes? And they are having a drink, because it's a really hot day today, isn't it? So, the little boy, he is reaching for the juice and do you know what happens next? Well, he knocks it over and spills it all over the floor. Oh no! So do you think you can tell me and show me what happens?
>
> *Jimmy*: What happens?
>
> *DW*: Can you tell me?
>
> *Jimmy*: A cow.
>
> *DW*: A cow?
>
> *Jimmy*: There's a cow. Get me the cow from the bag.

DW: I don't think the cow is in this story, is it?

Jimmy: My story, you said. The cow comes in. My hand is the cow. And the cow can fly.

DW: Yes. I see. What happens about the spilled juice?

Jimmy: There is no spilled juice. And it's dead.

DW: What's dead? Has the cow died?

Jimmy: The end. Well, not the end. The cow falls over, 'cos he's died, and he falls on the mummy. And the cow's bigger, isn't it? Than a mummy. So she dies as well. Squished.

DW: I see. So the cow dies and then mummy dies. Does anything else happen in this story?

Jimmy: No. Ended.

This particular extract shows examples of both catastrophizing (the mummy dying at the end) and of a bizarre response (the inclusion and subsequent death of the cow). In some of the other stories Jimmy told, there was evidence of 'good/bad splits' (describing alternating 'good' and 'bad' projected representations about the same figure, often in quick succession) in adults, especially the father figure. These markers gave an indication of the impact of neglect on Jimmy in terms of his lack of trust in the availability of adults to him at times of increased anxiety and need. In this sense, the story stems confirmed what we already knew (or thought we knew) and added to a wider body of evidence suggesting that Jimmy's parents were unable to provide a sufficient level of care for him at home; however, even more than this, the stories gave us an insight into Jimmy's home life 'behind closed doors'. As indicated above, the home in which Jimmy lived with his parents was very untidy and unclean in places. It was also very crowded, as his parents tended to hoard possessions and spent a significant portion of their income at car boot sales buying more and more things. This led to the home becoming very cluttered, with limited space for people to move around. It was notable in Jimmy's stories that the character of the male child often had trouble moving around and would bump and bang into things. One of the stories is about a 'bump in the night' after the child has gone to bed. It took Jimmy some time to understand this story, as he kept asking why the child had somewhere of his own to sleep and tried to bring him downstairs to sleep in the lounge with his parents. It took some persuading for Jimmy to continue with the story as intended. Whilst this was not new information *per se*, because various practitioners and I had been to the home and observed some of this for ourselves, it did provide further evidence of the difficulties Jimmy faced in everyday life and provided a unique child's-eye perspective of what it is like to live in a home where the layout and the quantity of possessions keeps changing from day to day.

Jimmy kept introducing the idea of a family dog in his stories (although there are no pets in this version). This was interesting because in real life, Jimmy's father owned a dog that was not very well cared for and often appeared to be quite ill. From observations and through talking to Jimmy (outside of using story stems), he seemed to have no interest in the dog; he did not talk about it by name, he never played with it and he seemed to view it more as a nuisance and as something with which to compete for space and his father's attention. However, in his story stems, Jimmy spoke about the dog and the male child as being friends and commented on how important the dog was to the male child. Although this might seem relatively insignificant, it prompted some further exploration with Jimmy around the family dog, and his social worker then tried taking the dog with them when they next went for a walk to the park. What she observed was completely different from what happened at home: Jimmy was clearly delighted with the dog; he played with him and threw sticks and balls for the dog to chase. Although this clearly had no bearing on the care plan for Jimmy – that he should live with alternative carers – it did affect the local authority care plan for contact and the 'life story' work subsequently completed with Jimmy, which both now included the family dog.

More immediately, the information obtained via this first story stem method informed the completion of the local authority court statements. As well as providing the court with evidence regarding Jimmy's school attendance, his success at school, the state of the home environment and Jimmy's poor presentation, we were able to go further than this and describe to the court how Jimmy had very little trust in adult carers to be a source of help and support for him and how this was affecting his behaviour in other settings, such as in school. Combined with evidence from the Adult Attachment Interview which was conducted with both his parents, this was instructive for the court, and the judge commented that they were not used to having such an insight into a child's life (as distinct from a description of their environment). Based on all the evidence the local authority was able to provide, the court issued an interim care order and Jimmy was placed with his paternal aunt and uncle, who had been assessed as suitable kinship carers. Six months after Jimmy was placed with them, I repeated the story stems with him. I undertook this work as part of a looked-after child review, and to help establish whether Jimmy's internal model of attachment had changed at all since his experiences at home with his parents. This second use of the method was not entirely unproblematic, not least because Jimmy partially remembered the story stems and, although he did not explicitly say so, it is possible that he also partially remembered his own original responses; however, Jimmy was very keen to repeat the story stems and certainly enjoyed the playful aspect of them. In this second session, as expected, Jimmy still told several stories with markers of catastrophizing and bizarre or atypical content, although it was notable that he no longer told stories with markers of 'good/ bad splits'. In this second attempt, Jimmy also included more elements of adults providing help and adults being aware of children being in distress. Both of these latter two markers are, in the full story stem assessment profile, coded as positive indicators of more organised attachment. Jimmy's stories on this second occasion also seemed to reflect the less chaotic home environment he was now becoming used to, so, for example, the male child in the story no longer seemed to have any difficulty in moving around and he was not bumping into objects, as he had done on the first occasion.

Conclusion

In conclusion, both examples demonstrate how the use of story stems with children of a suitable age can provide additional information to inform assessments. Although it was clear from other assessment work with the family that Aboyomi was in many ways a deeply unhappy boy, he did at least demonstrate a belief that he could rely on his parents to provide consistent and reliable comfort for him at times of increased anxiety or distress; therefore, through the use of the story stems with Aboyomi, we were able to form the view much more quickly than might otherwise have been the case that Aboyomi did not need to be made subject to a child protection plan or legal proceedings.

In the second case, with Jimmy, we already knew prior to the use of the story stems that he was being neglected but, as in many neglect cases, it was proving difficult to link descriptions of the poor caregiving environment and the actual impact on the particular child in question. The story stems that Jimmy completed provided this evidence and also helped inform the care plan in ways that would most likely not have occurred without them.

Chapter 10

Exploring Children's Inner Worlds

Fran Feeley

In Chapter 9, David Wilkins showed us how story stem or narrative work can be used to access a child's representational world, to offer insight into their experiences and, perhaps more significantly, their inner feelings and how they process attachment-related scenarios. Story stems could be said to build upon a wealthy tradition of play therapy, the common goal of this being to explore a child's inner world. In this chapter, I look at additional play-based techniques that can be used in direct work with children, the very work which should be at the heart of child protection practice. Such techniques provide us with the opportunity to better understand the inner world of the children we work with, not only in terms of how they view themselves, but also their understanding and representations of close relationships, be they with parents, carers or siblings. In working with children in this way, we are able to develop a more detailed picture of their life and experiences which can assist us to make better decisions and facilitate change.

There has been a shift away from the time spent carrying out direct work with families and more significantly children. The result of this has generally been attributable to the burden of increased bureaucratic and administrative tasks influenced by the ascendancy and dominance of managerialism. This could be said to have impacted not only on practitioners' time and capacity in being able to carry out direct work but also their confidence, as less time spent on meaningful direct work means many do not feel equipped or that they have the skills to conduct such work. This concern was echoed by Professor Eileen Munro in her review of the UK's child protection policy in which she expressed a belief that practitioners often lack the necessary skills, tools and teaching to develop effective and meaningful relationships with the children they seek to protect. Despite this apparent skills deficit, the policy guidance on the importance and need to communicate with children is extensive, as well as the legislative and statutory requirements to do so. This includes the Framework for the Assessment of Children in Need and Their Families, which stipulates that direct work with children, as well as recognizing their right to be involved and consulted about matters which affect their lives, is an essential part of assessment. This applies to all children, especially children with disabilities (DoH 2000). The Children Act 2004 also stipulates the duty of the local authority to ascertain the child's wishes and feelings and give them due consideration.

Serious case reviews in the UK repeatedly point to the failure of professionals to establish effective communication with children. However, we need to be mindful that children do not exist in isolation, but instead belong to wider family and social systems; therefore, in order for a child's voice to be heard within these systems and for practitioners to be able to make more informed decisions about a child's future welfare, it is important that time and focus be devoted to direct work with children.

Direct work with children needs to be done in the right setting as it involves more than simply asking a child, 'How are things?' Sometimes we may need different media, such as paint, pen and paper, clay, puppets or games, to help make sense of their wishes and feelings. In thinking about the setting, it is important to try to work with a child in a neutral, child-friendly place which is safe and quiet. When carrying out a specific piece of work with a child, it is preferable to meet them with their parent(s) or carer(s) the first time in order to provide a context for their behaviour and presentation, but subsequent sessions should involve the child on their own. Seeing the child alone is always important in child welfare practice generally, but is even more vital where there are concerns of maltreatment.

To gain an understanding of the child's world, we need to focus on developing a positive relationship with the child and wider family members. Munro (2011) made reference to this in her review when discussing the principles of a good child protection system, in terms of how 'the quality of the relationship between the child and family and professionals directly impacts on the effectiveness of the help given' (p.23); however, whilst it may seem obvious to state that 'the relationship' is central to effective social work practice, the building and development of such relationships is not without challenge (as we saw in Chapter 2). This relates not only to the time and bureaucratic restraints mentioned above, but also to the fact that we are predominantly working with children and families with a range of complex needs and difficulties who often struggle to develop positive and effective relationships in all aspects of their lives. Professionals need to develop trust by demonstrating honesty as well as reliability and continuity. In thinking about communicating effectively during direct work with children, it is also important to listen as well as demonstrate empathy and respect, to offer clear explanations, show understanding and take a genuine interest.

Techniques to help explore a child's mind

Below are some relatively straightforward ideas and techniques that can be used and adapted to explore and gain an understanding of a child's mind.

Puppets

Puppets are an effective technique to use with children in middle childhood, around the ages of six to eight years or under depending on the developmental age of the child, and can play a crucial role in helping to gain insight into a child's inner world. This is because in play-based puppet interviews, children project their thoughts and feelings onto the puppet, thus allowing the child some distance to communicate their feelings. You can invite the child to talk to the puppet, for example: 'Can you tell Benji Bear how you are feeling?' It is important to take eye contact *away* from the child so they can tell the puppet without inhibition. As well as providing both physical and psychological safety, it can often be easier for a child to talk to a puppet rather than about themselves, thus providing opportunities for greater self-expression.

Alternatively, you could encourage the child to talk 'through' the puppet. With this technique you can invite the child to play with you and your puppet theatre; you can improvise with the theatre using a box, chair or table for the child to use as a stage. Once the child has a puppet and is behind the stage, you can begin by asking the puppet if they know [child's name]. Then you can ask the puppet more specific questions about the child, such as what makes [child's name] happy or sad, or if [child's name] had one wish, what would it be, or 'is [child's name] ever angry?', 'What makes him/her angry?' or 'What do you think [child's name] does well/is good at?'

Another method is to work with the child to make their own puppet; it could be a simple sock or paper puppet. The focus is then on supporting the child to help develop a character for their puppet. Try asking questions about their likes and dislikes, such as what makes them happy or sad. For slightly older children you can simply get them to tell a story about their puppet. By developing a character and story for a puppet in this way, it enables practitioners to create the character over a number of sessions. This can be particularly helpful when working with children who appear withdrawn or guarded, as it provides a less direct or intrusive way of eliciting information by allowing the child to develop the story or character at their pace and time. Some children may struggle to talk to or for a puppet, and in this instance it is advisable to use your own puppet to try to support or encourage their puppet to speak. Other items, such as play sets containing dolls, teddies or animals, can also be used like puppets to encourage free play and role play with the child about aspects of their life, including home, school and peers.

On the whole, play-based puppet interviews not only allow us to understand a child's thoughts and feelings about themselves, but also offer insight into their attachment relationships if we consider that children develop representations of themselves (as well as their attachment figures) through parent-child interactions. For example, children who are being maltreated and not having their needs met consistently may develop negative beliefs about the 'self' and an internal working model where they are perceived as unlovable and unworthy. In working with puppets, a child may express this by talking negatively about themselves to or for the puppet, such as '[child's name] is bad, he/she never does anything right'. Whilst such negativity may be symptomatic of low-level insecurity in a child, or relating to a particular issue at home or school, it could also be indicative of something more worrying, including the child experiencing rejecting and hostile parenting; however, this would need to be examined in conjunction with other methods of assessment, such as the interviewing of caregivers and observations of the child at school and home.

I remember working with a seven-year-old boy who presented as being very guarded. When I met with him to undertake my first piece of direct work, he was reluctant to engage, throwing toys around before crawling under a table. The boy lay on his front with his head on his hands and I made a decision to crawl under the table with him, taking a puppet with me. I then used the puppet to try to encourage the boy to speak, using it to ask questions. The boy subsequently opened up under the table, telling the puppet he was sad because he missed his parents (he was in foster care), but that he did not like the fighting at home or his little brother, as they were always fighting, too, and this made him angry. He then punched the puppet away from him. Whilst this child was evidently expressing aggression towards the puppet, by the very fact of it being a puppet, the child was able to do so in a safe environment without risk of retaliation.

During my time working with the child, I became increasingly concerned about his welfare after a particularly worrying observation of contact between the child and his father. While waiting for his father to arrive at the contact centre, the child presented as excitable and highly aroused, looking out of the window for him, jumping up and down on the sofa; however, when his father arrived and came into the room, the child retreated onto the sofa, curled up into a ball, covered his face and began to cry. It seemed that the child's response to his father entering the room may have denoted 'fear without solution', the phrase used by Mary Main, as discussed elsewhere in the book, to describe situations when a child is anxious into which their caregiver enters.

The information gained from both observations of the child with his father, as well as the direct one-to-one work, including using puppets, the 'Islands' exercise (see p.133) and Story Stem Completion tasks, enabled me to gain a better understanding and insight into the child's inner world. The child was known to have been exposed to violence and aggression between his parents, with allegations of some physical chastisement towards him and his siblings. The child's often violent and aggressive reactions observed in my direct work with him could be seen as a representation of his lived experience within the family home, where he no doubt frequently felt anxious and frightened. I was then able to use this information to inform my assessment and make recommendations for the child's future welfare.

Islands

The three-islands technique is a drawing tool that can be used, as with puppets, to try to gain insight into a child's life without direct questioning. It is also a good way to engage with children and find out who they like to have close to them and why. The technique was developed by Kate Iwi, Young People's Services Officer at the charity Respect UK.

To carry out this exercise you need a piece of paper and some felt-tip pens. Draw the first island in the top left of the page. This is the 'Island of Always/Forever'. Explain to the child that this is a game and that in the game they live on the first island. Ask them to draw, write or tell you who or what they want on that island to be there, with them, forever.

Second, ask the child to decide who or what they want on a second island; these are people or things they might want to visit or be with them sometimes, but not all the time. This is the 'Island of Sometimes/ Visitor's Island'. It is drawn on the right side of the paper with a gated bridge between this island and the 'Island of Forever' and, again, tell the child that they have the key to the gate and control who visits, and when. You can explore further by asking the child when these things or people will be allowed onto the child's island. Now, ask the child if they can tell you about the things or people they are placing on this island.

Finally, draw a third island, the 'Island of Far Away/Never', at the very bottom of the paper, as far away from the other two as possible, and draw a sea between the bottom island and the other two. Ask the child to think about what or who they want to put on the 'Island of Far Away/Never'.

During this activity children use colour and/or pictures. The worker uses open-ended questions to find out what the positions, colours and pictures mean to the child, and why they have chosen to put a particular person or thing on a certain island. This tool provides practitioners with insight into a child's likes and dislikes, worries and concerns. It may also indicate something to explore further, such as a child living with their father but placing him on the 'Island of Far Away/Never', or a child placing a person we have not heard about before, such as a 'family friend', on the 'Island of Far Away/Never'.

It is also important to observe closely the child's body language when carrying out direct work, especially taking note of incongruence between verbal and body language, as well as behaviour. This can often be noted in children who may have been coached by their parents or who are experiencing confusion and anxiety. I observed this in a recent case when conducting the Islands drawing activity with a five-year-old boy. His father had moved out of the family home as a result of allegations of physical abuse against the boy. As our assessment progressed, the child was observed to ask if his 'daddy could come home' when in the company of his father at contact. We began to question if the boy was being coached or prompted, as he was not observed to talk about his father nor ask for him to come home at any other time. I decided to conduct the Islands exercise with him to try to get a deeper understanding of his close relationships. It was interesting to note that the child placed his father on the 'Island of Far Away/Never' commenting that he did not want to see him, drawing him in a seemingly angry manner, scribbling hard with his pencil. This was then able to be utilised in conjunction with detailed observations of parent-child interaction, to gain a deeper and more robust picture of the child's world and experiences. The observations of contact with his father showed a child experiencing a range of overwhelming and fluctuating emotions, including appearing eager to please his father at times, and presenting as compliant and apologetic; however, conversely, he was also noted as appearing angry during contact, hitting out at his father and telling him he hated him, and then crying and telling his father he loved him, repeating, 'Sorry, daddy'. By carrying out this direct work with the child on his own, I was able to gain a good insight into his thoughts and feelings and, as with the previous case study, use the information alongside observations of contact and the family history to inform my assessment and make recommendations for the child's future.

Happy, sad, angry

The aim of this exercise is to introduce the child to talking about feelings and to give permission to have certain feelings, such as anger or sadness. Like many play-based or drawing techniques, all that is needed are felt-tip pens and paper. For younger children, ask them to draw three different faces labelled 'happy', 'sad' and 'angry'. Then ask the child what makes them feel this way – for younger children you can ask them, 'When do you feel happy?' For older children, the task can be more abstract, for example, 'What makes you happy?' You can ask the child to draw or write their answers or support them to do so, depending on their age.

It is then possible to utilise their drawings or words as a basis for discussion, such as: Why did that make you sad? What would make it better? What makes you feel like that? What do you do when you feel like that? Why do you feel happy/sad/frightened? Always begin with a positive emotion (e.g. happy) and discuss each example given. When the negative feelings have been discussed, try to bring the child back to a more positive emotion before ending.

Most techniques in direct work can be adapted to suit a child's needs or age and stage of development. Variations of this technique could include other emotions such as 'worried' or 'confused'. Alternatively, it is possible to develop a simple board game, writing different emotions on different squares. You can then take it in turns with the child to roll the dice and give examples of when each of you have felt the particular feeling denoted by the square upon which a player has landed. It helps develop a trusting relationship with the child because it involves the practitioner and the child both sharing information, instead of just the child having to reveal information.

Three Houses

The Three Houses tool was first developed by Nicki Weld and colleagues in New Zealand and is also mentioned in Munro's final report (Weld 2008). All that is needed are paper and colouring pencils, and it can be used in a very practical way to help a child talk about what they may be worried about, what is working well and what needs to happen or change. It locates these key assessment foci in three houses – namely, the 'House of Worries', 'House of Good Things' and 'House of Dreams' – to try to help the child express these feelings in a child-friendly way.

When using the tool, start with either yourself or the child drawing one house outline on three different large sheets of paper. Then label the houses: 'House of Worries', 'House of Good Things' and 'House of Dreams'. Variations of this that can be used with slightly older children include: 'House of Vulnerabilities', 'House of Strengths' and 'House of Hopes and Dreams'. Begin by explaining to the child the three different houses and what they mean. It can sometimes be helpful to use word examples or pictures to try to engage the child in the session. Then ask the child which house they want to start with, although it can often be helpful to start with the 'House of Good Things', especially if a child is anxious or unsure. In this house, ask them to write or draw anything that makes them feel happy and positive. Then ask them to talk about the 'House of Worries', this time asking them to write or draw anything that makes them feel scared or concerned.

In the final 'House of Dreams' you could ask them a 'miracle' or 'wish' question, such as 'What would life be like if a miracle happened and you woke up in your dream world?' As the child draws or speaks, it can be helpful to write down their explanations at the side of the houses. Like most of the techniques describe above, the information gained can offer a powerful insight into a child's inner world and be used to help inform decisions about their future welfare.

What does the play in a session tell you?

When you have undertaken at least two to three sessions with a child, reflect on each of the sessions and take note of predominant themes and patterns such as 'good' versus 'evil', being kidnapped/rescued, loss/death or aggression/power. We are only looking for themes or patterns which can then be highlighted and referenced in our reports, rather than imposing our values or judgements.

With maltreated children, stories tend to end in disaster as they have not learned any means of conflict resolution. Such children tend to rely on magic or fantasy in their thinking in which the story may progress from disaster to having a wonderful time with the abusing parent. One way to help bring the work 'alive' in our assessments is to use the actual material (with permission) from the direct work, such as the child's picture from the Islands game, which can provide a very powerful visual representation of a child's inner world without the need for significant interpretation.

Conclusion

In conclusion, when carrying out direct work with children it is important to be mindful that whilst the focus of such work is often on the here and now, it must also be informed by a sense of the child's history in relation to the behaviour of the present. In addition, at an organizational level, if direct work is to be carried out effectively and confidently by practitioners, it requires the development of a culture within child protection agencies that promotes such work, as well as ensuring that time be protected to be able to do so; however, these techniques should not be employed as standalone methods nor be utilised to try to identify and assess attachment 'styles'. It is instead envisaged that they can be used in conjunction with other methods of assessment and investigation, such as parent-child observations and parent/carer/child interviews to provide a more holistic picture of a child's experience and therefore better inform decision making.

Chapter 11

Using the Child Attachment Interview

David Phillips

At the Moorfield Family Assessment Centre in Enfield, North London, we have been using ideas from attachment theory and techniques associated with the ADAM Project for several years. Attachment theory has provided a useful map to help us make sense of the human landscape of parent-child relationships and, in particular, understand the impact of maltreatment on young minds.

Whether undertaking court-directed assessments of parenting capacity where children are subject to care proceedings, or supporting families with children living at home with protection plans, a central theme of our work is trying to explore and understand the extent to which a child feels understood and held 'in mind' by their primary carers. Is the parent able to react to the child's intentions and behaviours accurately and not overwhelm the child? Without this experience, the child is unable to learn to recognise or regulate their feelings effectively and their emotional and behavioural development is likely to be significantly impaired.

For parents with infants and young children, we try to observe the micro-detail of their interaction, using video to explore the parent's capacity to read and respond sensitively to their child's signals and cues. For example, does the parent show 'mentalizing capacity', that is, a willingness, interest and ability to understand their infant's feelings and intentions as being different from their own? We also use guided parenting tasks to assess the parent's ability to manage and regulate more effectively their child's emotions and behaviour, as well as video-based feedback 'attunement' exercises to help assess the parent's capacity to reflect on, and make sense of, their child's world.

We do not currently use the Strange Situation Procedure in our work, but an understanding of it can still provide insights when assessing interaction between young children and their parents. For example, recently I chaired an initial meeting at our centre with a young woman with a history of heroin abuse and domestic violence, whose two-year-old daughter had attracted a child protection plan focused on neglect. When momentarily obscured from her mother's view, the child accidentally hurt her head whilst exploring a new toy in the corner of the room. She looked startled, upset and then immediately sought proximity with her mother, navigating her way past myself and my colleague to reach her mother. The child was quickly soothed by her mother's consoling response ('Oh, did you hurt yourself? Let mum make it better') and, after a few moments, confidently resumed her exploration of the toys at the other end of the room, having had her feelings of distress recognised and effectively managed. Such unplanned events can offer important attachment-related information, but to understand more fully the extent of a child's 'organised' versus 'disorganised' attachment behaviour, we would need to have observed reunion episodes.

Our work with the family has only just started, and we have yet to develop a formulation with the mother regarding the predisposing, precipitating, perpetuating and protective factors regarding her substance misuse and ability to ensure her safety and her daughter's safety; however, the interaction observed in the meeting suggested that the child viewed her mother as a 'secure base' and, so far at least, she had experienced her mother as available and emotionally responsive to her.

In our individual work with children and young people we incorporate attachment-based assessments to develop an understanding of the child's parenting, their feelings about themselves and whether they trust and feel secure with their parents or carers. For our court-directed parenting assessments we meet with a child for a minimum of three sessions and use a range of tools. For younger children, four to eight years of age, we use story stems in our first session. For children and young people nine to fifteen years of age we use the Child Attachment Interview (CAI).

This chapter focuses on three examples to demonstrate how we have applied the CAI to our work. The first example involves Jennie, a nine-year-old girl from a white English family who was living at home with her younger siblings on a child protection plan under the category of neglect. The second example features Patrick, a 13-year-old Congolese boy who was accommodated with a foster carer following his mother's formal detention in a psychiatric hospital. The third example involves Selma, an 11-year-old Turkish girl who was also subject to a child protection plan, under the category of emotional abuse.

Children's attachment security is a reflection of their expectation that their parents, or primary carers, are emotionally available and responsive to them when needed. Bowlby (1988) used the concept of a child's 'internal working model' to describe how children internalise these expectations, positive or negative. The CAI is concerned with revealing and exploring these representations of attachment figures and the extent to which feelings can be thought about and understood, contained and managed. In this way the CAI is like an archaeological tool, as it provides strong clues as to the child's caregiving history.

The CAI was originally developed as a research tool rather than as a clinical, diagnostic tool for work with individual children. In research a certain amount of error will not affect overall findings, but on an individual level, for example, in court proceedings, this could have major implications. Caution is therefore needed in the interpretation of an individual child's CAI (which, as we saw in Chapter 1, is true of each component in the Pathway Model).

Munro (1999) warned against the risk of practitioners' concrete thinking and bias when using a single hypothesis or method of assessment. In our attempts to establish what is least likely to be wrong in our assessments of child–parent relationships we use the method of 'triangulation' (a term originating from surveying to denote the geometric method of locating one point in space from the intersection of three or more different starting positions). This involves testing the validity of our findings by cross-checking them with, for example, information obtained from using other approaches to see to what extent they converge. The CAI is therefore just one of several techniques we use in our direct work with children, and these findings are combined with information from observations of parent-child interaction and direct work with parents.

The CAI is a semi-structured interview, originally designed for middle childhood (i.e. children eight to twelve years old), but it has been extended for use with adolescents up to the age of 15 years. As with the Strange Situation Procedure, it aims to activate mildly the attachment system and is characterised as a meeting between a child and a stranger in an unfamiliar setting. The interview takes approximately 30–40 minutes (and is preferably filmed). The interviewer asks direct questions. Practice is needed to elicit the right information by avoiding the use of leading questions and *not* pointing out contradictory statements. The interviewer needs to hold in mind the importance of assessing the child's view of their relationship with their attachment figure by exploring specific interactions or 'relationship episodes' between them.

Appropriate training is needed given the delicate nature of the interview, the vulnerability of the children and the importance of eliciting the right information and then making sense of it. Over the past three years, seven members of our team (including social workers, family support workers and our clinical psychologist) have attended the four-day training at the Anna Freud Centre in North London. This training includes learning how to review and analyse videotaped interviews using the coding manual. Many of the team have also attended ADAM Project training.

This chapter does not include detail about the coding or scoring system and makes reference only to limited sections of the protocol itself; however, in summary, the scoring system is based initially on identifying relationship episodes within the interview and then coding each episode individually. These codes form the basis for an overall attachment classification with respect to the child's mother and father independently. There are nine scales in the coding system, including 'emotional openness', 'preoccupied or involving anger', 'idealization' and 'dismissal and/or derogation of attachment.'

Emotional openness is concerned with the range of feelings the child describes and the extent to which they show an understanding of the relationship between emotions, mental states and behaviour. *Preoccupied anger* is concerned with the degree to which a child expresses anger or complaint that is uncontained and unresolved. *Idealization* refers to the extent to which the child's representations of attachment figures are distorted in a positive direction, while *dismissal and/or derogation* describes the extent to which the child adopts a strategy that aims to minimise the importance of attachment figures and relationships by active dismissal and/or derogation.

In our practice at the centre we rarely transcribe, code or score an interview to determine formally a child's attachment classification as being secure, insecure avoidant (or dismissing) or insecure ambivalent (or preoccupied.) Given that the proportion of the population with avoidant or ambivalent styles is around 40 per cent, this in itself is not that helpful; instead, we look for themes regarding the child's perceptions of their attachment figures' emotional availability and responsiveness. We also screen for markers of disorganised attachment behaviour and look to identify the child's ability to 'bring their mind' to the task of understanding and making sense of themselves and others.

We regularly watch videos of CAIs (as well as story stems, adult attachment interviews and films of parent-child interaction) together as a team or in smaller groups. This peer review of our work provides an external source of observation and guards against over-interpretation when analysing and attempting to articulate what we see. It also helps us develop our practise skills using the techniques. For example, could the interviewer have offered a different prompt or 'scaffolding' to the child here; was that a missed opportunity to explore a 'relationship episode'? Incidentally, colleagues report that regularly 'exposing' their filmed practise to team scrutiny has been a supportive and affirming experience and has helped promote learning and morale.

Examples of how we have applied the CAI

Example 1: Jennie

Jennie was subject to a child protection plan under the category of 'neglect'. She was nine years old, the second eldest of four children. Her family has a long history of involvement with Children's Services in several neighbouring London boroughs. Social work records show that five years prior, Jennie and her siblings were removed from their parents and placed in foster care for several months after a catalogue of concerns, including domestic violence, parental drug misuse, a chaotic lifestyle and non-engagement with helping agencies.

Despite the apparently poor prognosis for change, Jennie and her siblings had subsequently been returned to their parents' care on supervision orders and had since had several changes of address, the latest being to our area. The well-intentioned social work report that had originally recommended this return home had contained no information or analysis from the children's perspective about how they experienced their parents' care. The report did, however, contain positive and largely unsubstantiated self-reporting from the parents. Based on limited observations of family interaction during supervised contact, the report had also concluded that the parents 'both had a good attachment to the children', a meaningless – there is no such thing as a 'good' attachment – and, in this context, misleading phrase. The referral to our team for outreach support focused on the need to help the parents establish and maintain household routines, but it identified no particular concerns for Jennie's emotional or behavioural development. As part of our work with the family, I undertook a CAI with Jennie at our centre.

Children who have experienced their parents or primary carers as reliable, emotionally available and responsive tend to demonstrate a high degree of emotional openness and coherence when asked to reflect on their relationships with them. Experiences and relationships are assessed and valued, sense is made of conflict and vulnerability is acknowledged. By contrast, children who have experienced their parents' behaviour as unresponsive, unpredictable or frightening are not able to reflect on their feelings in an open, balanced or coherent way.

Whilst acknowledging some current difficulties with household routines due to problems with welfare benefits and temporary housing, both Jennie's parents insisted that they were providing a warm, loving and safe home environment for her. Apart from occasional poor attendance and an unkempt appearance at times, information from her new primary school did not contradict this view. Jennie was not reported as displaying any conspicuous difficulties in the classroom or playground. This apparently reassuring picture may have reflected what the school had been asked. Questions about Jennie's capacity to show empathy to her peers or her capacity to regulate her emotions may have revealed a different view.

If Jennie's parents were providing her with the emotional care they insisted they were, the hypothesis was that her CAI would support this. For example, Jennie would be able to provide specific, illustrative examples to support positive descriptions of what it was like to be with her parents and provide relevant examples of when her parents had responded to her needs. The following is an extract from the first part of Jennie's interview:

DP: I wonder if you can you tell me three words that describe yourself – not what you look like, but what sort of person you are.

Jennie: Crazy…hyper…and funny.

DP: Okay, great, I'll write them down. The first word you chose was 'crazy'. Can you give me an example of when you felt you were crazy?

Jennie: When I was in the playground I was crazy.

DP: And what were you doing in the playground that you felt was crazy?

Jennie: I was just being crazy…I don't know…just crazy, mad, that's it…

DP: The second word you chose was 'hyper'. Can you tell me about a time when you felt you were hyper?

Jennie: …Don't know…next question!

DP: Okay. Well, the third word you chose was 'funny'. Can you tell me about a time when you felt you were funny?

Jennie: I was…(long pause)…can't remember…

DP: Right, okay, now I'd like to ask you a different question. Can you tell me three words to describe what it's like to be with your mum?

Jennie: Happy…joyful…(long pause)

DP: Happy and joyful, right, that's two, that's great. Can you think of a third word to describe what it's like to be with mum?

(Long pause, Jennie looks out of the window)

DP: Not to worry. Do you want to start with these two and see if something comes up later?

(Jennie shrugs)

DP: Right, the first word you chose was 'happy'. Can you tell me about a time when you felt happy being with your mum?

Jennie: ...Mum and me had a girl's day. Mum buyed (sic) me trousers and a top...that's it.

DP: And how do you think your mum felt when she bought you the clothes?

Jennie: Don't know...this is boring, how long is it going to take?

DP: Well, I was hoping to talk with you for about another twenty minutes, if you're okay with that. Like I said before, it's not a test, there's no right or wrong answers, but I really want to know what you feel and think about your family. Now, the second word you chose was 'joyful'. Can you tell me about the last time you felt joyful being with your mum?

Jennie: Yesterday she let us go in the soft play room (at the centre.) That's it. She bought us food. That's it. Full stop.

DP: Okay, and can you think of a third word to describe what it's like to be with your mum?

Jennie: I don't know. I can't remember.

In the extract above Jennie showed a very limited ability or willingness to think about her own feelings or those of her mother. She frequently responded to questions with 'I don't know' or 'I can't remember', with little apparent effort to recall, as if wanting to block further discussion. She also appeared to idealise her relationship with her mother, as she struggled to support her very positive description of this relationship as 'happy' and 'joyful' with convincing illustrative examples. In fact, the limited examples that she did give, of being bought clothes and food, emphasised material rather than emotional comfort.

In the next extract from Jennie's interview, she was invited to think about a time of conflict with her mother and was also asked about her relationship with her father:

DP: What happens when your mum gets cross with you or tells you off?

Jennie: Don't know… she shouts.

DP: Okay, can you tell me about what happened the last time she shouted?

Jennie: Er, don't know…I can't remember.

DP: Do you usually know the reason that mum gets cross?

Jennie: Sometimes…(long pause)…I do know…I don't want to tell you.

DP: Well, how did you feel when mum got cross and shouted at you?

Jennie: Don't know…just normal, that's it.

DP: Okay, I'd like to ask you about you and your dad now. Can you choose three words to describe what it's like to be with your dad? I'll write them down.

Jennie: Fantastic…fun…(very long pause)…isolated…

DP: Right, the first word was 'fantastic'. Can you tell me about a time when it felt fantastic to be with your dad?

Jennie: Don't know…(pause)…I forgot…(pause)…Coffee!… He… he…he made me funny…

DP: The second word you chose was 'fun'. Can you tell me about a time recently that it was fun to be with dad?

Jennie: He…he took me to a funfair in London…(pause).

DP: Wow, a funfair, and what happened next?

Jennie: We went to London to visit the Queen…that's it.

DP: The last word you chose to describe what it was like being with your dad was 'isolated'. Can you start by saying what you mean by isolated?

Jennie: What's isolated?…I don't know…I can't think of another word…(long pause).

As in the first extract, Jennie's responses were very limited, and any exploration of feelings were quickly shut down (for example, by responses such as 'Can't remember' and 'Just normal'). It might be argued that, given the context of care proceedings, it would be understandable if a child like Jennie was wary about disclosing any information about their parents; however, as with her mother, Jennie's generally positive description of her relationship with her father appeared strongly idealised. Despite choosing some positive terms, she was unable to support them with any coherent or plausible examples.

Another theme of the interview was Jennie's difficulty in expressing any spontaneous feelings of need or vulnerability, and then only in response to specific prompts, such as 'How did you feel about that?' When Jennie did express feelings of vulnerability, this was in very limited terms. Emotions were labelled but, even with prompts, she was unable to elaborate further. For example, later in the interview, in response to being asked about a time when she was ill, Jennie stated, 'I watched TV. Mum and dad gave me a pillow and made me dinner. It was a shame I puked it all up. Next day Jennie was feeling better… that's it'. Asked about a time that she had felt hurt, Jennie again quickly replied, 'Can't remember…don't know' without any apparent effort to bring her mind to the task. With all of these examples, the practitioner needs to rule out that the child is not merely being un-cooperative or 'stroppy'; this can be established by comparing CAI responses with what the child would typically be like, both with the interviewer and with the parent(s) (but not with the child's peers).

I interpreted Jennie's interview as showing signs of an insecure-avoidant attachment strategy towards both her parents. This pattern is not associated with a child's home environment being emotionally available and supportive as Jennie's parents had portrayed, but rather a caregiving environment that is predictably unresponsive. But around 25 per cent of individuals are avoidantly attached, so it is not uncommon for people to find it difficult to discuss emotions.

Of further concern was that Jennie's interview also showed some behaviour or 'markers' characteristic of disorganised attachment behaviour, which is closely associated with children who have experienced maltreatment and/or a caregiving environment that is frightening. For example, although Jennie complied with the interview, there were times when she showed a rather controlling and withholding stance (e.g. 'Next question!', 'This is boring, how long is it going to take?', 'I do know…I don't want to tell you').

Also, although Jennie's account did not contain any catastrophic or bizarre imagery, her answers at times appeared rather disconnected and odd. For example, in response to being asked to give an example of when it had felt fantastic to be with her father, Jennie replied, 'I forgot…Coffee!... He...he…he made me funny…'. When describing a time when she was ill, Jennie also referred to herself in the third person: 'It was a shame I puked it all up. Next day Jennie was feeling better…'. Although not readily detectable from the dialogue, from watching the videotape it was evident that Jennie's mood during the interview fluctuated quite dramatically at times, from being very animated and rather theatrical to long periods of silence which did not appear to involve her thinking or trying to develop her answers.

Although it was used as evidence in the final court report (under the heading 'Direct Work with Jennie'), the CAI was not the deciding factor in the court's subsequent decision to grant interim care orders for her and her siblings and place them with alternative carers. Her parents' preoccupation with their own unmet needs and their inability to demonstrate that they could make any sustained positive changes to their parenting, despite the intensive help offered, provided more persuasive evidence to the court; however, the CAI did provide a way of exploring and starting to understand how Jennie experienced her parents' care. It strongly suggested that her home environment was not warm and responsive as her parents had maintained (and possibly believed). Due to their own unmet needs, Jennie's parents may have been unaware that their caregiving was not adequate; instead, the CAI indicated that Jennie experienced her parents' behaviour as consistently unresponsive, confusing and at times probably frightening, too. This view was subsequently confirmed during observations of family interaction during supervised contact, following Jennie's placement with her siblings in foster care. Both parents appeared enmeshed in their own relationship and consistently failed to respond to Jennie's cues. For example, on one occasion, as if replicating in real life one of the story stems used for younger children, Jennie attempted to present her father with a detailed drawing she had made of him at her foster placement. The gift was met with disapproval rather than delight ('That doesn't look anything like me!') and Jennie quickly retreated to the corner of the room to play quietly with dolls. A video-feedback exercise, similar to the one discussed in Chapters 6 and 7, where the parents watched footage of their interaction with Jennie and her siblings (and at regular intervals were invited to provide subtitles for what the children were feeling or thinking) further revealed their inability to recognise or respond to the children's mental states.

To conclude this account of using the CAI with Jennie, a second, follow-up CAI, perhaps 18 months into her placement and incorporating questions about her new carer as well as her parents, might provide important clues as to whether her attachment security had changed. The hypothesis would be that in a care environment where she is consistently held in mind, and feelings and behaviour are recognised, managed and made sense of, Jennie's attachment strategy would, over time, become more organised.

Pace *et al.* (2012) analysed the attachment patterns of 28 late-adopted children (placed when they were between four and seven years of age) using the Manchester Child Attachment Story Task. For children placed with adoptive mothers who were themselves assessed as 'secure-autonomous' using the Adult Attachment Interview, they found a significant change from insecure to secure attachment patterns within seven months of their placement. For older children like Jennie, it might be reasonable to suggest that their inner working models and attachment strategies would take rather longer to change significantly.

Example 2: Patrick

Thirteen-year-old Patrick and his two younger siblings had just been accommodated in foster care following their mother's formal detention in psychiatric hospital. The family had not been known to Children's Services prior to the mother's episode of disturbed behaviour, which had included the children having been beaten by her.

Undertaking the CAI with Patrick provided an initial way of assessing the impact of his family experiences on his emotional well-being and an opportunity to explore his understanding of his mother's mental health difficulties. The CAI was also used to explore Patrick's relationship with his non-resident father, who had recently made contact with Children's Services following his return from the Democratic Republic of Congo. In the following extract Patrick's ability to reflect on feelings of vulnerability was assessed by asking him to recall times when he had been upset, hurt and ill:

DP: Can you tell me about a time when you felt upset or misunderstood and wanted help?

Patrick: When my mum was…when she's ill sometimes…it puts me in a place that I have to look after my little sister and brother and try and tell them not to make too much noise or not to make too much trouble because my mum's ill, and to go easy on her…stuff like that.

DP: And can you tell me what happens when you're ill?

Patrick: Sometimes I feel sorry for my mum 'cos she has loads of jobs she has to juggle. She has to take my little brother and sister to school, look after me, sort the house…

DP: What does looking after you involve?

Patrick: Well, she'll make me a hot drink or something and see if I have any symptoms.

DP: Have you been ill when Dad has been at home too?

Patrick: Yes, he tried to cheer me up…like, just 'cos I'm ill doesn't mean I can't have fun, and I felt like I was getting better.

DP: What happens when you get hurt?

Patrick: Do you mean emotionally or physically?

DP: Either, what comes to mind?

Patrick: I don't know, I'm not usually in that situation. When I had chicken pox I had big lumps of spots and I had to stay out of school for a week and a few days and…uh…my mum and my dad tried to look after me and tried to think of a way to get me better. I had to go to hospital to check what it was, and eventually I got better.

DP: Has anything really big happened to you that upset or scared or confused you?

Patrick: Well, the first day I came into care really scared and worried me. It felt like it was a nightmare, or I thought I was still in a nightmare. It was very upsetting, but at the same time I was thinking what my mum would feel.

DP: Was your mum there at the time?

Patrick: Yeah, she was crying, she wasn't really saying too much to me, just to look after your brother and sister and stay safe.

DP: What about dad, what did he say about it?

Patrick: He wasn't there at the time, he was in Africa. My mum didn't have his number and social services were still trying to get numbers for him.

DP: What do you think will happen next?

Patrick: I don't know, I can't really get the picture of what's going to happen.

A number of themes emerge from Patrick's responses in this extract. First, in contrast to Jennie's CAI in example 1, Patrick showed no signs of anxiety or confusion; instead, he appeared calm and thoughtful and showed a willingness and ability to reflect on family experiences from his own and his mother's perspective in a balanced way ('It was very upsetting but at the same time I was thinking what my mum would feel'). He was also able to think about experiences from his younger siblings' perspective (' ...my foster carer...tried to make me feel, make us feel, that we're safe...').

Second, Patrick was comfortable to acknowledge feelings of vulnerability (' ...the first day I came into care really scared and worried me'). His answers also demonstrated an ability to reflect on his experiences. He gave coherent examples and responses that suggested that he valued his relationships with his mother and father. By contrast, children who have not felt understood by their parents, who have not had the experience of their vulnerable feelings being recognised and responded to, often have difficulty acknowledging vulnerability. Compare Patrick's answers with those given by Richard (below), a 14-year-old boy living at home with his parents with a child protection plan centring on neglect, who I interviewed shortly after Patrick. Richard's account was very dismissive of any feelings of vulnerability and instead emphasised self-reliance, suggesting that he had developed an avoidant or dismissing attachment strategy. This strategy was necessary to enable him to cope with a caregiving environment that the evidence would suggest was consistently unresponsive to his emotional-care needs. But, again, around 25 per cent of children and adults have an avoidant attachment organization, which does not necessarily indicate the possibility of maltreatment.

The following extract is from the CAI with Richard:

DP: Can you tell me about a time when you felt upset or misunderstood and wanted help?

Richard: Uh...my granddad went to hospital. Mum cried. I didn't cry, I never cry.

DP: And can you tell me what happens when you're ill?

Richard: I don't know. I'm never ill.

DP: What happens when you get hurt?

Richard: Nothing. I'm used to pain. Once I got hit by a car. I was on my bicycle and it hit my back wheel. I've been hit by a car three times, actually.

Returning to Patrick's CAI, his account of what happens when he is ill did not include any specific displays of emotional warmth from his mother; however, his account did suggest that he feels 'held in mind' by his parents ('My mum and my dad tried to think of a way to get me better'). This ability to reflect on, and make sense of, his family experiences strongly suggested that Patrick had experienced reasonably sensitive parenting in the past.

Young people with a parent(s) with mental health difficulties can often feel confused by their parent's behaviour, and feel responsible, blame themselves or believe they will become ill, too (Aldridge 2006). Patrick's interview highlighted that he felt worried and responsible for his mother's welfare and that he wanted to be given further information about her illness. Given that children's social workers often do not feel confident to explore parental mental health with children, and adult mental health workers do not feel qualified to talk with children, it was important that this issue was recognised.

Little was known about Patrick's relationship with his father. For example, his father's own account of having played an active parenting role with his children was contradicted by his mother, who insisted he was a largely absent and unreliable figure to the children, and the school had not had any contact with him. The CAI was helpful in exploring Patrick's relationship with his father. Having been asked for three words to describe what it was like to be with him, Patrick was then asked to provide recent examples to illustrate his choices. For many children we work with there is often a tendency to provide idealised descriptions of their relationships with their parents, as we saw with Jennie in example 1. Difficulties are denied or dismissed, but idealised portrayals (using descriptions such as 'fun' or 'fantastic') are subsequently not supported by specific examples, or sometimes even contradicted.

Patrick's three words for his father did not suggest any idealization; instead, they appeared quite balanced and he was able to support them by giving some specific and relevant examples without prompting, as the following extract demonstrates:

DP: Now I'd like to ask you about your relationship with your dad. Can you choose three words to describe what it's like to be with him?

Patrick: Uh…fun…strong-willed…and a problem solver

DP: The first word you chose was 'fun'. Can you tell me about a recent time when it was fun being with your dad?

Patrick: Well, sometimes he'll play with us on Xbox, he'll join in even though he doesn't know how to play it. It can be very fun!

DP: The second word was 'strong-willed'. Can you tell me about a time your dad was strong-willed?

Patrick: He's someone you don't really want to get on the wrong side of…if you did, you'll be in a whole lot of trouble…or something like that.

DP: Okay, the third word you chose to describe your dad was 'problem solver'. Can you think of a time when you felt that dad was a problem solver?

Patrick: He's the sort of person you can go to if you have an issue or problem…like when I was in trouble at school and it wasn't my fault. He told me that if somebody annoys you, you should ignore them. Just try it or move away from that person so they don't distract you…or tell the teacher; and that helped.

DP: And what happens when dad gets cross and tells you off?

Patrick: Well, because he knows that I'm not really a fan of homework, he'll probably set me some homework to do, like division or maths. If it was a big problem, he'd probably tell me off and send me to my room.

DP: Can you think of the time that last happened?

Patrick: He told me to come off the Xbox at a certain time – he didn't want me playing the game for too long – and when he came back downstairs I was still on it so he told me to turn it off and he set me some homework.

DP: How did you feel about that?

Patrick: I was kinda okay with it, maybe a little cross.

DP: And how do you think your dad felt about telling you off?

Patrick: At the time he tells me off it was probably in his head that yeah…*You deserved it, you're the one who put it on yourself*…but afterwards he tried to explain why it was the wrong thing to do and tell you to try not to do it next time.

Asking Patrick about times of conflict with his father ('What happens when dad gets cross and tells you off?') provided some reassurance about the quality of their relationship. Patrick's account was reflective and coherent, and showed no signs of anger, confusion or dismissal. He was able to acknowledge that he may have felt a little cross although, significantly, he did not show any signs of resentment or 'unprocessed' anger when recounting the incident. Patrick's reference to what was 'probably in his head' at the time also suggests a capacity to 'mentalise' or think about feelings from his father's perspective also, not just his own. This was my first CAI and, on reflection, it should have contained more open-ended prompts to explore the 'relationship episodes' contained in the first two examples Patrick gave to support his description of his dad being 'fun' and 'strong-willed'. (Note that watching the video of the interview afterwards always shows how much you missed at the time.)

Patrick's ability to support a positive portrayal of his relationship with his father contradicted his mother's account that the children had little previous contact with their father. This information was highly relevant when subsequently assessing his father's capacity to provide alternative long-term care to Patrick and his younger siblings. Patrick's representation of his father as a 'secure base' in his CAI was subsequently supported by observations of parent-child interaction during supervised contact. Patrick and his younger siblings appeared open and comfortable with their father, and he in turn demonstrated a willingness and ability to 'tune in' to their mental states and effectively manage their emotions and behaviour.

The CAI also identified that Patrick felt protective and responsible for making his mother feel better, that he was worried about the future and he wanted help to make sense of his family's situation. Using materials from *Being Seen and Heard: The Needs of Children of Parents with Mental Illness* by Alan Cooklin (2006), his father was subsequently helped to talk together with Patrick and his siblings about their mother's mental illness. (Their mother remained too unwell to take part in this process.) Patrick and his siblings moved to their father's full-time care, and they continue to have regular contact with their mother.

Example 3: Selma

The final example involves Selma, an 11-year-old Turkish girl. Selma is the eldest of three siblings, all subject to child protection plans under the category of emotional abuse following a 'transfer-in' meeting from a neighbouring borough. Concerns for the children's welfare centred on reports that their parents argued constantly in front of them and that their mother showed little emotional warmth towards them. There had also been an incident when, having been left at home together, the children had started fighting and Selma had bitten her younger brother, bruising his arm.

Our service had been requested to provide outreach work in the family home, and a CAI was arranged with Selma in the initial stage of the work to explore her relationships with both her parents and assess the impact of her family life on her well-being. Although not specifically designed to gather biographical information, Selma's CAI proved very helpful in identifying important themes for the outreach work to focus on with her parents.

The following is an extract from near the beginning of the interview:

DP: I'd like you to choose three words that describe what it's like to be with your mum.

Selma: Sometimes embarrassing…loving…and…I can't remember…I don't know…sometimes boring.

DP: Okay, right, the first word, or phrase, you used was 'sometimes embarrassing'. Can you think of a time when you felt it was embarrassing being with mum?

Selma: I don't know…like sometimes when she can't explain things correctly it's a bit embarrassing. When she's trying to return something to a shop to get a refund and she can't explain it properly 'cos like her English isn't that amazing. Then it's a bit embarrassing.

DP: Okay, the second word you chose was 'loving'. Can you think of a particular time when it felt loving to be with mum?

Selma: I can't remember…At the end of the day I think everyone loves their mum, so that's why.

DP: Right, but can you tell me about a particular time it felt loving to be with her?

Selma: I can't remember…when we go to the shops and she buys me stuff that I want…I'll tell her I like something and then if she likes it too, then she'll buy it. First she'll look at the price tag and then she'll buy it.

DP: How does that make you feel?

Selma: Happy.

DP: And how do you think your mum feels?

Selma: Don't know…a little annoyed that she wasted money.

DP: The third word you chose was 'boring'. Can you tell me about a recent time when it felt boring being with your mum?

> *Selma*: When we go shopping, yeah, and then my mum like takes ages and I have to go with her and I have to wait, and waiting for me is quite boring.
>
> *DP*: What happens when mum gets cross with you and tells you off?
>
> *Selma*: She shouts and stuff.
>
> *DP*: Could you tell me about the last time mum got cross with you?
>
> *Selma*: Hmmm, I think about a month ago…
>
> *DP*: And why was she cross?
>
> *Selma*: I think it was because she had a lot on her plate and I wasn't helping her and she got cross with me. She was like, 'Please help me' and I said, 'Okay, okay, I'll help you', but then I didn't.
>
> *DP*: Was it fair that your mum got cross with you?
>
> *Selma*: Yes,'cos I said yes I would help, but I didn't.

Selma's representation of her relationship with her mother as sometimes embarrassing, loving and boring appeared quite balanced, although somewhat negative. She was able to provide examples to illustrate her choices, with limited prompting, and had little resentment or anger towards her mother. In response to the question about what happens when her mother becomes cross, Selma demonstrated some capacity to reflect and think about her mother's feelings ('I think it was because she had a lot on her plate and I wasn't helping her'). Her capacity to make sense of her experience and mentalise in this way was reassuring, as it suggested that she had experienced some degree of sensitivity and of having her own feelings understood by her parents.

It was also reassuring that Selma's account did not include any markers of disorganised attachment behaviour, which might have been expected if she had experienced her parents' behaviour as frightening. For example, she did not say anything that appeared nonsensical, bizarre or catastrophic; she did not appear controlling and she showed no sudden changes in mood or lapses into long silences.

In the next extract Selma was asked about her relationship with her father:

DP: Can you choose three words to describe what it's like to be with your dad?

Selma: I think it's fun…and boring.

DP: And do you have a third word?

Selma: Annoying.

DP: Okay, the first word you chose was 'fun.' Can you tell me about a time that it felt fun to be with dad?

Selma: It was fun because he says that I watch rubbish shows, like 'The Only Way Is Essex' and stuff like that, but in the end he joins in and watches it and he laughs at it as well.

DP: And the second word you chose was 'boring'. Can you think of a time when it felt boring?

Selma: He like, he like wants me to do all homework and I don't like doing homework. He's like, 'Yeah, doing homework is more important than watching TV' and I'm like, 'No!' He asks me sometimes, 'Is education more important than TV?' I usually say TV. I don't really mean it, but I say it 'cos it's more entertaining.

DP: Okay, and the third word you chose was 'annoying' Can you think of a time when it felt annoying to be with dad?

Selma: Once, my brother and sister were fighting and he said, 'No TV!' I was like, 'I didn't do nothing' and he said, 'I'm not going to bring the TV to your room so you can watch it on your own!' I said, 'It's not fair, I didn't do nothing' and he was really annoying!

DP: What happens when dad gets cross and tells you off?

Selma: He shouts at me.

DP: What does he get cross with you about?

Selma: Getting into fights with my brother…

DP: What do you fight about?

Selma: You're going to laugh at this…we fight about the remote control because we watch two different things. He likes cartoons and stuff like that and I prefer reality TV.

DP: Then what happens?

Selma: Dad says, 'No one is watching', or sometimes he says, 'Let your brother watch…', he says, 'Say sorry', and then I say sorry and it's finished…kind of…I don't really get a punishment or my brother doesn't get a punishment, that's what I think. I don't think sorry is enough, it's just a word that you say.

DP: What sort of punishment do you think your dad should give you?

Selma: Well, I'd like to say none, but he could turn the television off and stop us watching the programmes.

DP: Is it fair that dad gets angry and tells you off?

Selma: It's not fair on him, really…he gets stressed out.

As with her mother, Selma's three words to describe her relationship with her father were balanced, if a little negative ('fun', 'boring' and 'annoying'). Her ability to provide illustrative examples to support her choice of words suggested that she was able to make sense of her relationship with him. In the description of what happens when her father gets cross, for example, following arguments with her younger brother about the television, Selma described experiencing her father's attempts at resolving conflict as rather ineffectual ('I don't think sorry is enough, it's just a word that you say').

Selma's subsequent comments about her father providing firmer boundaries and managing disputes with her younger brother more effectively was later used in feedback to her parents. Her father acknowledged that he was not confident to do this and selected learning how to do so as one of the goals for the outreach work to target. (Information on motivational interviewing, setting targets for change and goal-attainment scaling, and the techniques used with Selma's parents can be found in Hamer 2005.)

In the next fragment from Selma's CAI, she was asked to recall examples of what happened when she was upset, hurt and needed help. She was asked directly whether she felt loved by her parents and also asked about what happened when her parents argued:

DP: Can you tell me about a time when you were upset and wanted help?

Selma: I don't think I…I don't think so…I don't think ever…

DP: You've never felt upset or misunderstood?

Selma: I have…but I can't remember…

DP: Do you ever feel that your parents don't really love you?

Selma: I don't know.

DP: If you did know, what might you say?

Selma: I think…I know they love me, but I think they don't act like it sometimes…like when my dad supports my brother and not me, that's how I feel, but deep down I know…

DP: What happens when you get hurt?

Selma: I get really upset.

DP: Can you tell me about a time when you got hurt?

Selma: I felt heartbroken…this girl was really rude to me. I didn't like it, but I didn't tell the teacher 'cos she has to sit next to me and would call me snitch and stuff.

DP: Did you tell anybody about it?

Selma: No.

DP: What about your mum and dad?

Selma: No.

DP: What would have happened if you'd told them?

Selma: They'd have gone to the school and said what the girl did and got in a massive row.

DP: Do your parents sometimes argue?

Selma: Yeah.

DP: Can you tell me about the last time they argued?

Selma: Two days ago. My dad works like fourteen hours but only brings thirty pounds and my mum said, 'What the hell are you doing then? You work fourteen hours and only get nothing'. My mum thinks he's giving it to another lady, that's from my point of view, but I don't really know.

DP: How do you feel when they argue?

Selma: Annoyed, 'cos not everybody's parents are like that…well, I just think that.

DP: You think other parents don't argue as much as yours?

Selma: Yeah…I think they do argue, but not as much.

DP: Do your parents know how you feel when they argue?

Selma: I think they do know, but my mum doesn't take it into consideration.

DP: How does that make you feel?

Selma: Annoyed. I think she should ask how I feel.

DP: And if she did, what would you say?

Selma: I think I'd say, 'I'm quite upset that you argue all the time'.

DP: And what would happen if she knew that?

Selma: I think she'd try not to argue so much with dad.

Selma initially appeared unwilling to acknowledge feelings of vulnerability when invited to recall a time when she was upset and needed help, but when asked about what happens when she gets hurt, she readily described an incident when she was upset by another girl calling her names at school. Selma did not tell either parent about her distress and did not appear to trust them to resolve the difficulty. At first sight, this might suggest that Selma did not experience her parents as a secure base; however, it is not uncommon for children not to tell their parents about school problems, because they fear their parents will react in a way that, however well-intentioned, gets them into more trouble. It is therefore important not to over-interpret children's responses and ideally to identify repeated themes which offer a better understanding of their underlying internal working models.

In response to the question 'Do your parents sometimes argue?' Selma made it clear that she felt upset and annoyed by her parents' frequent arguments. Her comment that her mother thinks her father is giving money to another woman suggested concerns regarding parental boundaries and information sharing, and that Selma was being exposed to sensitive adult information that could lead her to be anxious about the stability of her family.

Selma was also able to express the view that her own feelings were important and should be taken into consideration, and furthermore, that if her mother did know how she felt, she would try to argue less. With Selma's permission, her parents were later shown episodes from her CAI, including the sequence above where she described not telling her parents that she was upset and her feelings about their frequent arguments. Both her parents were responsive to this exercise and agreed that they wanted to improve their relationship and reduce their arguing. Subsequent video feedback of early-evening family interaction, and a parenting task to play the 'Nurturing Game' (see 'Resources' at end of Bibliography) together with the children, was also used to help the parents recognise their children's signals and respond more consistently to them.

Following positive reports from a range of sources, including Selma herself, the Child Protection Review Conference held several months later took the decision that the children no longer needed a protection plan. Selma's CAI proved a useful tool in understanding how she experienced her parents, and helped them become more emotionally available and responsive to her and her younger siblings.

Conclusion

Is using the CAI ethical with vulnerable children? Given that a guiding principle of our work with children and their families is 'Do not do any harm', it might be argued that it is unethical for an adult stranger to ask direct, anxiety-provoking questions to a vulnerable child deliberately designed to arouse and activate their attachment system, albeit mildly. My response to this concern is that a sensitively managed interview will be nothing like as traumatic as the child's lived experience. As with any other direct work with a child or young person, if they become distressed, we stop the interview, acknowledge that the questions are difficult and only continue if the child is comfortable to do so. At the end of all CAIs I say something like the following:

> Thank you very much for talking to me about your family. That was really helpful. Some of the questions were very tough and I wonder if you might want to talk to somebody later if our interview has stirred up difficult feelings or other questions? We're going to meet up again next week so we can talk some more then, but shall I let [name of carer, teacher, family member] know that I've asked you some very hard questions today?

For children already exposed to maltreating and neglectful parenting, it is delay that is most damaging. Timely and purposeful assessments are in the child's best interest, and in our experience the CAI is a useful tool to help with this process.

Chapter 12

Working with Children and Families to Promote a Secure Base

Claire Denham and Jo George

In working to promote a secure base for children, we seek opportunities to highlight and encourage shared positive emotions between parents and children. This work also supports adults in reducing levels of conflict in their close relationships and their relationships with children, and helps foster a sense of connectedness between primary caregivers and the children in their care.

We explore ways to increase adults' empathy for children, seeking to explain behaviours in an attachment-focused manner (where the need for comfort and reassurance might be present), by providing adults and children with activities that promote calm, positive emotional engagement to encourage warm, loving, but non-intrusive, touch between adults and children through sustained eye contact. We also seek conversations with adults which help them identify ways in which they emotionally engage with children, but more importantly, the ways they emotionally *disengage*, for example, at times of acute stress or emotional arousal.

These methods are useful in helping build a secure base because they focus on emotional regulation, developing adults' understanding of the internal world of the child, as well as increasing emotional warmth, emotional availability and attunement to children's cues for comfort and reassurance. They also stress the need for children to explore safely the world around them.

Much of the work takes place where there are concerns about parenting within a broader context of managing risk in the home, and where there is an overriding goal of promoting resilience and sensitive care to foster and sustain the child's sense of security.

Case studies

We describe and discuss four families in which the Pathway Model was used to assess and help the parents and children of those families.

Case 1: Arri

In the first family, we applied the Pathway Model using the strange situation and observation techniques with a two-year-old girl. An Adult Attachment Interview (AAI) was also carried out with the mother, and this was followed by direct work sessions between the mother and her child.

Arri was two years old when Children's Social Care became involved with her family. Her mother, Lisa, a young British Bangladeshi, had been married to Bruce, a white Scottish man with schizophrenia, older than Lisa by about ten years. Arri was made the subject of a child protection plan because we were concerned that she could be experiencing significant harm as a result of extremely insensitive parenting, witnessing domestic abuse and emotionally distressing interactions between her parents, as well as experiencing physical neglect in relation to feeding, nurturing and warm touch. Cleanliness was also addressed as a concern, as well as a lack of supervision. Arri was observed to become 'frozen', especially when her father was around, and it was noted that she did not turn to her mother for protection and comfort. The mother was noted to be irritable in her responses to Arri. Lisa appeared not to be physically or emotionally available to Arri and she told us that she was sleeping during the day.

At the time of our intervention Bruce had been asked to leave the family home following an incident of domestic abuse. Subsequently all contact was suspended between he and Arri following a contact session where the father aggressively shook Arri when he insisted that she was staring at him. But despite the father being out of the family home, there remained many concerns for her emotional welfare. Her 'frozen' behaviour suggested she was traumatised by exposure to her father's volatile and aggressive behaviour, the arguments between her parents and the failure of either parent to protect her from, or respond to, her distress. She also showed delayed development, suggesting chronic under-stimulation. Due to Arri's age, most of the assessment was conducted through observation in addition to an AAI with Lisa.

Subsequent work with the mother focused on increasing mentalization and attunement.

A Strange Situation Procedure (SSP) was conducted to gain a better understanding of Arri's attachment behaviour. Arri did not know us at the time of the procedure but did not show any physical or emotional distress when Lisa left the room. She stood and turned to look towards the door. When Lisa re-entered the room, Arri stared at her blankly. Lisa moved across the room and sat down on a nearby chair. Arri did not move; she stood and stared at her mother. It was thought that Arri presented with signs of significantly insecure, but not disorganised, attachment behaviour during this procedure, especially given her unresponsiveness to her mother's departure and that neither Arri nor Lisa sought physical contact on reunion. Avoidantly attached children tend not to overtly seek physical contact and often avoid their carer when distressed. Arri appeared to adapt to this rejecting caregiving by downplaying and inhibiting her need for comfort and reassurance.

Throughout the observations it became clearer that Arri was unaccustomed to positive interaction, for example, by not having her feelings noticed or attended. We observed that Arri did not seek comfort and reassurance by openly crying or complaining. Different practitioners felt that Arri repressed her distress at being ignored, keeping her feelings inside. Arri was unable to comfort herself, as she did not have her attachment figure to help her regulate feelings of distress, fear and insecurity.

Arri's distress was particularly evident in one observation of her response to her mother collecting her from nursery. When Lisa entered the nursery, Arri remained expressionless; she appeared slightly nervous and stood in one place, staring blankly at her mother whilst rocking side to side. She seemed to distance herself from her mother upon reunion and did not seek physical closeness. Throughout this interaction, Lisa did not speak to Arri or look at her. It was as if Arri was invisible. There was no warm greeting but instead an expectation that Arri should follow her out of the room. Arri did not complain or demand attention, and she followed Lisa out of the nursery. This could have indicated the possibility of disorganised attachment behaviour, but as this was not a controlled SSP, we could only speculate on what we had observed. Although we had not seen disorganization upon reunion when we conducted the SSP previously, these serendipitous observations made us question whether Arri's insecurity might be more severe than we first thought.

Although Lisa was hurried at the time, we surmised that a primary attachment figure who often interacted positively and with sensitivity to their child would not hold back as much as we witnessed; moreover, a child used to regular positive interaction would know how to elicit a nurturing, attentive response from their attachment figure, especially when reunited after being apart for several hours. Arri's behaviour was in great contrast to when the practitioner came into the nursery room. In this instance, Arri's response was more animated. Upon the practitioner's arrival, Arri's face brightened with a smile and she wanted to give the practitioner a cuddle.

The two observations of Arri heightened concerns about her emotional and social development, and provided us with insight into her experiences of being cared for and the impact this could be having on her development. Arri's behaviour struck us as an adaptive strategy developed in the context of her immediate caregiving environment. It suggested that Lisa's responses did not help her understand and cope with the world and what was happening around her. When she looked worried and in need of reassurance, this appeared to go unnoticed by Lisa. Arri did not try to engage her mother and seemed surprised when her mother *did* pay her attention. We wondered whether Lisa's own feelings surfaced when she herself felt overwhelmed or upset. Throughout our observations, Lisa appeared expressionless and spoke in a monotone voice; in response, Arri was withdrawn, disengaged and understimulated. Consequently, we decided to complete an AAI with Lisa.

Lisa grew up in a family where her mother suffered from chronic depression and where she and her siblings had to look after themselves. Lisa reacted to this experience by giving up any expectation that her mother would meet her needs, just as Arri seemed to be doing in her care. Lisa was assessed as having low mentalizing capacity. She engaged with the interview yet was flat and showed little emotion when describing loss and a deprived childhood. Lisa showed limited capacity to reflect on her experiences of being parented and what she would do differently with Arri. (She showed very little appreciation of Arri's thoughts, emotions or experiences.) Our assessments concluded that Arri presented with markedly insecure attachment behaviours with the possibility of some disorganization, which led us to conclude that:

- Lisa was passive and did not initiate contact or interact with Arri. There was little direct eye contact or verbal interaction between them. She preferred to observe Arri rather than interact with her.

- Arri was unusually quiet and she did not seek interaction with her mother. We felt that this was because she did not have an expectation that Lisa would respond to her.

- Arri's social skills appeared delayed for her age, as she showed little interest in other children when her mother was present. (Arri appeared more interested in other children and adults, however, when she attended nursery on her own.)

- Arri was more able to respond to interaction and praise from nursery staff but was unresponsive when her mother attempted to carry out mentalization tasks with them (see below).

Our intervention would need to help Arri learn to trust caregivers before she could take steps towards becoming more securely attached to Lisa. If we were to help Arri to feel more secure, we would need to understand whether or not Lisa would be able to hold Arri 'in mind'.

We undertook a 'mentalizing' task with Lisa. Direct work was focused on helping her develop better attunement to Arri's emotional needs whilst at the same time being able to contain Arri's insecure feelings and anxious behaviour. This was achieved by helping focus Lisa's mind on Arri's mind, first of all by encouraging her to try to understand that Arri actually possessed a 'state of mind'. For example, we asked Lisa what she thought was in Arri's mind when Lisa came towards her. We asked Lisa what she thought Arri might be thinking when she started to cry and looked at her mother. We also asked what she felt Arri might be thinking when someone she had not encountered came into the room (and why Arri looked nervously at her mother).

We also encouraged Lisa to look at Arri's face, and watch her behaviour, whilst we talked to Lisa as if *Arri* was speaking to her mother – 'speaking for the child' – framing Arri's behaviour in the language of attachment. When Arri went towards Lisa with her arms outstretched, we would say 'Look mummy, I'm not sure about this situation and I'm a bit frightened. I'm going to come to you because it makes me feel safe' thereby helping Lisa connect Arri's proximity-seeking behaviour with asking for safety, and reinforcing Lisa as a safe haven for her daughter. Our work with Lisa and Arri continues.

Case 2: Charlie

Charlie was 18 months old when Children's Social Care become involved with his family. He had been taken into police protection after attending a hospital Accident and Emergency department with unexplained multiple bruising, bite marks and severe bruising on his big toes. There were also concerns about neglect, and especially his very low weight. There were also subsequent concerns about the attachment of Charlie to his mother, Emma. The suspected perpetrators for these injuries were his mother and her current partner, Michael.

Emma, a young white British woman, had a relationship with a white British man with learning difficulties, Alan, who was Charlie's father, prior to her relationship with Michael. This relationship with Alan did not last more than a few months and Emma had a history of brief relationships with men who were abusive to her. Charlie was living with Michael and Emma at the time of his hospital attendance.

Both Michael and Emma had histories of mental health problems. Charlie was known to Children's Services in another part of the UK following reports of domestic abuse, Michael's difficulties with drugs and alcohol, and concerns for Emma's history of self-harm. The couple were also in an unstable housing arrangement and they had financial difficulties, too.

Friends of Emma subsequently raised a number of concerns about her never eating with Charlie, not providing appropriate food, nor paying attention to Charlie – instead being distracted by excessive Internet use – and that Charlie was not provided with play or activities. Her friends had raised their concerns with Emma regarding Michael having recently been released from prison, providing ineffective care to Charlie and smoking cannabis around him. Emma dismissed their concerns. They reported that Michael had stayed with Emma for two to three weeks after a court hearing.

Following Charlie's visit to the hospital casualty department, he was removed to foster care where he remained throughout the care proceedings. The foster carers reported that Charlie did not appear to know how to play, so they were encouraged to support him to play with toys in a creative way to promote his development. Work with Emma included raising concerns about Charlie's very poor weight gain. She told us that she fed Charlie three meals a day, and that he ate a lot of fruit. Charlie would pick at his food, but, she said, 'he was always eating... sometimes he scoffed his face all day long', whereas 'on other days he would not want to eat'. Emma connected this to her own experience and reflected that some days she did not want to eat much, whereas on other days she would become very hungry and have to get something to eat.

An AAI was carried out with Emma in order to explore how she reflected on her childhood history and to consider her capacity to be 'mind-minded' and mentalise others. Emma's account of her childhood overall was not congruent with the actual events and her narrative lacked coherence. She initially reported a positive childhood with a close and loving relationship with her mother, feeling loved and safe; however, as the interview unfolded, it became clear that Emma had experienced significant abuse from her sister and that her mother had not been able to protect her. Emma also recalled that she did not share problems with her mother, either about the abuse or when she encountered other life difficulties, and that she did not want to talk to her mother as she did not want to upset her. Through the course of the interview it appeared that Emma had a somewhat idealised view of her childhood which is in marked contrast to experiences which remain unresolved for her.

At times Emma appeared to jump from one subject to another and it was hard to follow her account or understand the reasons for her oscillation. Disordered and fragmented logic in a person's thinking can be an indicator of unresolved loss or trauma. This was perhaps most striking when Emma spoke of the loss of her friend who died in childhood, which she has referred to as having been traumatic for her at different times. Emma also stated that Charlie had her friend's eyes, and she appeared to become somewhat vacant at this time in that she was no longer 'present' during the AAI; she also became incoherent and illogical, but without 'correcting' the narrative.

For the last part of the interview Emma sat still, with an apparently 'harsh' and rigid expression on her face, staring out of the window. She did not make any eye contact for the remainder of the interview. Her answers were flat, or clipped, which, whilst not *said* angrily certainly left us with a strong impression of anger, resentment or distrust. If Emma had experienced periods of stress or depression, this might be how she had physically presented at those times. If Charlie has been exposed to this, it would help explain some of his attachment difficulties, and in particular how, when he first came into care, he found it very hard to look at his mother on contact visits.

When observing Charlie's interactions during contact with his mother, he often sought to move away from her, and he would run off rather than give her a cuddle goodbye, whereas with his carer he often responded with positive physical affection without having to be asked.

Charlie appeared to find it hard to accept either help or praise. Advice was given to Emma to remain close to Charlie during contact visits, but not to crowd him or to force eye contact if he clearly did not want it. Emma was advised to try to remain close to, and alert to, Charlie, and when *he* chose to look to her or seek her attention, she should respond positively and warmly.

In reviewing the recordings of these observations with Emma, we drew attention to interactions which showed Emma as a secure base for Charlie. For example, we walked Emma through what happened when Charlie was playing on the floor and picked up a building block. Emma was distracted on her mobile phone at the time. We commented on how Charlie waved the building block about and then turned around and thrust it towards Emma's face. We commented 'Look, mummy, this block is really interesting. I need to count on you to share my world with me to help me feel secure. When I feel secure, I want to show you the things I'm discovering'.

Case 3: Grace

Jessica was a white British mother of newborn Grace. Jessica's own mother died when she was a young girl. Following the death of her mother, there were concerns about her father's ability to care for Jessica and her siblings. Her siblings were removed and placed in foster care. Jessica remained with her father. Jessica reported that she experienced physical abuse and that her father had frequently locked her in her room. Often, she was not allowed to leave the house and her father kept her from school because he believed that she would become sexually promiscuous. Jessica had experienced loss and trauma, and her overall experience of the significant attachment figures in her life was characterised by a lack of care or nurture and deprivation of warmth and security. Jessica's partner, Darren, was white British and had been in the care of the state. His childhood experiences were marked by a number of placement breakdowns. He had witnessed domestic abuse, was physically abused by his father and had experienced the death of his mother when he was young.

Both Jessica and Darren had moderate learning difficulties. Jessica, Darren and Grace were placed in a foster placement together. At the time of our involvement there was increasing concern about bonding and attachment patterns between Grace (at two months) and her mother. Jessica repeatedly stated that she did not think that Grace was 'bonding well' with her but that Grace was 'bonding more' with Darren.

She felt that 'Grace did nothing but scream and cry', that Grace did not love her and that she was a 'daddy's little girl'.

Jessica's handling of Grace was rough: she would bounce her up and down whilst she was feeding, and would force-feed her when she was not hungry. She would also lay Grace on her stomach, on her lap, but without supporting Grace's head. Jessica's parenting was also intrusive and insensitive, and she would often misread Grace's cues for comfort and proximity. When Grace twitched or made facial movements whilst sleeping, Jessica would clap her hands in Grace's face or shake her hand forcefully to wake her, as she thought she was having nightmares. There were also concerns that Grace was inappropriately dressed for the weather, an example being the child wrapped up in fleece in extremely hot weather, *because Jessica was feeling cold* – another likely indication of low mentalizing capacity.

Grace appeared fearful when she was picked up by her mother. She would go rigid or curl her legs up into the foetal position. Grace was noted to cry for long periods of time and was not easily soothed by Jessica. She started to avoid her mother's eye contact which, at that age, can signal concern (unless there is another explanation, such as a problem focusing on near objects). There were several occasions throughout the duration of the assessment and intervention that led us to question Jessica and Darren's bond with Grace and commitment, as well as their ability to regulate their own feelings and emotions or develop insight into how their behaviours could affect Grace's emotional development.

The parents were often misattuned to Grace's needs, and this was particularly notable when they became distracted by their own relationship difficulties. At such times they were inconsistent in responding to Grace's efforts to interact with them. There were also a number of occasions when Jessica stated that she regretted having Grace and she thought that Grace hated her and would cry to torment her. Again, these statements are suggestive of low mentalizing capacity as well as indicative of 'persecutory attributions'. We became concerned about Grace's emotional presentation during direct work sessions. Jessica was often in a low and agitated mood and this affected the emotional care offered to Grace. Jessica often lost patience, and she would shout and swear at Grace. Darren was quiet and did not attempt to interact verbally with Grace to soothe her. Both parents were visibly frustrated.

We also noted that the parents had unrealistic expectations of Grace, and this was observed particularly in the first few sessions at the placement. The first instance was when Jessica told Grace off for dribbling and drooling. Jessica stated that it was 'gross'. We asked Jessica to reflect on whether Grace could control her dribbling. Jessica replied, 'Yes, she knows what she is doing and she does it on purpose to wind me up'. Jessica and Darren also displayed difficulty reading Grace's cues. During one observation they had fed Grace and then made another bottle despite Grace already having had a substantial feed. Grace clearly was not hungry and did not want another bottle. Both parents persisted in feeding Grace despite continued protestations and ongoing cries of distress.

The parents' own histories of being parented were filled with inconsistency, neglect, loss and physical abuse. Their relationship with their families and each other were fraught with persistent arguments and violence. It was feared that this perhaps was being replicated in their relationship with their daughter which, in turn, was impeding their ability to bond with Grace. If the parents were unable to display consistent emotional warmth and had continued to be erratic, rough and intrusive in their responses to Grace's needs, there was a fear that she could eventually develop disorganised attachment behaviour along with developmental delay. On the other hand, when Grace received consistent, calm and sensitive care, she quickly transformed into a smiling, happy baby, responding with coos and babbles. When in the care of the foster carer, Grace was not a demanding baby and could readily be comforted when in distress, so long as the care provided was responsive, warm and sensitive.

Through our observations and direct work with Jessica and Darren it became apparent that the likelihood of them being able to provide a consistently sensitive, warm and responsive approach in handling Grace was doubtful. On the contrary, Grace was too frequently being exposed to unsettling, uncomfortable and unreliable experiences. Although we came to the conclusion quite rapidly that we could not support a long-term plan for Grace to return to the care of her parents, it was important for us to remember that, even where there are no plans for rehabilitation, helping to promote secure attachment enables a child to be better equipped to manage transitions and losses, in this case a transition from foster care to an adoptive placement.

We were able to help support and direct contact sessions with the parents, but we were not able to achieve progress, we believe as a result of violent domestic abuse that continued unabated. Given that contact was required to continue, we wanted it to be as positive an experience as possible for Grace as well as for her parents.

Case 4: Ashanti

The fourth family comprised Nelly, a young black Caribbean single mother, her eight-year-old daughter, Ashanti, and six-month-old son, Benton. Ashanti had been hit by her mother with a kitchen implement and coat hanger, causing physical injuries. Following this incident, both Ashanti and her brother, Benton, were taken into police protection and subsequently spent time in a foster placement while a police investigation took place. Benton later returned to his mother's care, but Ashanti went to live with her father following a child protection medical examination which corroborated Ashanti's account of what had happened.

Nelly met Ashanti's father, Anton, through friends and they had a relationship for approximately five years, but it broke down at the time of her unplanned pregnancy with Ashanti. Although Ashanti had regular contact with her father, the relationship between Ashanti's parents was strained with Nelly antagonizing Anton, and Anton being non-responsive. There were concerns that Ashanti was being regularly hit by her mother, and that Nelly had denied Anton any contact with his daughter, particularly when Nelly was resorting to physically chastising her daughter. There were also concerns about Nelly's emotional unavailability to her daughter, and that she was often observed to be hostile to her daughter, ignoring her and talking on the telephone when Ashanti greeted her at the end of a school day. She would also become highly critical of her daughter, often talking to the practitioner about how lazy and selfish she was, that 'she won't amount to anything' and that 'she's only achieving national expectations at school, where she should be getting better marks'. Nelly also focused on how Ashanti was like father and found it very difficult to show her warmth and any physical affection. Nelly refused to tell her daughter that she loved her in spite of Ashanti's repeated attempts and requests for reassurance and physical care. Ashanti would often ask her mother, 'Mummy, do you love me?' This question would be ignored.

The Pathway Model was applied in several ways, first by family history taking and the use of the AAI to explore with Nelly her own difficulties of being parented and then by hypothesizing about sites of struggle and blind spots in parenting. For example, it became apparent that, during times of distress, Nelly's grandparents had often been dismissive of her feelings or denied them. Interestingly, Nelly had little memory of her mother – or any caring experiences from her mother – yet felt abandoned by her at a very young age, and that she had not been a good mother. In turn, Nelly had learned to self-regulate uncomfortable feelings or feelings of distress by denying or dismissing them, particularly in relation to Ashanti, who seemed to trigger Nelly's attachment system. We encouraged her to concentrate on the emotional experience and the expression of such feelings, and tried to help her look for ways to make connections with Ashanti when she was feeling upset, anxious or frightened. We often did this by posing questions about how Nelly might comfort or reassure Ashanti, or what Nelly noticed about other people comforting and reassuring important people in their lives and if there was anything she could take from that to help her comfort and reassure Ashanti. We asked Nelly to think about what she thought was 'caring', and how she felt looked after when things got tough or when she was anxious or ill. We focused on encouraging and helping her incorporate such responses into her interactions with Ashanti when her daughter was distressed or in need of care. (We encouraged Nelly to think back to positive experiences of being cared for to help with this process.)

The information from the AAI was used to plan the direct work sessions which focused on building skills for Nelly where her own experiences of being parented had been impoverished. We helped Nelly think about alternative ways to react to Ashanti's attempts at closeness and comfort and, as practitioners, we modelled mind-minded explanations to Nelly about what was happening, encouraging her to think about explanations for the world around her daughter and talked through how Ashanti's attempts to connect with her mother were not intended to irritate her or deliberately 'wind her up' but that she was asking her mother, 'Is everything okay? Are you okay with me and do you still love me?' We explained patiently and on many occasions to Nelly how Ashanti would continue to ask this of her mother as she had in her mind a version of herself as unloved – and maybe unlovable – following her previous experiences of being hit and criticised.

In one recorded session when Nelly left the room and then came back a little while later, Ashanti appeared to sulk, ignore her mother and kick a wall. Nelly was very negative about this behaviour, commenting on how naughty she was and that she had no respect for things around her. She became quite angry when seeing this. We took this opportunity to comment on Nelly's emotional state, taking care to soothe her and empathise with her in order to support Nelly towards being more mind-minded. We then reframed Ashanti's behaviour, explaining that what possibly happened when Nelly left the room was that Ashanti got anxious and unsure, and then missed her mother. By kicking the wall Ashanti was trying to distract herself from feelings of worry and loss.

With Nelly and Ashanti, direct work sessions focused on simple play and nurture tasks which encouraged physical proximity, touch and sensation that could be experienced by both Ashanti and her mother, such as encouraging Nelly to rub cream into her daughter's hands and talking to Nelly about what Ashanti might be feeling and experiencing by this close and tender demonstration of love from her mother. In one instance we introduced a bag of feathers into a session with Nelly and Ashanti, encouraging both of them to pick out feathers to run gently over each other's faces and feet and concentrate on thinking about what the sensations might be for each other, encouraging and praising warm eye contact and helping Nelly to see how she was enabling her daughter to feel safe in her care.

Conclusion

Families where parents have had poor experiences of being parented themselves, or where there is loss and trauma, often distrust attempts to offer comfort, reassurance and warmth, especially from child protection practitioners. Through persistence, consistency and empathy, and by offering to help make connections between behaviours, feelings, words and what each person is thinking, it is possible to create warmer and 'softer' relationships between carers and children. Parents can then think about children's internal worlds and help them relate in an emotionally responsive way, thereby laying the foundation for secure relationships.

Chapter 13

Attachment to People and Place with Traveller Families

Melanie Hamilton-Perry

I have been incorporating the framework and methods outlined in the ADAM Project model when working with children and families from Traveller communities, and have become aware of some interesting cultural variations, which can be transferred to other minority ethnic groups and first-nation individuals. For example, studies looking at the bonding and attachment of Australian Aboriginal children have evidenced some similarities in child-rearing habits and attachment behaviours to what I have observed within the Traveller communities (Yeo 2003). In this chapter I present a general overview of some of the cultural implications I have become aware of when incorporating the ADAM Project model when working with children and families from the Gypsy, Roma and Traveller communities. This is followed by two case studies of how the model has been used to help assess and understand parenting capacity. While respecting the diversity of all of the various Gypsy, Roma and Traveller groups, I refer to all groups simply by the term 'Traveller' unless specification is necessary.

It is widely acknowledged that the Gypsy, Roma and Traveller communities are some of the hardest to reach, deprived, socially excluded, marginalised and discriminated-against groups within the UK (Bennett and Hamilton-Perry 2010; Cemlyn 2008; Clark and Greenfields 2006; Richardson 2006). The exact number of Gypsies, Roma and Travellers living in the UK is not known. Estimates have been quoted from 82,000 (Kenrick and Clark 1999) to 300,000 people; these figures do not include families living in homes of bricks and mortar (Clark and Greenfields 2006). This makes Gypsies, Roma and Travellers some of the largest ethnic minority groups in the UK. Nevertheless, professional knowledge and understanding of the Gypsy,

Roma and Traveller traditions, culture and child-rearing practices appear limited or misunderstood.

I have been working with families from the Gypsy and Traveller communities in various roles, ranging from teaching assistant to my present role as child protection social worker, over the past ten years. During this time I have noticed that many Traveller children have been reported as having 'insecure attachments' to their parents. This may be the case with some of the Traveller children; however, when reading the files it is often apparent that professionals lack cultural awareness of the Traveller lifestyle and the role that the extended family plays in traditional family life.

Traveller families were traditionally self-employed, moving in family groups from town to town, following the harvests and working as agricultural workers. Employment options were seasonal and time-constrained; therefore, to provide for the family and put some money aside for the winter months, all the able-bodied family members worked together. From an early age, Traveller children worked alongside their parents to earn enough money to put food on the table. Children who were too young to work alongside their parents were cared for by older siblings, grandparents or extended family members (those who were unable to work due to illness or old age). This pattern of children working alongside their parents and family is sometimes evidenced in Asian countries and communities. During the winter months Gypsy families earned their living hawking (selling) their wares, fortune-telling and entertaining.

Traveller families traditionally are larger than those from the settled communities. It is not uncommon for families to have ten children or more, which results in the mother being constantly pregnant or recovering from childbirth; therefore, all the female members within the family often share the responsibility of caring for the children. The eldest female child within a family often plays an important role in caring for her younger siblings. This can result in Traveller children's attachments to their parents *appearing* insecure; however, these children may have a secure attachment or multiple attachments to the eldest sister, grandmother or aunts. Traveller men rarely play a role in caring for the children.

Traveller society is a matriarchal culture that delineates male-female roles clearly, with strict sexual morality (Hawes and Perez 1996, p.8). A woman could not discuss gender-related personal problems with a male professional, or vice versa, and a woman caring for a man could not undertake personal care (unless they are husband and wife). Children are highly valued and kept on a tight rein. They are taught their parents' trades and to behave in a respectful manner to elders; they are expected to obey orders quickly (Bennett and Hamilton-Perry 2010).

Methods used from the ADAM Project model

The methods used were the Strange Situation Procedure, story stems and the Adult Attachment Interview.

Strange Situation Procedure

Although I am well known within the Travelling communities, I have been unable to find Traveller mothers who are willing to participate in the Strange Situation Procedure. There is traditionally a lack of trust between the Travelling community and multi-agency professionals, particularly Children's Services, which centres on Travellers' cultural experience of having their children taken into care, as they see it, just because they are Traveller children (Bennett and Hamilton-Perry 2010; Clark and Greenfields 2006). Most Traveller children do not leave the care of their family until they reach five years of age, when it becomes a legal requirement to send their children to school. Traveller women are reluctant to leave their children in the care of a *gorgia* (a person from the non-Traveller community) even for a few minutes, and for many families the struggle between schooling and 'learning the Traveller way' persists, with the former perceived by some as a means of assimilation, which they do not desire.

Story stems

I have had some interesting responses from children from the Travelling communities when I have introduced story stem work with them. I attempted one of the modified[1] ADAM Project story stems, as given below:

---

1   *Note from the editors*: for practical reasons it was not possible to use all the stories, so we incorporated a slightly different design for busy practitioners.

Mum and dad are just ready to leave on the family holiday when mum says to (younger brother/sister) 'Can you get Snuggles (cat) so that I can feed her before we go. I can't find Snuggles anywhere'. Can you show me and tell me what happens next?

The Traveller children's response has been consistent. None of the children could understand why the family would even feed a cat, let alone keep a cat as a pet. Romani culture has many beliefs and taboos about pollution connected with all things *mochardi* (unclean). Dogs and cats are seen as *mochardi*, i.e. dirty animals. (Similar problems of 'cultural translation' might also occur with the full 13 stories, which include animals but not pets.)

Dogs are kept as working animals if they have some financial value, but they are not viewed as pets. Many of the children spoke about leaving the dogs behind if their families were threatened with eviction because the dogs would not come when called. Cats were described as 'valueless'. The only positive comment about the value of cats was made by a child living on a Traveller site which had an ongoing rat problem.

Adult Attachment Interview

When I have asked individuals from the Traveller communities to describe their relationship with their mother as far back as they can remember, or to give me five words to describe their relationships with each of their parents, I have become aware that most individuals have struggled to find words to describe their *emotional* relationships with their parents. Finding practical words to describe their relationships appears to be easier. One Traveller woman, when asked these questions, stated, 'She worked hard to feed us'. After a discussion about her memories of her mother working hard, I asked her if she had felt loved as a child. She informed me that they do not talk about love.

Both of the mothers discussed later in this chapter spoke about not having the words to talk about their relationships. Sally explained that there are few words in the Romani language to express emotions. It is often assumed that as Travellers speak English, no language barrier exists; however, while a form of English is spoken, often with a strong dialect involving different words and meanings, it decreases the likelihood of Gypsies and Travellers making immediate sense of what is being said to them unless talking within their own community. This can result in difficulties processing verbal information, as on occasion several sentences can be lost, leading to misunderstanding. Many Gypsies and Travellers find it difficult to express themselves because they do not have the right words and, rather than lose face, they simply do not try, especially in front of a person unknown to them.

The Romani language is believed to originate from Sanskrit and comprises a number of different dialects belonging to the family of Indo-European languages. Romanichals (English Travellers) speak an ethnolectal variety of English, which is referred to as Romani, which may contain between a few hundred down to a few dozen Romani-derived words (Hancock 2010). Shelta is a language spoken by many Irish Travellers (particularly in Ireland, but also in Britain).

Case studies

Case 1: Kim

Kim and Sally are from a dual-heritage background. Their maternal family are English Travellers while their paternal family are *gorgia*. When I first met 16-year-old Sally and her 7-month-old daughter, Kim, there were many concerns for Kim's well-being. Kim was deemed to be a 'child in need of protection' under the categories of neglect and physical abuse. Sally's parenting was immature and inconsistent, and she did not know how to care for Kim or herself. Sally was still very much a frightened child in her own right.

I had watched Sally with Kim, and the way that Sally responded to Kim suggested to me that Sally had both the emotional capacity and the mentalizing abilities to parent Kim appropriately. When Sally thought that she and Kim were not being observed, she visibly relaxed. Sally sat Kim on her lap facing her and spoke to her softly, mirroring Kim's facial expressions. Kim's hand touched and explored Sally's face. Sally smiled and laughed with Kim when she put her fingers in Sally's mouth and up her nose.

In the Adult Attachment Interview (AAI) with Sally, the narrative of her childhood evidenced unresolved trauma and loss, which helped to explain why at times she displayed extremely insensitive parenting and low mentalization. Both Sally and Kim presented with behaviours that suggested that they were experiencing unresolved trauma and loss and/or post-traumatic stress. Sally seemed to be oversensitive to stress and unable to regulate her emotions. She often displayed a tendency towards hyper-arousal and vigilance. Nevertheless, Sally's patience with Kim was generally remarkable. Sally prioritised Kim's needs above her own, to the point where she was not looking after herself properly; however, I had noted that Sally would sometimes handle Kim roughly, or she would make a scary face at Kim for no apparent reason. As we have seen previously, parents who have experienced unresolved trauma and loss can display frightening, or frightened, parental behaviour and thus seriously overlook their children's emotional needs. When I first started working with Sally and Kim, Sally presented with offensive and defensive behaviours. Sally's communication style appeared to be rather immature; her speech was also deeply influenced by Romani dialect and mannerisms. At times of stress Sally would verbally attack before she was attacked, which resulted in her appearing to be aggressive. This perceived aggression heightened some professionals' concerns about the level of risk to themselves (Ferguson 2009, 2010) as well as to Kim.

After a home visit when Sally had a disagreement with Jane, another young person in the house, I asked Sally, 'What do you think Kim might have been thinking, watching you shout at Jane?' Sally shrugged and said she did not know. I sat on the floor next to Kim and said, 'I think that Kim would say that watching mummy shout at people makes her feel frightened'. Sally replied, 'She watches people when they argue and stops chatting to herself. Do you think she really is frightened?' Sally seemed surprised that Kim would have her own thoughts and feelings.

The AAI highlighted that Sally struggled to understand what had happened to her as a child and her difficulty making sense of her situation. Sally also had difficulty finding the words to explain her feelings and emotions. I believe that Sally's low level of literacy and language capacity also affected her capacity to process her memories and emotions. Sally noted that she never had the chance to settle anywhere as a child, as the longest that she remembers staying in one place was six months. She said that she did not feel that she belonged anywhere. She said she had learned through experience that she and her extended family were not wanted by the settled society. The constant evictions left her feeling unsettled and insecure and her own parents stressed and angry.

Case 2: The T family

Whilst using the AAI with some Traveller families has not always proved to be helpful, the *skills* required to undertake an AAI effectively have proved to be invaluable. I had just been allocated a new family of Traveller children who were parked in a muddy lay-by next to a busy rural road. A member of the public had contacted Children's Services with concerns that the children were being excessively chastised.

The family comprised Mr and Mrs T and their four children. They were living in a 20-foot touring caravan with no mains services. All four children were under the age of five years, and while they appeared to be slightly grubby, all seemed well fed and physically sustained. The caravan was spotless. Mrs T presented as a calm and organised mother for most of the time; however, if one of the children stepped out of line or did something wrong, her whole persona appeared to change and she switched from being a kind and caring mother to a shouting, swearing and frightening figure. When we discussed her way of disciplining the children, Mrs T could not accept or understand why Children's Services had concerns and why I was telling her that if she continued to beat the children, they could be removed from her care.

Mrs T stated, 'I've got to teach them; they have got to learn'. There were no other concerns about the care the children received. In all other aspects of her parenting Mrs T demonstrated thoughtful and sensitive caregiving, but she struggled to suppress her explosive and sometimes violent tempers when she felt that the children had done, or were about to do, something wrong. I felt that a possible explanation for Mrs T's frightening behaviours could be connected with unresolved trauma and loss; therefore, I decided to undertake the AAI with her. I was aware that Mrs T did not have any family nearby to look after the children while I conducted the interview. With Mrs T's consent, I brought along a selection of age-appropriate videos from home, gave her five litres of diesel for the generator and settled the children in front of the family's television.

At the beginning, progress was slow and Mrs T struggled to articulate what she wanted to say; however, her narrative was spoken in such a way that indicated that her attachments to her mother and grandmother were organised. When asked if she had any memories of frightening punishments as a child, Mrs T seemed to freeze and her face paled. She nodded and burst into tears. After ascertaining that she felt happy to continue, I gently asked Mrs T for an example. She explained that once, when she was a little girl playing in the yard with her younger brother, they had seen something that caught their eye in the men's work area. They had gone over to explore, knowing that they were not allowed to play there. Mrs T stated that she could not remember exactly what had happened, but somehow her little brother had been run over by their dad's lorry and had subsequently died. Her parents did not beat her or even shout at her for taking her little brother to the men's work area. Her mum simply sat her down after the funeral and told her that he would not have died if she had done as she had been told and had looked after her brother next to the trailer. Mrs T states that she is not sure if her dad ever spoke to her again after her brother died. She said afterwards that she had almost 'forgotten' about her brother's death; it was certainly something that was never discussed. She acknowledged that she lives in constant fear of one of her own children being hurt or killed. Living in lay-bys at the side of the road meant that they were always at risk from passing cars. The lack of a safe place for the children to play is a constant concern for her.

Conclusion

In conclusion, by using the AAI, I gained an invaluable insight into the possible reasons for Mrs T's behaviour towards her children and I was able to work with her to develop other ways of disciplining them. It provided me with the tools to explore Mrs T's life experiences in an effective and unchallenging manner. I am not sure if Mrs T would have spoken about her brother's death if I had simply worked with her using a question-and-answer assessment procedure.

Chapter 14

Introducing the ADAM Project Across the Entire Children and Families Department in Enfield, London

David Wilkins

In late 2011, senior managers in the Children's Services department in the London Borough of Enfield took the decision to undertake a comprehensive implementation of the ADAM Project. This decision would involve training every social worker and manager in the theory, research and methods related to disorganised attachment behaviour and, at the time of writing (July 2013), over 200 members of staff have between them attended training days, workshops and received individual mentoring in their work with individual children and their families. These staff work across the Referral and Assessment team, the Child and Family Support team (working with children subject to child protection or child-in-need plans), the Adolescent Support team (working with teenagers on the 'edge of care'), the Family Centres (providing contact support and parenting assessments) and the Children with Disabilities team. In addition to this, staff from the Looked-after Children teams, the Adolescent and Leaving Care team, the Youth Offending Service and the Parent Support Service are also undergoing the same training. This investment in the ADAM Project is key to the department's commitment to implementing the Munro reforms and is part of a strategy to build and develop further our focus on children's experiences and understanding of their own situations. In this chapter, I explain the rationale behind the decision to implement the ADAM Project across an entire department, as well as the training programme being used, and I summarise the ongoing evaluative work around this decision.

Enfield's rationale for implementing the ADAM Project

The rationale behind the decision to invest 'wholesale' into the ADAM Project was dependent on a number of different aims. First, although we have an excellent group of social work practitioners in Enfield, from our passionate, newly qualified social workers to our experienced, advanced practitioners and Family Centre workers, we wanted to develop something of a shared methodology and approach to practice. As argued in the Munro report into child protection 'Good professional practice is informed by knowledge of the latest theory and research' (Munro 2011, p.23), and in Enfield, we wanted to take this principle seriously and develop an approach to practice that we could claim as the 'Enfield brand'. In other words, as children move through 'the system' we have created – of the Referral and Assessment team, Child and Family Support team, potentially the Adolescent Support team, and the Looked-after Children teams and potentially beyond – we wanted to ensure that they experienced a degree of consistency in the service they received. This is not to say that other theoretical approaches are not welcome; indeed, as Munro has previously argued, there is no compulsion on practitioners to adopt only one theoretical approach, as:

> ...we are more often choosing between theories that are complementary rather than conflicting. One intervention may focus, for example, on improving an abusive mother's parenting skills, while another may be trying to reduce her social isolation. The effectiveness of one does not rule out the value of the other. (Munro 2002, p.469)

So, for example, the Adolescent Support team in Enfield has developed a very effective 'strengths-based' approach to their work, but in addition to this they make use of methods such as the Adult Attachment Interview to help them understand the motivations of the carers they work with, their own experiences of being parented and what might be 'getting in the way' of their ability to implement change. Similarly, in the Family Centres in Enfield, staff have been trained in the skills of motivational interviewing as a form of 'guiding to elicit and strengthen motivation for change' (Miller and Rollnick 2009) amongst the carers with whom they work; therefore, whilst the introduction of this methodology is not designed to prevent the use of different approaches, the aim is for the ADAM Project to provide an underpinning for all social work in Enfield, to encourage a focus on the child's relationships with their close carers and a focus on an understanding of the child's experiences of being cared for through an understanding of these relationships.

Second, we wanted to develop through the ADAM Project a greater set of skills and resources for social work practitioners to engage in direct work with children and families. Again, the Munro report into child protection highlights the 'centrality of forming relationships with children and families (in order to) understand and help them', although Munro also says that this centrality has 'become obscured' by a focus on compliance with 'prescription and keeping records' (p.7–8); therefore, part of the rationale for introducing the ADAM Project across the entire Children's Services department in Enfield is to complement our other attempts to reduce the focus on 'prescription and compliance'. In other words, we realised that as well as seeking to streamline our processes and our bureaucracy, we also needed to take positive steps to ensure that social workers felt confident and able to spend more time directly working with children and their carers. The development and training opportunities for social workers in Enfield are generally considered to be excellent, but no training programme is perfect and we wanted to increase the amount of training available in the kinds of direct work tools included in the ADAM Project, such as story stems and guided parenting tasks.

The training programme in Enfield

Given the considerable investment of time and money by Enfield into the ADAM Project model, careful consideration was given at the outset as to the best way to ensure that social workers and others were able to: (a) access the training; (b) receive ongoing support in their use of the theory, research and methods related to disorganised attachment behaviour; and (c) use their new knowledge and skills effectively in practise with children and families. We also wanted to ensure that this new training programme took account of the varying current knowledge base and skills of our practitioners and managers, and to offer a way for individual members of staff to access as much of the training as they felt they needed. In other words, whilst all members of staff are expected to become knowledgeable about the theory and research related to disorganised attachment behaviour, we recognised that not all members of staff would need to develop the same skill set or knowledge base in terms of actually using the various methods with children and families. For example, a Head of Service would be unlikely to undertake a story stem with a child directly but would need to understand the concept in order to either offer supervision or undertake informed case-audit work; therefore, we planned for a range of different 'training pathways' to meet the needs of staff members in a range of different roles (see Table 14.1).

Table 14.1 Outline of the various training components implemented in Enfield

Training component	Description	Purpose
Core training	Two days[1] in a 'traditional' training style, with a group of staff (15–25 individuals) attending a seminar-style training day, led by David Shemmings or Yvonne Shemmings	To ensure staff were knowledgeable about the theory and research related to disorganised attachment behaviour and related caregiver characteristics such as unresolved trauma and loss, and disconnected and extremely insensitive parenting; to further ensure that staff were familiar with the methods of the project, such as story stems and guided parenting tasks
Journal of Social Work Practice in Enfield	An in-house journal launched in November 2013 and produced three to four times per year by practitioners for practitioners, containing examples of good practice (including but not limited to use of ADAM Project methods and ideas) as well as a notice board to update staff on any relevant developments	To enable good practice to be shared between colleagues, most notably across team boundaries; accessible to all members of Children's Services in Enfield
ADAM Project website	An open-access website containing general information on attachment theory as well as password-protected access to training materials	To provide staff with quick access to information on the key ideas of the ADAM Project and individual refresher training on the use of specific methods

1   This has now reverted to the full four-day programme.

Training component	Description	Purpose
Workshops	For each method of the ADAM Project, staff were offered small-group workshops (for between four and eight individuals) during which they could practise with colleagues, receive feedback from more experienced colleagues and watch videos of the methods being used with children and carers	To enable staff to feel confident in using the methods with children and carers, provide a safe environment for them to practise, ask questions and watch other people using the methods via videotapes of actual sessions with children and carers
Access to in-depth training courses for particular methods	A small number of staff have been encouraged to access in-depth training courses, on particular methods, at the Anna Freud Centre in London. For example, a number of staff have attended four-day training on the Child Attachment Interview and the Story Stem Assessment Protocol. One Head of Service has trained at Leiden University in the Netherlands in the use of Video-based Intervention to Promote Positive Parenting	To ensure that a number of staff within the department are able to achieve an expert level of proficiency in individual methods and then be in a position to support the development of their colleagues
Individual mentoring	Staff were offered the chance to work alongside more experienced colleagues which could include three-way supervisions to discuss particular casework, shadowing home visits, requesting more experienced colleagues to complete particular methods and being observed completing the methods directly	To support the transfer of the knowledge and skills obtained via the other training components into practice; to provide feedback to staff on their implementation of the methods

Of the training components highlighted in Table 14.1, a number of staff have accessed each one, whereas other social workers may only have attended the core training and perhaps one workshop on a particular method of interest to them in their field of practice. For example, social workers in the Adolescent Support team may not frequently need to use methods such as guided parenting tasks, but they are more likely to use methods such as adult or child attachment interviews, given their focus on work with teenagers.

The inclusion of training components focused on mentoring and on the practice and observation of the use of the methods can be understood as drawing on the research of Joyce and Showers (2002) regarding the extent of practical implementation as a result of various training initiatives. They found that just 5 per cent of learners transfer a new skill to practice as a result of learning a theory; 10 per cent of learners transfer a new skill as a result of learning a theory and seeing a demonstration in a training environment; around 20 per cent of learners transfer a skill as a result of learning a theory, seeing a demonstration and practising the new skill themselves in a training environment; and 25 per cent of learners are likely to transfer a skill as a result of learning a theory, seeing a demonstration, practising the new skill and receiving corrective feedback in a training environment. However, 90 per cent of learners transfer a new skill into a practice context as a result of learning a theory, seeing a demonstration, practising the new skill, receiving corrective feedback in a training environment and then receiving 'on-the-job' coaching within a mentoring relationship. Thus, the inclusion of individual coaching and mentoring, in addition to the other components listed above, was considered a crucial component in ensuring that the majority of staff who attended the training were then able to start using their newly acquired skills and knowledge in practice.

Evaluation of the ADAM Project in Enfield

An evaluation programme for the ADAM Project in Enfield was developed right at the start. A series of potential outcome measures were considered including the collection and collation of staff views, as well as case-file audit alongside analysis and feedback from other professionals, such as health visitors and independent reviewing officers. Feedback on the training programme was also collected using learner evaluation sheets at the end of training sessions and three-monthly reviews by managers as to the impact of the training on the social workers they supervise. Anecdotally, social workers and managers provided the following comments on the implementation of the ADAM Project in Enfield:

- 'Helpful to know the background in terms of supervisory content and discussion with staff' (team manager, Referral and Assessment team)

- 'I have completed a story stem and am planning to do a Child Attachment Interview shortly' (Family Centre worker)

- 'I have managed to undertake one Adult Attachment Interview with a mother I am working with and I have another one planned…tomorrow' (social worker, Child and Family Support team)

- 'Thanks very much for yesterday's workshop, which was very, very useful' (social worker, Disabled Children's team)

- 'I am going to use a guided parenting task this afternoon' (social worker, Child and Family Support team)

However, whilst this anecdotal evidence is positive, in order to ensure a robust analysis, a random selection of participants were asked to complete a Q study, involving Q sorts which were subsequently analysed using Q methodology (Shemmings and Ellingsen 2012). Q methodology is a method of social science research in which participants are asked to sort a number of statements related to the topic being studied. Participants read a series of statements and then sort them into a grid (see Figure 14.1) depending on how strongly they agree or disagree with each one. Examples of the kinds of statements that the participants were asked to sort are given in Table 14.2.

Table 14.2 Selection of the statements that social workers in Enfield were asked to sort (by expressing agreement or disagreement) in order to evaluate their views on the ADAM Project in Enfield

Using methods related to disorganised attachment and associated caregiver characteristics such as adult and child attachment interviews, story stems, guided parenting tasks and strange situation procedures allows social workers to investigate the reality of family relationships.

Understanding theory, research and methods related to disorganised attachment can make decision making more complicated. Methods related to disorganised attachment and associated caregiver characteristics such as adult and child attachment interviews, story stems, guided parenting tasks and strange situation procedures feel intrusive to families.

Theory, research and methods related to disorganised attachment offer social workers a helpful general framework for thinking about children and families.

Using theory, research and methods related to disorganised attachment helps social workers understand the motivations and behaviour of carers.

Using methods such as adult attachment interviews, related to associated caregiver characteristics such as unresolved loss and trauma, is a good way of involving carers in social work assessments.

Using methods related to the theory of disorganised attachment and related caregiver characteristics such as adult or child attachment interviews, story stems, guided parenting tasks and strange situation proceduvres helps child protection social workers feel more confident about doing other direct work with children.

There is too much focus on attachment theory in social work, to the exclusion of other theories that may also be helpful.

Using ideas and methods related to disorganised attachment fits well with wider social work practise with children.

-6	-5	-4	-3	-2	-1	0	1	2	3	4	5	6

Figure 14.1 A number of participants in Enfield were asked to sort a series of statements related to the ADAM Project into a grid such as this one

The purpose of using a Q study was to allow a quantitative analysis of the subjective views of the social workers and reduce the risk that positive views may have been unduly accentuated. Having collected a number of Q sorts, the way in which the statements are arranged is analysed using a dedicated computer programme.[1] The results are then further interpreted to reveal common but distinctive perspectives or viewpoints expressed.

Using the Q method revealed three distinct viewpoints regarding the ADAM Project in Enfield.

The first of these viewpoints suggested that using ADAM-related knowledge and skills enhanced assessments of children, made it easier to understand the behaviour and motivations of carers and children, and enabled more insight into families. The second viewpoint was less enthusiastic and indicated that a number of social workers felt that the analysis of methods such as story stems and guided parenting tasks was too complicated and they would be concerned about being cross-examined in court. These social workers were also worried that they may be viewed as 'unqualified' to use such methods when compared with psychologists and psychiatrists. The third of these viewpoints was something of a mixture between the first two, indicating that a number of social workers felt that although the ADAM approach enabled them to more easily involve carers in assessments, gain greater insight into families and that it increased their confidence in using other direct work tools, they also felt some concern about being cross-examined in court and about whether other professionals would view them as 'unqualified'.

Based on these findings, it is possible to see how some social workers in Enfield have enthusiastically embraced this training approach and are actively using it and finding it useful in practice. They feel confident enough to 'defend' their approach, if required, in a court setting. A second group is perhaps lacking in the requisite confidence when using the methods in practice, and further examination of their case files indicates that they are not really attempting to do so. The third group is more tentatively using the approach and the specific methods but retain some level of concern about how this work might be viewed by others,

---

1   Q method: see http://schmolck.userweb.mwn.de/qmethod

especially in a court arena; however, they do seem to be developing their confidence and skills in using other direct work tools (such as the 'Three Islands' or 'Three Houses', and 'emotion cards' or board games; see Chapter 10). The next stage of the evaluation involved comparing social workers with different views and examining what might explain these differences. From this analysis, it was noticeable that the social workers in the first group had accessed more of the individual mentoring components of the training programme in a way that most of the social workers in the second group had not (although this was not the case for every single one). Most of the social workers in the third group had accessed some individual mentoring, but only relatively recently, prior to their completion of a Q sort. What this suggests most clearly is that, as Joyce and Showers' (2002) research suggests, the ultimate transfer of new skills from a training setting to a practice setting is highly dependent on the use of coaching and mentoring *in practice*.

Conclusion

In conclusion, the implementation of the ADAM Project in Enfield is at the time of writing well underway, and a growing number of staff are completing the training and putting the knowledge and skills acquired into practice. Where social workers have utilised the approach in practice, they are generally reporting that it has helped improve their practise and increased their confidence, both to continue using the ADAM approach and to try other direct work tools as well. As the sense of a shared methodology grows and develops in Enfield, we are hopeful and confident that families and children will start to notice our common focus on the importance of close relationships and will therefore find it easier to make the transition between teams and individual social workers; however, this is not to suggest that other methodologies and methods will be phased out. As indicated above, different teams are more than capable of reviewing their own needs for complementary approaches, depending on their own specialist areas of practice. Equally, individual social workers will never practise in a routine way, nor should they. What works for one social worker and for one family may not work for another. Nevertheless, whilst individual approaches to practice are to be encouraged, the importance of a shared knowledge base should not be underestimated.

Chapter 15

Introducing the ADAM Project in Lewisham

Tania Young

The ADAM Project was introduced to Lewisham in 2010 to promote better outcomes for children and improve the quality of safeguarding practice. It was hoped that adopting the approach would facilitate more effective and timely social work interventions where maltreatment was suspected or known, as well as help identify children about whom the level of concern may not be warranted. The approach was to train social workers and team managers in the theory and methods of the ADAM Project with the objective of enhancing the quality of assessments of children in need in Lewisham. Cases where there was uncertainty about the level of harm the children may be experiencing were the ones that were prioritised for the use of this intervention.

Social workers were trained in the theory of disorganised attachment behaviour and its relationship to maltreatment. The training provided social workers with a series of methods that enabled them to identify disorganised attachment behaviour in children. It also enabled social workers to identify in adults the presentation of extremely insensitive or disconnected parenting, unresolved trauma and loss, and very low mentalizing capacity. They also learned the assessment methods incorporated in the Pathway Model and, wherever possible, these techniques were recorded using video for quality assurance purposes. This was because in order for the ADAM Project tools to be used properly, workers had to learn to interact in a somewhat counter-intuitive way. For example, it was critical that children were not led and that workers did not indicate agreement or give praise during the techniques (such as the Child Attachment Interview), as this would have compromised the validity of the tools; therefore, the use of video allowed for a more accurate analysis. Nevertheless, when workers gain confidence in using the methods, it has proved possible to analyse the material later because only very specific and precise information is being observed.

ADAM Project training was intended to support and supplement 'traditional' social work methods, rather than replace them. ADAM Project methods enabled social workers to collect relevant information more quickly, and to provide a framework for assessing families without needing to rely on question-and-answer sessions with carers and ongoing monitoring to see how things develop.

How the teams were trained

The pilot team for the ADAM Project was a small team of eight social workers within Family Support and Intervention (FSI). Practitioners in this team became very confident in the techniques; subsequently, all other FSI teams and the Family Centre were trained followed by the Referral and Assessment teams. The pilot team, who by this stage had developed confidence in the use of the tools, then became mentors for other social workers within the department.

Regular practice in the use of the methods was essential for practitioners to achieve a reasonable level of competence and confidence. Managers therefore ensured that practitioners were regularly making use of the methods in which they had been trained. The expectation was that social workers would not report their findings until the videos had been quality assured, either through workshops or by their manager or project leader having reviewed the piece of work first. Social workers analysed their own videos and the manager or leader would increase inter-rater reliability. This approach protected the integrity of the project as well as provided ongoing training and support. Particularly complex videos are reviewed by David Shemmings and/or Yvonne Shemmings.

Social workers were reminded by supervisors that even where the analysis revealed disorganised attachment behaviour, unresolved loss and/or trauma, low mentalizing capacity or other potential difficulties, this was not definitive in terms of abuse or maltreatment. Whilst the ADAM Project tools proved to enhance social work assessments significantly, they were not used in isolation from other social work methods.

In order to be most successful, ADAM Project methods and ideas became a core component of what practitioners did, rather than an 'optional extra'. Furthermore, ADAM Project training soon became the core of Lewisham's training in child protection. Although Lewisham piloted this project and became the most advanced in its application, a number of other local authorities were also taking up the training. Because of the widespread interest, Lewisham had a responsibility to ensure the continued integrity of the project. It could have adverse consequences if practitioners were to implement the ideas and methods in an inappropriate way and draw inappropriate conclusions about children, young people and their parents.

Social workers across the department embraced the training with enthusiasm and passion. There was a sense that social workers were eager, even desperate, to find new tools to allow them to assess and work with families in a different way. Historically, social work training seemed to be much more theoretical and social workers were delighted by the chance to learn tangible skills that actually made a difference to the quality of their assessments and their ability to keep children safe.

A subsequent and unexpected outcome that followed from this work was a team of social workers who felt empowered, skilled and positive about their job. There was a stronger sense of job satisfaction and pride in relation to the level of expertise that they now had. They spoke in child protection conferences and in court with more confidence about their assessments. Other professionals took them more seriously. There were several examples of child protection conference chairs and professionals from other agencies making positive notes about the quality of assessments and a noticeable improvement in social work practise within the department.

How the Project affected assessments

One of the aims of FSI has always been to ensure that its most vulnerable children have their individual needs identified and addressed in such a way that improves future outcomes. The problem, however, is that even with the best intentions, the needs of vulnerable and maltreated children are, at times, either overlooked by different professionals or are such that the child protection training and subsequent practise are inadequate to assess thoroughly such complex needs. The case in the UK of the death of Peter Connelly (Baby 'P') has been a tragic example of how, in spite of the best intentions and achieving the performance indicators, the system at times still fails children and families. The reliance on children to develop a trusting relationship with a social worker in order to disclose is an approach that is still heavily relied upon in assessing children at risk. It is time-consuming and arduous, especially when some parents work so hard to prevent it.

The introduction of story stem work is one of the methods that has helped overcome some of the difficulties we face regularly when working with children where we suspect maltreatment. In some cases the use of story stem profiles has enabled a more trusting relationship to develop between the social worker and the child. It has also enabled us to tap into children's perceptions of family roles, attachments and relationships without the need to ask them any questions at all. There are many examples of children being anxious during social work visits or very wary of being asked anything about their family life. The benefit of using story stem assessments is that the child does not necessarily appreciate that they are telling you so much about their family life without having to mention their family specifically; therefore, this can significantly reduce feelings of anxiety and apprehension that we frequently observe during interviews with children. The safe atmosphere, in and of itself, builds upon the child's relationship with the social worker and provides the child with an opportunity and space to disclose. One might say that this is an example of standard social work practice and this may be true. In my view, however, it is the mere use of playing (in the child's mind) that enhances that opportunity for further disclosures.

Second, and more importantly, this technique allows for the identification of disorganised attachment behaviour. Once identified, and combined with the evidence collated by the standard social work tools for investigation such as observation, interviews, police checks and history gathering, it can strengthen and add weight to the overall assessment of need. It often tells us something that we would have no way of finding out through the standard methods of assessment. In an internal survey of the use of the ADAM Project training in Lewisham, in over 75 per cent of cases where one or more of the methods were used, social workers reported the discovery of new information from the use of these methods that they had not learnt before. Social workers reported that it enhanced their overall assessment in 100 per cent of the cases where the methods were used.

On the other hand, it provides an alternative tool to reassure us that maltreatment may be less likely when there is no evidence of disorganised attachment behaviour. There have been examples since we have been using these techniques where we have had significant concerns that were counter-indicated by the use of these methods. What we got in contrast was a rather reassuring picture that home life was more settled than we had understood. The techniques help practitioners gain a deeper understanding of life at home for children and act in ways that facilitate the process of change by providing them with therapeutic support that will help lead to attachment behaviour becoming more organised or, alternatively, it can be used in the evidence-gathering process at the commencement of care proceedings.

Resistance to being filmed

Initially it was thought that most parents would refuse to give consent to either themselves or their children being filmed. We anticipated this to be the main stumbling block but, to our surprise, this was not the case. Almost every parent who we asked to be filmed agreed to it. In contrast to our expectations, parents in particular relished the opportunity to share their story and be listened to in a manner that they had not previously experienced. Anecdotal feedback from parents and children was that they found the approach helpful. One father said after doing the Adult Attachment Interview (AAI) that it was the first time he had ever felt properly heard. Strikingly, his family had had a social work service for many years. The approach has facilitated parents' engagement in the child protection process and this was particularly encouraging.

Case studies

Case 1

A 12-month-old infant (female) is referred to social care by her health visitor as there are concerns about family discord, the behaviour of two older children in the family, alongside the mother's potential misuse of alcohol and the infant's general presentation. The referral is progressed to an assessment and a social worker from Intake and Assessment visits.

They complete the initial assessment and a core assessment is initiated. The older two children in the family are 7 and 13 years of age and both present with some behavioural problems and relatively poor school attendance; the older child, Nathan, is also known to local police for committing various minor offences.

The social worker decides that, although there are some clear risk factors for the children, it is not clear whether any of them are being significantly harmed or at risk of significant harm. The social worker decides to complete an AAI and guided parenting task with the mother and the father. The AAI with the mother reveals quite marked unresolved loss and trauma and fairly low mentalizing capacity. From the guided parenting task, it becomes clear that although her parenting is not significantly insensitive, she does show quite marked signs of disconnected parenting. Whilst worrying, this reassures the social worker to some degree that the infant is not at imminent risk of physical harm due to rough handling; however, there are now more grounds for the health visitor's concerns. The discovery of the unresolved loss and/or trauma provides some explanation as to why the mother might be consuming a fairly high amount of alcohol. After discussing this openly with the mother, the social worker discovers that her father died unexpectedly in a car accident just before the infant was born; however, given the challenges of caring for a newborn baby, the mother never felt able to talk openly about her loss. Because of the social worker's informed and open approach, the mother feels understood rather than judged and so feels able to admit her drinking might be a problem and agrees to attend a local alcohol support service.

The AAI with the father does not reveal any particular markers of concern, although it is noted using the guided parenting task that his basic play skills are not well developed. This helps the social worker to plan an effective intervention by way of some basic parenting classes. The AAI with the father also provides some reassurance that the child does have at least one adult in the home with whom she might reasonably be expected to form an organised attachment.

The infant is on the threshold of the age for the Strange Situation Procedure, so the social worker decides to use it to see what happens. As might have been predicted from the AAIs, the infant does not display any behaviour suggesting disorganised attachment behaviour towards the father, but upon reunion with the mother, the infant does seem to freeze slightly. Whilst the behaviour is not marked, it does suggest to the social worker that there may be a potential difficulty in the relationship between the infant and the mother.

The social worker now decides to assess the older children. With the seven-year-old Rebecca, the social worker completes a story stem assessment. The child's stories are not particularly positive but show no markers of disorganization. This reassures the social worker that, whilst things may be far from optimal, the child is not thought likely to be experiencing significant harm at home.

The social worker also completes a CAI with 13-year-old Nathan and becomes aware that the father of the infant and Rebecca is not the biological father of Nathan. Nathan seems to have an organised attachment to his mother, but when talking about his biological father, he displays several markers for disorganization. This alerts the social worker to the possibility that the older child may be experiencing maltreatment, but not by an adult in the family home. The social worker asks the mother about contact and is informed that Nathan and Rebecca frequently have overnight contact with Nathan's father. Until recently, he used to pick them both up from school one night a week.

The social worker completes an AAI with the biological father and he shows marked evidence of dissociation and unresolved loss and trauma. This raises the social worker's concerns that he may have maltreated Nathan and potentially Rebecca as well.

Based on the above information, the social worker is now in a position to talk more openly with Nathan about what she thinks has happened to him. This insightful approach allows Nathan the relational space to disclose to the social worker that his father physically beats him and this is why he has been reluctant to go to school, because he thinks his father might meet him afterwards. Nathan confirms that Rebecca was not hit, but he thinks she must have heard and seen what was occurring. Nathan said that he did not tell his mother as she was obviously struggling with the infant and the loss of her own father. He says he encouraged Rebecca to skip school as well, in case his father went to meet her.

The social worker refers the matter to the police, who conduct an Assessment of Best Evidence[1] interview with Nathan. He reaffirms the disclosures and is able to give specific dates and times. Rebecca is also interviewed and, although she is less specific, she corroborates much of what her brother has said. Nathan undergoes a medical examination, which reveals evidence of recent physical abuse, and the police subsequently arrest his father.

Because the two older children now appear to be much safer than before, the social worker focuses attention back on the infant. Although it seems unlikely that the infant is currently experiencing abuse, there is still a risk of maltreatment in the future. The social worker refers to the Family Centre and requests that a video-based intervention be implemented for the mother and infant. Although initially it seems that the mother struggles to understand her infant's mind, after just eight sessions her mentalizing capacity has increased, and over the next few weeks the infant's physical condition begins to improve as well. By now, the father has completed the basic parenting course, and when the guided parenting task is repeated, it is evident how much his play and communication skills have improved. The father is also more aware of the physical care needs of infants and is observed to be more active in helping the mother in this respect.

The case is soon closed after a brief period of monitoring when it is noted that not only has the infant's physical presentation improved, but also the older children's school attendance is improving. Their behaviour remained challenging at the point of closure, but both children were involved in School Action programmes and the schools were confident that things would continue to improve over time.

Case 2

A six-year-old girl has been known to the service for several years and has been the subject of a child protection plan for much of that time under the category of sexual abuse. The mother is a single parent who was the victim of sexual abuse as a child and her daughter was the product of a relationship with a man whom she saw as a father figure (although not blood-related). The child has a history of soiling which

---

1   An interview to ensure that evidence is not 'contaminated' by leading questions, etc.

leaves professionals feeling very concerned. They are of the strong opinion that the child has been sexually abused. The mother is vulnerable in her own right and is assessed as being unable to distinguish between safe and unsafe individuals. The child has never made a disclosure but has undergone child protection medicals, including a child sexual abuse medical, although they have not revealed any evidence of harm, sexually or otherwise. Little progress has been made with respect to the child protection plan, partly because professionals are so convinced that this child is suffering sexual harm that they are waiting for a disclosure. The social worker completes a story stem assessment with the child. The child's stories are strikingly secure apart from one story where there is some indication that this child may have come into contact with unsafe individuals. There is no evidence of disorganised attachment behaviour. Her stories are warm, secure and safe. This is not the presentation of a child who may have suffered maltreatment, in particular sexual abuse.

The social worker completes an AAI with the mother, who shows signs of low mentalizing capacity. Further medical investigation reveals that the child's soiling was a physical problem, not an emotional response to harm. A therapeutic social worker is allocated to the family with the aim of carrying out work with the child around 'keeping safe' and confidence building, and work with the mother of a similar nature but with a focus on how to identify unsafe adults. Now that the focus of the child protection plan is no longer investigatory, targeted intervention is put in place with an emphasis on prevention. Both mother and child have a number of individual and joint sessions over several months and significant progress is observed. The multi-agency team is satisfied that the child is not suffering from significant harm (namely, sexual abuse), and the child is removed from a child protection plan. The case is closed shortly afterwards with confidence that the child is safe.

Conclusion

In conclusion, both cases illustrate how the ADAM Pathway Model and associated methods helped us 'see the wood for the trees' more quickly than we would have using other assessment methods. They also indicate the open-mindedness needed on the part of practitioners, because we have found time and again that, used carefully, the model can confirm or disconfirm the initial information, intuition and, in many cases, suspicions. (Chapter 16 explores the notion of contra-indication in more detail.)

Chapter 16

Using Pathway Model Components as Counter-indicators in a Complex Child Protection Referral

Henry Smith

It is known that some practitioners in the ADAM Project have found the model to be as useful in *disconfirming* the presence of its key components. I now describe and analyse a situation when we used the Pathway Model in this way.

Case study

Case: Tracey

Police officers were called by Mrs Green's neighbour because the neighbour's daughter saw Tracey (three years of age), Mrs Green's daughter, alone outside her home just before midnight on 25 December 2012. Mrs Green said that during the evening she had drunk two cans of strong lager and said she had ended up feeling 'very low'. She described how she tried to call her mother to talk to her about how she was feeling, but there was no answer. (Mrs Green's mother later informed me that she had left her phone in her car, which was why she missed the message.) Mrs Green stated that she had called a friend and asked him to come for a chat. When the friend arrived, Mrs Green informed him that Tracey was staying with her family, when she was in fact asleep in her bedroom. Mrs Green stated that they then went to a pub which she said was open late that evening, and that she drank about six pints of lager. When she returned from the pub at around two a.m., Mrs Green found a note from the police stating that Tracey had been taken into their care.

She subsequently said that she had thought at the time that if she had contacted the police straight away, it would have only made things worse as she was drunk. Mrs Green described how she 'cried and cried' before going to sleep that night. When she woke in the morning, she contacted her mother and they went to the police station together. The police then placed Tracey in her grandmother's care.

A core assessment was started following this serious incident. Given the risks to Tracey identified by her mother's actions, I felt that the assessment needed to weigh the chance of Mrs Green leaving Tracey alone again, and the safety measures that could be put in place, against the emotional damage that could be caused to Tracey by removing her from her mother's care.

London Borough Y's records indicated that the incident that led to this referral was not the first time that Tracey had been taken into police protection. Previously, Tracey (then two weeks old) had been taken into police protection as a result of Mrs Green leaving her in the care of Tracey's godmother, and the house subsequently being entered forcibly by the police in a drugs operation. (Tracey's godmother lived in a shared house; it was raided as another tenant was suspected of dealing drugs.) Mrs Green stated that both she and Tracey's godmother were unaware of this prior to the arrival of the police. London Borough Y's records indicate that Mrs Green was interviewed by a senior social worker following the incident who concluded that Mrs Green was capable of meeting Tracey's needs, so Tracey was returned to her care.

Initial interactions

When I asked Mrs Green what was going through her head when she left Tracey alone that evening, she initially struggled to express it. She said that she had thought about this herself but could not come to a conclusion. She found it hard to contemplate and said that it was not in her nature to hurt a child. She described how she had suffered a 'breakdown' a few weeks earlier after her best friend had died very suddenly. (She had seen him the night before, and shortly after she left him, he died after being in a diabetic coma.) He was found by his children, and Mrs Green described how she was wracked with guilt, wondering if there was anything she could have done, and that she never got the chance to say goodbye to him. She also described how earlier that week she had had an argument with her manager and had walked out of work. As a result, she was suspended at the time of the referral, pending disciplinary procedures.

From talking to Mrs Green it would appear that she has experienced several losses of significant people in her life during the previous few years. In addition to the loss of her friend, her maternal grandfather died in 2011 following a long illness. She recalled that prior to his death, her stepmother had fallen out with her as Mrs Green was in a relationship with a man from a different culture. As a result, she said, she was not allowed to be involved in the funeral arrangements or attend the wake.

Mrs Green explained to me that, following the death of her friend and her suspension from work, feelings of depression and hopelessness had increased. She stated that in retrospect she should have talked to someone and asked for help, and that she could not believe that she had 'let things get to this'. She described herself as someone who struggles to talk about her emotions and said that she did not recall ever talking to her family about 'stuff like that'. Mrs Green revealed that when she is upset, her attitude is to 'keep it in and carry on'.

When I asked Mrs Green what she thought might have happened to Tracey, she sobbed and replied, 'Anything. She could have been taken by someone or hit by a car'. I again asked her to try to identify the thought processes that had led her to make the decision to leave Tracey alone, and she sobbed and again stated that she could not identify them. I asked her if the decision had been motivated by a feeling of 'to hell with it' or a feeling that she would be able to get away with going out without Tracey waking up, and Mrs Green stated that it was probably a bit of both. Given that Mrs Green had left Tracey alone, I wondered if this might indicate the presence of components of the Pathway Model which, if that was the case, would emerge if we conducted an Adult Attachment Interview (AAI). I also wondered whether Mrs Green's actions indicated a situation of disconnected parenting, which we could assess by asking her to take part in some guided parenting tasks. Perhaps she had experienced unresolved loss and trauma at some point in her life, and her leaving Tracey was a result of the processes outlined in the Pathway Model.

The AAI demonstrated no indications of unresolved loss and trauma. Mrs Green talked openly, and coherently about her family history. She had grown up with her mother and father in London. She described her early relationship with her mother as 'happy', 'besotted' and 'secure', and she recalled wanting a lot of attention from her. She described how her father worked as a long-distance lorry driver and how this meant that she did not see him for long periods. She described her early relationship with him as 'happy' and 'comfortable', and she said that she was 'daddy's girl'. She remembered feeling more attached to her mother when she was young, but that when her father was home, her mother would give him more attention than her. Because her mother worked night shifts in a care home, and because her father was often away, Mrs Green recalled that her older sister would be responsible for looking after her. The narrative and her descriptions contained richly recollected events and memories evoked with ease.

Mrs Green recounted that her parents separated when she was ten years old and that following this, her father moved to a rural part of eastern Europe to set up a business with his new partner, whom she described as her stepmother, despite his not speaking any of the local language. Mrs Green remembered spending summer holidays visiting her father and his partner. She said that things were very basic where they were staying (there was no running water, for example). She did not remember her parents' separation having much emotional impact on her at the time, feeling that this was probably due to the fact that her father was regularly working away so, for her at least, it did not feel like such a big change. Her father died in 2011, following a long illness, and she stated that she is 'currently very close to her mother'. Although some parts of her account were somewhat 'matter of fact' and defended, there were no indications of *unresolved* loss or trauma.

Mrs Green described herself as a 'nightmare rebellious teenager' and said that when she was 13 years old, she was expelled from school after fighting and, in her words, 'bullying' her fellow students. As a result, her mother sent her to the north of England to live with her maternal grandmother, who was the headmistress of a convent in which Mrs Green enrolled. She stayed there for a year and said that it was a 'total nightmare' as her maternal grandmother was extremely strict and she had no friends in the area. She recalled her father coming to visit her when he was back from eastern Europe and that she had pleaded with him to bring her back to London (which he did). Again, parts of her account seemed somewhat 'cold' and distant, so possibly it was indicative of an avoidant attachment organization. However, as we have seen, this pattern of attachment exists in around 20–25 per cent of individuals; hence, it was not thought to be particularly relevant.

Mrs Green recalled that when she was 18 years old her stepmother and father had their first child, and that her stepmother experienced postnatal depression. She therefore went to live in eastern Europe to support her stepmother and remained there until she was 21 years old. Following a problem with her immigration status, she was given ten days to leave the country by the authorities. She returned to London, where she met Tracey's father. She described how they were in a relationship for seven months before she became pregnant with Tracey. Three months later their relationship ended. Mrs Green recalled how, when she phoned Tracey's father to inform him of the pregnancy, he asked her to phone him back after he had finished watching a football match. Tracey's father saw her when she was three months old but not again until he visited on Christmas morning in 2012. (Mrs Green requested that I did not contact him, as she does not feel that he is a positive influence on her daughter's life.)

After transcribing the interview, I felt that an interesting pattern had emerged of Mrs Green and her parents resorting to what appeared to be sudden and drastic 'flight' behaviours at times of acute stress. I felt that this was evidenced by: (a) Mrs Green's father's decision to move to eastern Europe shortly after the breakdown of his marriage; (b) Mrs Green being uprooted and sent to a convent after getting in trouble at school and, less seriously perhaps, her walking out of work following an argument with her manager; and (c) Mrs Green leaving Tracey with her godmother when she was two weeks old when she felt that she needed a break.

Given that Mrs Green also left Tracey alone on Christmas night, I feel that this pattern may have been an example of a 'learned impulsive behaviour' rather than indicative of *unresolved* loss or trauma (though clearly she had experienced both loss *and* trauma). Perhaps this pattern of 'flight' behaviours had been learned by Mrs Green as a result of her parents' actions. Given the stress that Mrs Green was under, which may have been compounded by an unannounced visit of Tracey's father, perhaps her actions were a 'flight'-like escape from this stressful situation. This would appear consistent with the feelings that she herself identified as a mix of 'to hell with it' and her thinking that she could 'get away with it' if she left Tracey.

Observing the guided parenting tasks, I noted that the interactions between Mrs Green and Tracey appeared to be very natural. For example, Tracey seemed familiar and at ease with her mother's way of playing with her. I was particularly interested to see if, using the Pathway Model, Mrs Green showed any signs of disconnected parenting. One of the tasks involved her not allowing her daughter to play with an enticing toy, and I felt it would be particularly interesting to see how this was managed. Throughout the session, I observed that Mrs Green was able to maintain boundaries with Tracey. She told Tracey that she was not allowed to play with a particular toy, which the child accepted. During the last stage, she supported Tracey in tidying up but reminded her that she should help and would not be allowed to play with other toys if things were not put away. Equally, she used praise with Tracey at each stage, telling her that she was doing very well and how clever she was for getting her colours right. I noticed a high level of emotional warmth throughout the session and observed nothing that would be indicative of disconnected parenting.

Discussion

From talking to Mrs Green there was little doubt in my mind that she was aware of the seriousness of this incident and that she was angry with herself for her behaviour. I felt that she was appropriately upset by the risks to which she had exposed Tracey, and the fact that she was able to describe them to me was encouraging. Whilst I felt that it was promising that she could identify these risks, and that she was, in my opinion, 'upset for the right reasons' – in as much as she was worried, albeit in retrospect, about the risks to her child, rather than the impact on herself – she still had placed Tracey in a position of what she herself eventually recognised as extreme danger.

Aside from the two incidents where Mrs Green left Tracey, the assessment did not identify any other concerns regarding her parenting. In fact, her care of Tracey suggested quite attuned and sensitive parenting responses. Consequently, I did not feel that it was in Tracey's interest to be removed from Mrs Green's care, so long as an appropriate safety plan was put in place to prevent her from being left alone again.

I felt that the safety plan needed to take two forms. First, as a period of acute emotional stress has been identified as a causal factor in Mrs Green leaving Tracey, she would benefit from counselling to help her address and resolve the emotional impact of many of the distressing events outlined in the assessment. Second, as the assessment had identified a pattern of sudden and drastic 'flight'-like behaviours, a contingency plan for the care of Tracey would be necessary, as it was not certain that the pattern would not be repeated in the future. Mrs Green and her own mother both confirmed that she had tried to ask for support on Christmas night, but that her mother had left her phone in her car and had therefore missed Mrs Green's call. I was concerned that whenever she felt 'very low' again, Mrs Green would have a support network limited to her mother, as had been the case the night she left Tracey. I felt that a family group conference should be arranged, and that Mrs Green should identify friends and family members who could form a formal support network in such a crisis. If the participants in the family group conference could talk frankly about what had happened and come up with a robust safety plan, this should prove sufficient in safeguarding Tracey were this to happen again.

Conclusion

In conclusion, the Pathway Model was helpful in several ways. The AAI helped me to assess the family's history and functioning, and it uncovered information that a conventional interview would probably have missed. This led to my observing the pattern of quick and drastic 'flight' behaviour that I felt was key to this case.

The guided parenting tasks helped me in two ways. First, I observed none of the disconnected or extremely insensitive parenting behaviours defined very specifically in the Disconnected and extremely Insensitive Parenting scale. Second, on the contrary, I noted quite attuned and sensitive parenting alongside other strengths in Mrs Green's caregiving. This helped me to demonstrate that removing Tracey from her mother's care would not be in her best interest. This was achieved by systematically ruling out the different components of the Pathway Model.

Chapter 17

'Fake It Till You Make It'

Can Deliberately Adopting Secure Attachment Behaviour Lead to Secure Attachment Organization?

Sonja Falck and David Shemmings

Introduction

The idea that acting as if something were true could cause it to *become* true goes back at least as far as 350 BC when Aristotle wrote that we acquire a particular quality by constantly acting in a particular way: '[W]e become just by performing just actions, temperate by performing temperate actions, brave by performing brave actions'.[1] The question for our purposes is: could we become *secure* by performing *secure* actions? Some of the preceding chapters invite this possibility.

Research by social psychologist and Harvard Business School professor Amy Cuddy indicates that even making the simple change of deliberately adopting a more open and confident body posture for a few minutes actually affects our brain chemistry, by increasing our testosterone levels (the 'power' hormone) and decreasing our cortisol levels (the 'stress' hormone; Baron 2012; Buchanan 2012; Cuddy 2011, 2012; Venton 2012). Adopting a more confident body posture not only makes us appear more confident on the outside, it also alters our brain chemistry, which in turn changes how we feel on the inside. So whilst it is possible to act confident as a result of already feeling confident, it may also be possible to acquire a *feeling* of confidence as a result of deliberately acting confident.

---

1   *Nicomachean Ethics, Book II*. Translated by W. D. Ross. Edited by Paul A. Boer Sr. Kindle edition: Veritatis Splendor Publications (2012).

Cuddy also shows how acting confident and therefore being perceived by others as *being* confident leads to an increase in positive social outcomes that are rewarding, such as being successful at a job interview (Halverson 2010). When actions are rewarded they become reinforced; hence, we are naturally drawn to repeating those actions because of the positive result we have associated with them. This is known as operant conditioning (Skinner 1938). It is clear how, in this way, the positive feedback loop shown in Figure 17.1 gets set up.

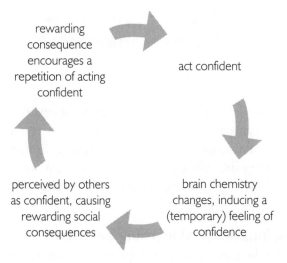

rewarding consequence encourages a repetition of acting confident

act confident

perceived by others as confident, causing rewarding social consequences

brain chemistry changes, inducing a (temporary) feeling of confidence

Figure 17.1 Cycle of acting confident

When regular repetitions of any kind of action are performed, what happens neurologically is that a substance called myelin becomes wrapped around the brain circuitry that is used to perform that action (Coyle 2009). Myelin essentially acts as an insulator, causing nerve impulses that move through a myelinated circuit to move along that circuit with less effort and more speed and precision: it is like the difference between having to find a new path through a forest for the first time and moving along a well-worn, fully cleared path that you have passed along many times before and that might even be paved and well lit. It is the difference between having to think about how to do something with conscious effort to make it happen and doing something that comes to you naturally, without conscious effort. What this means is that after someone has gone through many repetitions of the above cycle of acting confident in a given context, the person will no longer be *acting* confident, but will have actually *become* confident (which might also become generalised to other contexts) as demonstrated in Figure 17.2.

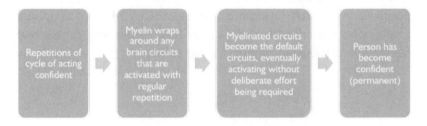

Figure 17.2 Process of becoming confident

Confidence is only one of several indices associated with secure attachment organization; however, the other indices could similarly be broken down into the kind of process detailed above. To assist people who are experiencing difficulties in their lives associated with disorganised attachment, how might we help set in motion the above process?

Utilizing innate social learning behaviour

For at least as long as human beings have been interested in storytelling and play-acting, people have been interested in observing how others respond to, and deal with, the various situations in which they find themselves, taking from their observation of others information, guidance and even direction for how to deal with their own life situations. If it were not the case that hearing about others' behaviour and its results naturally influences one's own behaviour, 'primitive' cultures would not have been able to establish the oral tradition of sharing fables as an effective method of passing on, and perpetuating, their social customs (Bauman 1986). The idea that on seeing what others do we spontaneously reflect on what we ourselves do is utilised by Shakespeare in *Hamlet* as though it is already – and this was written more than 400 years ago – an accepted wisdom. In Act 2 Scene 2 it is decided that the way the ruling monarch can best be induced to pay attention to, and reflect upon, his own behaviour is by causing him to witness others behaving as he has behaved. It is contrived that he becomes the unwitting audience to others staging a dramatization of his own actions: 'The play's the thing, wherein I'll catch the conscience of the king'.[2]

The principle described here was formalised into a theory explicated by psychologist Albert Bandura, initially called Social Learning Theory and later Social Cognitive Theory, which explains how people learn by watching what other people do and then copying that behaviour. This is also known as 'modelling' (Bandura 1962, 1986). In contemporary neuroscience, the discovery of mirror neurons has provided some physiological evidence of how this works. It turns out that merely by watching someone else perform an action, in our own brain the neurons fire that would be required for us to perform that same action ourselves (Keysers 2011). A person can improve their skiing, for example, simply by watching someone else doing it well: the requisite brain circuits are activated just through observation, preparing that person to be able to do better at it themselves when they next have the opportunity to try. Mirror neurons are also the basis of how empathy works – that simply by hearing about or seeing the situation someone else is in, we can find ourselves feeling the same feelings they are feeling within their situation. (But is the feeling yours...or mine? The first case is *em*pathetic and the second *sym*pathetic, the word 'pathetic' in each case deriving from the Greek pathos denoting an 'evocation of compassion'.) An important aspect of modelling, however – in accordance with operant conditioning as mentioned above – is that we will only be motivated to copy a behaviour that has been observed to attract a positive result. Practical examples of these principles in action are evident in schools where it has been demonstrated that children's prosocial behaviour with peers (Fabes *et al.* 2012) and their on-task performance in the classroom (Richards, Heathfield and Jenson 2010) can be improved by exposure to positive peer modelling.

The fact that people are inherently affected by watching and hearing about others' behaviour, that they naturally and spontaneously engage in comparing what they see in others to themselves and learning by such observation and that they are inclined to copy and repeat behaviour that they have associated with a positive result is thus well documented, from cultural practices through to modern psychological theories and contemporary neuroscientific research.

---

2   The Complete Works of Shakespeare (1958), pp.945–980. London: Hamlyn.

Research into the function and development of the brain is moving into new territories. No longer simply interested in right-versus-left hemispheric activity when subjects perform simple to complex cognitive tasks, neuroscientists have become fascinated with how two or more brains in proximity each co-regulate the emotional and social perceptions of the others; therefore, it is the affective synchrony, resonance and the 'social' brain that are now of particular interest. Naturally, prime categories for newer studies are empathy, projection, transference and counter-transference, because such psychosocial constructs are heavily rooted within ideas about inter-subjectivity and 'theory of mind'. Allan Schore comments that when two or more people are attuned, the following occurs:

> ...each recreates an inner psychophysiological state similar to the partner's...moment-to-moment state sharing... . In contexts of 'mutually attuned selective cueing', the infant learns to preferentially send social cues to which the mother has responded, thereby reflecting 'an anticipatory sense of response of the other to the self, concomitant with an accommodation of the self to the other'. (Schore 2001, p.31)

In other words, 'neurons that fire together, wire together'. In terms of the way the brain can *re*wire itself when in an empathic relationship, these findings may constitute one of the explanatory mechanisms of our notion of 'fake it till you make it'. Below we propose a model for utilizing what we know about this to set in motion the acting/ becoming process already explained.

Explication of an 'Act→Become' model ('act secure until you become secure'): how might it work?

Exposure

The starting point would be to provide people who are manifesting behaviours associated with insecure or disorganised attachment (whom we will refer to as 'participants') with opportunities for observing types of situations that are familiar to them from their own lives and in which they can hear about or see people manifesting ways of functioning associated with insecure or disorganised attachment (mirroring their own tendencies of behaviour) as well as ways of functioning associated with secure attachment (role models). This exposure to alternative behavioural models could occur through reading or hearing stories (storytelling), by watching video footage, by experiential immersion in live situations either through role play (play-acting) or in a naturalistic setting or by using computer-based, 'immersive' simulations. Exposure could be arranged for participants in groups rather than on an individual basis. In order to have the greatest control over gaining access to examples for observation that are of maximum relevance, using stories, films, role play or computer-based 'immersive' simulations would be more reliable than using a naturalistic setting. People could also be more receptive to thinking about behaviour that is initially represented to them at a remove from themselves, e.g. through stories or films, rather than if they are invited to think about their own behaviour, which can feel threatening and provoke defensiveness against, rather than openness to, engaging in discussion. An example from the field of family work of material that participants could be exposed to is a situation in which a father is in the supermarket with his ten-week-old baby in the trolley in the car seat. The baby has been crying since entering the shop 15 minutes ago and is red in the face and crying hard. Dad is seen walking slowly down the aisles, slowly choosing meat at the fresh meat counter, smiling at the assistant. He then moves to the magazine section and browses them. The baby continues to cry.

Observation

We have established that upon exposure to other people's behaviour there is a natural tendency to observe it and compare it with one's own; however, to accelerate the learning that someone could take from their observation of others' behaviour, following the exposure an opportunity should be provided for discussion of what has been observed. This discussion could also take place in a group, with a facilitator who would encourage and highlight comparisons made between the contrasting kinds of behaviour observed. All discussion should be conducted in a manner that is neutral, not showing judgement of any of the behaviours discussed, but encouraging an attitude akin to scientific experimentation, showing curiosity about different possibilities of behaviour in the same situation and what results ensue from the different actions. Bearing in mind the principles of operant conditioning, discussion should include a specific focusing of attention on what has been observed regarding the results of the different behaviours. Depending on the skill of the facilitator and to what extent the atmosphere within the group is one of safety and openness, participants might begin to talk about comparisons they are making between the observed behaviour and their own behaviour (e.g. 'That's the sort of thing I would do' or 'I never do that' etc.).

This group discussion could end with the facilitator giving a short presentation that identifies and groups together the behaviours that have been observed which are associated with secure attachment, explaining what secure attachment organization involves and what it may look and feel like in the contexts under consideration. The facilitator could invite comment on what the participants think about secure attachment organization as described and how they believe it might affect their lives if that was the way they functioned.

The facilitator then sets the participants a homework assignment of watching out in their own lives, between then and the next meeting, for examples of secure behaviours noticed (in anyone, in any context) and to make a note of them and any observations about them in a journal. Contrasting behaviours from the field of family work can be seen in the following example:

> A 14-year-old boy comes home from an evening out. He was expected home at an agreed time of 9 p.m., but he arrives at 1.30 a.m. He has not phoned his parents to let them know. In the first situation, the parents have waited up and are very worried. When he arrives they say, 'We were so worried and upset when you did not arrive home at 9 o'clock and have been wondering if something bad might have had happened to you, as you didn't call us to say you'd be later than we'd agreed. It was thoughtless of you not to have done that. It has made us feel we cannot trust you. We need to talk about this another time, though, as we are all tired now. We should all go to bed, but we will talk tomorrow'. Now contrast this 'fair but firm' response with what happened in a different household. This time, when he comes home, they yell, 'Where the hell have you been? We've been up all night worried sick that you had been murdered! You are so thoughtless – you never think about us! We've given you everything and this is what you do to us! Well, that's it, you are grounded for a month; and don't think you can wheedle out of it! It's no use you trying to explain, just get to bed, we don't want to hear'. This continues with them both shouting through the closed bedroom door.

At the next group meeting, the facilitator leads group discussion about what participants have noticed in their own lives and recorded in their journals. This can be followed by further story and/or video observation and discussion as outlined above.

Emulation

Following the second group meeting, participants could be met on an individual, one-to-one basis to be helped to identify for themselves specific target *secure* behaviours in particular situations that they consider would be beneficial to adopt in their own lives. The facilitator can help the participant to link observed behaviours with observed results and discuss why they think the behaviour leads to that sort of result, as well as why they might wish to try a different behaviour for themselves (i.e. in an attempt to produce the kind of result they want). The facilitator then describes the homework assignment to be undertaken, which will entail the participant starting to try the behaviours for themselves in their own lives. The focus is on the participant trying and practising outward manifestations of secure functioning, regardless of what they are feeling inside, and to observe the results (including any impact on their feelings). Each participant keeps a journal in which instances of practising with emulating specifically identified target secure behaviours are noted and described together with a record kept of the observed results.

Assimilation

A further two or three individual sessions can be conducted, during which the facilitator works with participants to learn about their experiences and observations as recorded in their journal and link these observations back to how the participant is feeling. The aim is to track how the practice of simply emulating the outward manifestations of secure functioning – regardless of what one is feeling or thinking – might produce beneficial results that impact on, and cumulatively change, what one is feeling. Each session is structured to ensure that the facilitator supports the participant to:

- observe and process (make sense of) their observation of models of secure functioning

- make links with how these models differ from their own current functioning

- engage in a comparison of results of the different ways of functioning

- track the impact that deliberately behaving differently has on how they feel.

During these sessions the facilitator works with the participant to augment his or her capacity for awareness of their own processes, such as using mindfulness techniques. Exercises in mindfulness helps individuals to practise non-judgemental observation of their own feelings and behaviour, becoming more self-aware, more in control of their own actions and more empowered to make choices about how to respond differently (Tan 2012). The facilitator can also focus on improving mentalization (Allen and Fonagy 2006), using techniques for encouraging reflection on the possible motivations and states of mind underlying others' behaviour. As we have seen in other chapters, the essence of mentalization lies in the recognition of the existence of others' minds and how different they may be from one's own, which can help individuals become more imaginative about, and empathetic towards, what others' situations might be, diminishing tendencies to be rashly reactive to others' behaviour or to take others' behaviour personally.

Drawing on the tenets of attachment-based psychotherapy (Costello 2013), during the process of these sessions the facilitator can be said to be acting as a secure base for the participant from which the participant can explore alternative behaviours creatively between the sessions, trying different ways of functioning, and returning to the facilitator to 'refuel', and being able to use the facilitator as a safe haven for comfort, reassurance and processing of what has been experienced during exploration.

Consolidation

During the final two meetings, the focus is for the facilitator to track with the participant how the performing of manifestations of secure functioning is starting to be self-perpetuating as a result of the beneficial results it yields, and how by repetition this new kind of functioning is starting to come naturally rather than having to be consciously effected, i.e. it is becoming habit-forming (Lally *et al.* 2010).

These ending sessions should also include discussing with the participant his or her strategies for self-maintenance of the newly learned functioning by the end of the series of sessions. This can include teaching of the technique of 'security priming', which has been found to be effective in encouraging secure behaviour (Mikulincer and Shaver 2007). An example of security priming is the creation of a mental image as a reference point that can be returned to that reminds the participant of feelings she or he has experienced of security or models of secure functioning with which she or he has been impressed. Conjuring such images can actually make a person feel more secure and can support him or her to choose a more secure way of behaving in any given situation.

Further 'supervised' practice (optional)
A further resource that could be provided to help maintain newly learned functioning is an ongoing drop-in support group, which participants could attend on a voluntary basis. The format of this group could include group discussion and participation in role play which provides valuable opportunities to further experiment with different behaviours and practise with them.

Summary of model

Exposure: two group meetings providing presentation, film/story and facilitation of group discussion

Observation: same as above

Emulation: first individual meeting

Assimilation: two to three further individual meetings

Consolidation: two individual meetings

Further supervised practise (optional): voluntarily attended drop-in support meetings offering facilitated group discussion and role play

---

Conclusion

The emphasis is on emulating behaviours that are associated with secure attachment organization in sample situations, regardless of what the person is feeling inside, and noticing the external and internal results of having behaved that way. This has similarities to cognitive behavioural therapy (CBT), in which the history and root causes of a disadvantageous behaviour are not explored but, instead, attention is focused on how to adapt that behaviour to something more advantageous. In CBT homework, tasks are also set and journals are kept (Sweet 2010).

The sequential stages of the 'Act→Become' model presented above are compatible with David Kolb's experiential learning theory (Kolb 1983). He posited a cycle of experiential learning that we all go through repeatedly, involving experiencing, reflecting, thinking and acting. This cycle of learning involves four stages: (a) *concrete experiences*, which provide a basis for (b) *reflective observation*. The person's observations and reflections are assimilated and distilled into (c) *abstract concepts* that have implications for action with which the person can actively test and experiment. This (d) *active experimentation* leads to the creation of new experiences, and the cycle goes round again (see Figure 17.3).

Figure 17.3 Kolb's cycle of experiential learning

In the 'Act→Become' model, emphasis is placed on the importance of practice, based upon the notion that new or unfamiliar ways of being cannot be incorporated without regular practice. This is the concept on which the Shyness Clinic (located in Palo Alto, California) is based. There clinically shy people are supported both to role play within the clinic and try in their lives outside of the clinic behaviours that would not normally come easily to them (such as asking someone for a date). The approach is not about paying attention to the origins of the participants' shyness but rather giving participants the opportunity to keep rehearsing different and more adaptive behaviours – supported with coaching and feedback – until they progressively feel more comfortable with them and find that they become a more 'second nature' part of their daily lives (Coyle 2009). Participants there are motivated to keep performing the new behaviours because the positive results they experience provide their own reward. As described above, the process by which a new behaviour becomes established as 'second nature', or as a habit, is through the myelination of the requisite brain circuitry: the more often new behaviours are practised, the more they are strengthened.

Attachment research has shown that it is certainly possible for a person's attachment organization to change (Magai 2008). This chapter has detailed some of the mechanisms involved in such change and proposes a model for how to deliberately promote and accelerate it. In essence, the way this works is to: (a) expose participants to behaviours associated with both insecure and disorganised attachment (mirroring their own tendencies) as well as secure attachment organization (role models); (b) assist participants to reflect on, and make sense of, what they observe during exposure and (c) encourage and support practice of modelled secure behaviours in their own lives and noticing of the results. It is possible that individuals experiencing chronic unresolved loss and/or trauma may need additional help during the 'Act→Become' process, but there does not appear to be any reason why the approach could not be effective for people who have experienced abuse or other extremely frightening events in the past.

Afterword

David Shemmings and Yvonne Shemmings

The ADAM Project works by helping parents understand, if there are concerns around child protection, more precisely what the key mechanisms are and how they can address them. Practitioners support the family throughout this process openly and sensitively, but also firmly, with intelligent kindness, unsentimental compassion and non-directive curiosity. Central to the approach is helping parents to appreciate what it is like for their child to be parented by them. For parents who are abusing or neglecting their children, this can be very difficult to do and requires patience and skill from practitioners.

The project continues to develop, with many different authorities and organizations seeing the potential of the Pathway Model to improve assessments and help families, and, on occasion, to protect children by removing them. We write this Afterword at the time of the conviction in the UK of Mariusz Krezolek and Magdelena Luczak for the death of Luczak's four-year-old son, Daniel Pelka, who was tortured and starved. At the time of his death Daniel weighed around 30 pounds (13.6 kg), the average weight of a typical 18-month-old child. Daniel was force-fed salt, held under water until unconscious, beaten and locked up. Clearly, there are some children who must be removed from their family. Although in retrospect there were worrying signs of neglect and maltreatment, they may not have been sufficient *at the time* for professionals to have removed him.

There are two points at which we believe the use of Pathway Model could have helped in this case (as well as in the cases of Peter Connelly and Khyra Ishaq). First, because this child would have been terrified of both adults, he almost certainly would have shown marked disorganised attachment behaviour if professionals had known how to use and interpret story stems. Second, the type of mentalization-based prompts used with the mother and stepfather described in Chapter 2 would have revealed a considerable amount of detail about the internal worlds of both Krezolek and Luczak towards her son. Such information almost certainly would have supplemented the concerns different professionals had at the time. This knowledge could have deepened and strengthened their enquiries. But the model is not a panacea, and it cannot and should not replace the more fundamental practice of listening to and talking with the child and examining every room in the family home; however, these can be difficult and sometimes dangerous tasks for child protection professionals, because police officers cannot always accompany them.

New directions

Since beginning the project in 2010, a number of other applications of the model's potential have been brought to our attention by different professionals. First, those in the field of adoption and fostering have told us that indicators of disorganised attachment behaviour in children placed with foster carers can augment other outcome measures, especially if completed at different points in time. Similarly, undertaking an Adult Attachment Interview with prospective foster carers and adopters could be useful to screen applicants to see if they demonstrate significant amounts of *unresolved* loss and trauma and/or low mentalizing capacity.

Second, given the alarming increase in child trafficking and child sexual exploitation – these are now the second fastest-growing crimes across the globe – we are starting to work with different organizations to see whether children and young people subjected to such treatment would also show signs of disorganised attachment behaviour. (An element of doubt exists because, in the case of child sexual exploitation, they may be living within secure family settings.) What we are learning from studies of these more recently discovered forms of child maltreatment is that the abusers and gangs understand how to deliberately manipulate the attachment needs of young people; they seem uncannily accomplished at grooming and gaining the trust of young people, often in very devious and planned ways.

Third, because it is well known that there are limits to relying on group-based training as the sole medium for changing practice, we are now offering direct 'coaching' and mentoring using mobile technology. Small numbers of committed and skilled practitioners are offered 20 remote-coaching sessions, each lasting for one hour, scheduled in advance for the coming year. Depending on local permissions, procedures and mobile communications compatibility, these sessions provide participants 'live' coaching on ADAM Project skills and techniques using Skype or FaceTime platforms. (The practitioner wears an earpiece so that we can provide synchronous commentary on an audio or filmed session.) Participants are sent freely available contemporary Internet-based articles and discussion papers, and they share their experiences in secure, theme-based chatrooms. They are also invited to contribute to articles, publications, conferences and events concerned with the development of the ADAM Project (as each of our contributing authors in this volume has done). The expectation is that participants will champion the ADAM Project within their organizations by becoming coaches and mentors for their colleagues. In other words, we want them to 'pay it forward'. This is because lasting change is 'caught' – like a virus – between practitioners working at the same level in an organization. Rather than senior managers trying to implement change hierarchically through layers of the organization, their efforts are needed to concentrate on helping their best staff become 'infectious'.

As a result of our experience over the past three years, we believe we are a lot clearer about the qualities we need in child protection practitioners. At one level, to be effective and resilient they need: critical and analytical skills, a commitment to evidence-based practice and a keen interest in applied theory; intelligent kindness and unsentimental compassion, as well as non-directive curiosity; and a talent for inspiring confidence in others, as well as an infectious enthusiasm for the transformational potential of their profession to change the life chances of children and families.

To offer the kind of help and support families need, child protection practitioners have to become a temporary secure base and safe haven for parents and children before the process of change – often, painful change – can begin. To do so, practitioners need to be reliable and unshakeable in their commitment. But such qualities are shown by actions, not words: they are embodied in the everyday practice of being on time for appointments, by wanting to be with, and work with, parents and children – and by hanging in there and not giving up on them while there is a realistic hope of lasting change. So here is the challenge to educators and managers: how can you ensure that child protection practitioners are well prepared and nurtured to carry out such an onerous task without becoming cynical and burned out?

Answer: you and the organization in which you work have to model those qualities with the practitioners who do the face-to-face work with children and families.

Contributors

Lissil Averill completed her first degree in social policy at Trinity College Dublin. After a few years working in adults' social services in Dublin and London, and then volunteering in children's community services in Bolivia and Mexico, she went on to complete a master's in social work in the National University of Ireland, Galway. She has been a social worker in inner London since 2008, in child protection, looked after children, and duty and assessment teams. She is currently employed by the London Borough of Camden as a social worker at Great Ormond Street Hospital, and is studying towards a diploma in systemic family therapy.

Alice Cook is a Family Assessment Practitioner who has been working in child protection for four years. She completed a BA in Psychology and Education at Durham University. Alice is completing a PhD on Unresolved Trauma at Royal Holloway University. She has published work in Child and Family Social Work and Children England. Alice has worked with Community Care on providing social workers with effective direct work techniques. She has delivering training and presentations on the ADAM Project to a number of organizations in the UK.

Claire Denham currently holds a position as an Independent Reviewing Officer (IRO). Prior to this position she practised as front line social worker in child protection for eight years. Claire holds a Bachelor of Social Work from Ryerson University, Toronto and additionally has completed the consolidation module in Child Care for the Specialist Post Qualifying Graduate Diploma and the Post Qualifying Award in Social Work with Children and Families at Royal Holloway, University of London.

Sonja Esterhuyse Falck did her first degree in Clinical Psychology at the University of Cape Town, South Africa, and later obtained an MA in Psychoanalysis at Middlesex University. She is a UKCP and BACP Senior Accredited psychotherapist who has been in private practice in Central London since 1999. She is also a Tavistock-trained executive coach. Sonja designs and teaches adult education courses and workshops including the Psychology of Attachment at City Lit, Covent Garden, and she is currently undertaking a Doctorate for which she has been working with Mensa to research the attachment styles and workplace interpersonal relationships of gifted adults.

Yvalia Febrer qualified from the University of London following her undergraduate degree in Russian and Italian at Oxford University. She is a Media Spokesperson for The College of Social Work. Following her time in child protection, she now works as Programme Director of Frontline, the UK's newest recruitment and training scheme for children's social workers. Yvalia is currently undertaking a PhD at Royal Holloway University into secondary trauma among social workers.

Fran Feeley is a qualified social worker and practice teacher working in child protection. She has extensive experience of assessing children and families, with a particular interest in carrying out direct work with children. This has seen her develop and deliver online lectures in this area for the University of Kent's MA in Advanced Child Protection. Fran currently works in a specialist multidisciplinary court team for parents misusing drugs and alcohol.

Jo George has been involved in child protection since 2007 when she began working in a long-term child protection team in an Inner London borough. She is currently a Senior Therapeutic Social Worker and Systemic Psychotherapist and works also as a Child and Adolescent Mental Health Practitioner, with children and families, providing systemic consultation to a family centre. She also runs a domestic abuse project aimed at helping couples overcome violent and conflictual behaviour.

Melanie Hamilton-Perry graduated from Anglia Ruskin University with a master's degree in social work. She also holds a BA in social policy. She is currently undertaking a PhD researching attachment and Traveller communities at the University of Kent. During the past ten years Melanie has specialised in working with members from the Gypsy and Traveller communities in various roles, Melanie is currently employed as a locum safeguarding social worker for Norfolk County Council.

David Phillips qualified as a social worker from University College, Cardiff in 1992. He is currently manager of the Moorfield Family Assessment Centre in the London Borough of Enfield. This provides parenting assessments and outreach support for vulnerable families where children are subject to care proceedings and protection plans.

Henry Smith is a senior practitioner in the London Borough of Richmond upon Thames's Initial Response Team. He qualified as a social worker at Durham University in 2008 and went on to work in a Family Intervention Project before moving into statutory children and families social work in 2012. He is currently preparing to undertake a small scale research project in the occupied Palestinian territories comparing and contrasting social work practice with children and families there with practice in the UK.

Michelle Thompson is a qualified counsellor and service manager of the Young Mums and Young Dads outreach team for St. Michael's Fellowship in London. She has over 13 years' experience of working with young parents in the London Borough of Lambeth where her service has been highlighted on TV and radio as an example of best practice. Working in the fields of child protection, domestic abuse, gangs and child sexual exploitation, Michelle has a keen interest in providing good quality Personal, Social, Health and Economic Education (PSHE) to young people. She is currently studying for a master's degree in Education.

David Wilkins has worked in social care since 2000 and qualified as a social worker in 2007 following the completion of his master's degree in social work. David is currently the Principal Child and Family Social Worker for the London Borough of Enfield. He is also about to complete his PhD at the University of Kent. His research focuses on the use of theory in social work practice. He has previously worked as a senior lecturer in social work at Anglia Ruskin University.

Tania Young was a Team Manager in the London Borough of Lewisham's Family Support and Intervention Team. After gaining her degree in 1998 she went on to study social work at the University of Tasmania and qualified in 2000. She currently manages a team of social workers working in child protection. Tania has now returned to Australia to live and work.

Bibliography

Ainsworth, M., Blehar, M., Waters, E. and Wall, S. (1979) *Patterns of Attachment: A Psychological Study of the Strange Situation.* Mahwa, NJ: Lawrence Erlbaum Associates.

Aldridge, J. (2006) 'The experience of children living with and caring for parents with mental illness.' *Child Abuse Review* 15, 79–88.

Allen, J. G. and Fonagy, P. (eds) (2006) *Handbook of Mentalization-Based Treatment.* Chicester: John Wiley and Sons.

Allen, J.G., Fonagy, P. and Bateman, A.W. (2008) *Mentalizing in Clinical Practice.* Arlington, VA: APP.

Bakermans-Kranenburg, M.J. and Van IJzendoorn, M.H. (2004) 'No assosication of the dopamine D4 receptor (DRD4) and -521C/T promotor polymorphisms with infant attachmet disorganization.' *Attachment and Human Development 6*, 211–18.

Bakermans-Kranenberg, M.J. and Van IJzendoorn, M.H. (2007) Research review: 'Genetic vulnerability or differential susceptibility in child development: the case of attachment.' *Journal of Child Psychology and Psychiatry and Allied Disciplines 48*, 1160–1173.

Bandura, A. (1962) *Social Learning Through Imitation.* Lincoln, NE: University of Nebraska Press.

Bandura, A. (1986) *Social Foundations of Thought and Action: A Social Cognitive Theory.* Englewood Cliffs, NJ: Prentice-Hall.

Baron, N. (2012) *Power Poses: Tweaking Your Body Language for Greater Success,* accessed on 3 December 2013.

Baron-Cohen, S. (2011) *Zero Degrees of Empathy: A New Theory of Human Cruelty and Kindness.* London: Penguin.

Bauman, R. (1986) *Story, Performance, and Event: Contextual Studies of Oral Narrative.* Cambridge: Cambridge University Press.

Belton, B. (2010) 'Knowing Gypsies.' In D. Le Bas and T. Acton (eds) *All Change! Romani Studies Through Romani Eyes.* Hatfield: University of Hertfordshire Press.

Bennett, S. and Hamilton-Perry, M. (2010) *Health Needs Assessment of the Gypsy and Traveller Community in Bedfordshire (Excluding Luton).* Bedford: NHS Bedforshire.

Bowlby, J. (1988) *A Secure Base: Clinical Applications of Attachment Theory.* London: Routledge.

Brandon, M., Sidebotham, P., Bailey, S. and Belderson, P. (2011) *A Study of Recommendations Arising from Serious Case Review 2009–2010.* DFE-RR157. Available at www.education.gov.uk/publications/eOrderingDownload/DFE-RR157.pdf, accessed on 10 December 2013.

Bretherton, I., Ridgeway, D. and Cassidy, J. (1990) 'Assessing Internal Working Models of the Attachment Relationship: An Attachment Story Completion Task for 3-Year-Olds.' In M. Greenberg, D. Cicchetti and M. Cummings (eds) *Attachment in the Preschool Years: Theory, Research and Intervention.* Chicago, IL: University of Chicago Press.

Bronfman, E., Parsons, E. and Lyons-Ruth, K. (1993) Atypical Maternal Behaviour Instrument for Assessment and Classification (AMBIANCE): Manual for Coding Disrupted Affective Communication, unpublished manual. Cambridge, MA: Department of Psychiatry, Cambridge Hospital.

Buchanan, L. *Leadership Advice: Strike a Pose,* accessed on 3 December 2013. www.inc.com/magazine/201205/leigh-buchanan/strike-a-pose.html.

Butler, I. and Drakeford, M. (2012) *Social Work on Trial: The Colwell Inquiry and the State of Welfare.* Bristol: Policy Press/BASW.

Carkhuff, R. R. (1969) *Helping and Human Relations Skills* (vols. 1 and 2). New York, NY: Holt, Rineholt, Winston.

Carlson, V., Cicchetti, D., Barnett, D. and Braunwold, K. (1989) 'Disorganised/disoriented attachment relationships in maltreated infants.' *Developmental Psychology 25*, 525–531.

Cemlyn, S. (2008) 'Human rights and Gypsies and Travellers: an exploration of the application of a human rights perspective to social work with a minority community in Britain.' *British Journal of Social Work 38*, 153–173.

Clark, C. and Greenfields, M. (eds) (2006) *Here to Stay: The Gypsies and Travellers of Britain*. Hatfield: University of Hertfordshire Press.

Cohen, J.R., Asarnow, R.F., Sabb, F.W., Bilder, R.M. et al. (2010) 'A unique adolescent response to reward prediction errors.' *Nature Neuroscience 13*, 669–671.

Cooklin, A. (2006) *Being Seen and Heard: The Needs of Children of Parents with Mental Illness* (DVD). London: RC Psych Publications.

Corby, B., Shemmings, D. and Wilkins, D. (2012) *Child Abuse* (revised, 4th ed.). Maidenhead: Open University/McGraw-Hill.

Costello, P. C. (2013) *Attachment-Based Psychotherapy: Helping Patients Develop Adaptive Capacities.* Washington, DC: American Psychological Association.

Coyle, D. (2009) *The Talent Code.* New York, NY: Bantam.

Crittenden, P. M. (2008) *Raising Parents: Attachment, Parenting and Child Safety.* Portland, OR: Willan.

Crittenden, P., Farnfield, S., Landini, A. and Grey, B. (2013) 'Assessing attachment for family court decision-making.' *Journal of Forensic Practice 15*, 4.

Cuddy, A. (2011) 'Boost power through body language.' Harvard Business Review Video (blog). Available at http://blogs.hbr.org/video/2011/04/boost-power-through-body-langu.html, accessed on 6 April 2011.

Cuddy, A. (2012) 'Your body language shapes who you are.' TED talk. Available at www.ted.com/talks/amy_cuddy_your_body_language_shapes_who_you_are.html, accessed 18 October 2013.

Cyr, C., Euser, E.M., Bakermans-Kranenburg, M.J. and Van Ijzendoorn, M.H. (2010) 'Attachment security and disorganization in maltreating and high-risk families: A series of meta-analyses.' *Development and Psychopathology 22*, 1, 87–108.

Dale, P. (2004) 'Like a fish in a bowl: parents' perceptions of child protection services.' *Child Abuse Review 13*, 2, 137–157.

DoH (Department of Health) (2000) *Framework for the Assessment of Children in Need and their Families.* London: The Stationary Office.

Dingwall, R., Eekalaar, J. and Murray, T. (1983) *The Protection of Children: State Intervention and Family Life.* Oxford: Blackwell.

Egan, G. (1986) *The Skilled Helper: A Problem-Management Approach to Helping.* Monterey, CA: Brooks/Cole.

Emde, R.N., Wolf, D.P. and Oppenheim, D. (2003) *Revealing the Inner Worlds of the Young Children.* Oxford: Oxford University Press.

Fabes, R. A., Hanish, L. D., Martin, C. L., Moss, A. and Reesing, A. (2012) 'The effects of young children's affiliations with prosocial peers on subsequent emotionality in peer interactions.' The *British Journal of Developmental Psychology 30*, 4, 569–585.

Fauth, R., Jelicic, H., Hart, D., Burton, S. *et al.* (2010) *Effective Practice to Protect Children Living in 'Highly Resistant' Families.* London: Centre for Excellence and Outcomes in Children and Young People's Services.

Ferguson, H. (2009) 'Performing child protection: home visiting, movement and struggle to reach the abused child.' *Child and Family Social Work 14*, 471–480.

Ferguson, H. (2010) 'Walks, home visits and atmospheres: risk and the everyday practices and mobilities of social work and child protection.' *The British Journal of Social Work 40*, 4, 1100–1117.

Fonagy, P. and Target, M. (2005) 'Bridging the transmission gap: an end to an important mystery of attachment research?' *Attachment and Human Development 7*, 333–343.

Forrester, D. (2012) *Parenting a Child Affected by Parental Substance Abuse.* London: BAAF.

Forrester, D., Kershaw, S., Moss, H. and Hughes, L. (2007) 'Communication skills in child protection: how do social workers talk to parents?' *Child and Family Social Work 13*, 1, 41–51.

Forrester, D., McCambridge, J., Waissbein, C. and Rollnick, S. (2008) 'How do child and family social workers talk to parents about child welfare concerns?' *Child Abuse Review 17*, 1, 23–35.

Forrester, D., Westlake, D., McCann, M., Thurnham, A. *et al.* (2013) *Reclaiming Social Work? An Evaluation of Systemic Units as an Approach to Delivering Children's Services: Summary report of a comparative study of practice and the factors shaping it in three local authorities*: Tilda Goldberg Centre, University of Bedfordshire.

Galvan, A. (2010) 'Adolescent development of the reward system.' *Frontiers in Human Neuroscience 12*, 4–6.

Gaughan, K. and Kalyniak, S. (2011) 'The Centrality of Relationships.' In S. Goodman and I. Trowler *Reclaiming Social Work*. London: Jessica Kingsley Publishers.

George, C., Kaplan, N. and Main, M. (1985) *The Adult Attachment Interview*. Unpublished manuscript. Berkeley, CA: Department of Psychology, University of California at Berkeley.

Goodman, S. and Trowler, I. (2011) *Reclaiming Social Work*. London: Jessica Kingsley Publishers.

Green, J., Stanley, C., Smith, V. and Golwyn, R. (2000) 'A new method of evaluating attachment representations in young school-aged children: The Manchester Child Attachment Story Task (MCAST).' *Attachment and Human Development 2*, 48–70.

Halverson, H.G. *Feeling Timid and Powerless? Maybe It's How You Are Sitting.* www.psychologytoday.com/blog/the-science-success/201010/feeling-timid-and-powerless-maybe-its-how-you're-sitting, accessed on 3 December 2013.

Hamer, M. (2005) *Preventing Breakdown: A Manual for Those Working with Families*. Lyme Regis: Russell House Publishing.

Hancock, I. (2010) *Danger Educated Gypsy. Selected Essays*. Hatfield: University of Hertfordshire Press.

Hawes, D. and Perez, B. (1996) *The Gypsy and the State: The Ethnic Cleansing of British Society* (2nd ed.). Bristol: The Policy Press.

Hesse, E. and Main, M. (2000) 'Disorganised infant, child and adult attachment: collapse in behavioural and attentional strategies.' *Journal of the American Psychoanalytic Association 48*, 4, 1097–1127

Hesse, E. and Main, M. (2006a) 'Frightened, threatening, and dissociative parental behaviour in low-risk samples: description, discussion and interpretations.' Development and Psychopathology 18, 309–343.

Hodges, J., Steele, M., Hillman, S. and Henderson, K. (2003) 'Mental Representations and Defences in Severely Maltreated Children: A Story Stem Battery and Rating System for Clinical Assessment and Research Applications.' In R. Emde, D. Wolk, C. Zahn-Waxler and D. Oppenheim (eds) *Narrative Processes and the Transition from Infancy to Early Childhood*. New York, NY: Oxford University Press.

Howe, D. (2013) *Empathy: What It Is and Why It Matters*. Basingstoke: Palgrave Books.

Howe, D., Brandon, M., Hinings, D. and Schofield, G. (1999) *Attachment Theory, Child Maltreatment and Family Support: A Practice and Assessment Model*. London: Macmillan.

Joyce, B. and Showers, B. (2002) *Student Achievement through Staff Development*. (3rd ed.). Alexandria, VA: Association for Supervision and Curriculum Development.

Juffer, F., Bakermans-Kranenburg, M.J. and Van IJzenboorn, M.H. (eds) (2008) *Promoting Positive Parenting: An Attachment-Based Intervention*. New York: Lawrence Erlbaum/Taylor and Francis.

Kenrick, D. and Clark, C. (1999) *Moving On: Reconnecting Frequent Movers*.

Keysers, C. (2011) *The Empathic Brain*. Social Brain Press.

Kolb, D. (1983) *Experiential Learning: Experience as the Source of Learning and Development*. London: Prentice Hall.

Lakatos, K. Nemoda, Z. Toth, I., Ronai, Z. *et al.* (2002) 'Further evidence for the role of the dopamine D4 receptor (DRD4) gene in attachment disorganization: interaction of the exon III 48-bp repeat and the 511 C/T promotor polymorphisms.' *Molecular Psychiatry 7*, 27–31.

Lally, P., van Jaarsveld, C. H. M., Potts, H. W. W. and Wardle, J. (2010) 'How are habits formed? Modelling habit formation in the real world.' *European Journal of Social Psychology 40*, 6, 998–1009.

Lyons-Ruth, K. (1996) 'Attachment relationships among children with aggressive behavioural problems: the role of disorganized early attachment patterns.' *Journal of Consulting and Clinical Psychology 64*, 32–40.

Lyons-Ruth, K. and Jacobvitz, D. (2008) 'Attachment Disorganization: Genetic Factors, Parenting Contexts, and Developmental Transformation from Infancy to Adulthood.' In J. Cassidy and

P.R. Shaver (eds) *Handbook of Attachment: Theory Research and Clinical Applications* (2nd ed.) New York: Guilford.

Madigan, S., Bakermans-Kranenburg, M.J., Van IJzendoorn, M.H., Moran, G., Pederson, D.R. and Benoit, D. (2006) 'Unresolved states of mind, anamalous parenting behaviour, and disorganized attachment: a review and meta-analysis of a transmission gap.' *Attachment and Human Development* 8, 89–111.

Magai, C. (2008) 'Stability and Change in Attachment Styles.' In J. Cassidy and P. R. Shaver (eds) *Handbook of Attachment.* New York, NY: The Guilford Press.

Main, M. and Hesse, E. (1998) *Frightening, frightened, dissociated, deferential, sexualized and disorganized parental behaviour: a coding system for parent-infant interaction* (6th ed.). Unpublished manual, University of California at Berkeley.

Main, M. and Solomon, J. (1990) 'Procedures for Identifying Infants as Disorganized/Disoriented During the Ainsworth Strange Situation.' In: M. T. Greenberg, D. Cicchetti and E. M. Cummings (eds) *Attachment in the Preschool Years: Theory, Research and Intervention* (pp.121–160). Chicago, IL: University of Chicago Press.

Maiter, S., Palmer, S. and Manji, S. (2006) 'Strengthening social worker–client relationships in child protective services.' *Qualitative Social Work 5*, 2, 167–186.

McMahon, L. and Farnfield, S. (2004) 'Too close or too far out: learning to hold the role of the observer.' *Journal of Social Work Practice 18*, 2, 239–246.

Mikulincer, M. and Shaver, P. R. (2007) 'Boosting attachment security to promote mental health, prosocial values, and inter-group tolerance.' *Psychological Inquiry 18*, 3, 139–156.

Miller, W.R. and Rollnick, S. (2002) *Motivational Interviewing: Preparing People to Change* (2nd ed.). New York: Guilford Press.

Miller, W. R. and Rollnick, S. (2009) 'Ten things that motivational interviewing is not.' *Behavioural and Cognitive Psychotherapy 37*, 129–140.

Munro, E. (1999) 'Common errors of reasoning in child protection work.' *Child Abuse and Neglect 23*, 8, 745–758.

Munro, E. (2002) 'The role of theory in social work research: a further contribution to the debate.' *Journal of Social Work Education 38*, 3, 461–470.

Munro, E. (2011) *The Munro Review of Child Protection: Final Report – A Child-Centred System.* London: Department of Education.

Niner, P. (2003) *Local Authority Gypsy/Traveller Sites in England.* Office of the Deputy Prime Minister. www.odpm.gov.uk/pub/516/LocalAuthorityGypsyTravellersitesinEnglandFullReportPD985Kb_id1153516.pdf, accessed on 10 August 2006.

Out, D., Bakermans-Kranenburg, M. and Van IJzendoorn, M. (2009) 'The role of disconnected and extremely insensitive parenting in the development of disorganised attachment: validation of a new measure.' *Attachment and Human Development 11*, 5, 419–443.

Pace, C.S., Zavattini, G.S. and D'Alessio, M. (2012) 'Continuity and discontinuity of attachment patterns: a short-term longitudinal pilot study using a sample of late-adopted children and their adoptive mothers.' *Attachment & Human Development 14*, 1, 45–61.

Perry, D. and Szalavitz, M. (2008) *The Boy Who Was Raised as a Dog and Other Stories from a Child Psychiatrist's Notebook: What Traumatized Children Can Teach Us About Loss, Love and Healing.* New York, NY: Basic Books.

Platt, D. (2008) 'Care or control? The effects of investigations and initial assessments on the social worker–parent relationship.' *Journal of Social Work Practice 22*, 3, 301–315.

Richards, L. C., Heathfield, L. T. and Jenson, W. R. (2010) 'A classwide peer-modeling intervention package to increase on-task behavior.' *Psychology in the Schools 47*, 6, 551–566.

Richardson, J. (2005) 'Talking About Gypsies: The Notion of Discourse as Control.' *Housing Studies 21*, 1, 77–96.

Richardson, J. (2006) 'Workshop 8 – Housing and social theory. An examination of the treatment of Gypsies and Travellers: human rights in an expanding Europe?'.

Richardson, J. and Ryder, A. (eds) (2012) *Gypsies and Travellers: Empowerment and Inclusion in British Society.* Bristol: The Policy Press.

Rogers, C. (1951) *Client-Centered Therapy: Its Current Practice, Implications and Theory.* London: Constable.

Rooke, J. (2012) 'Stories Lived, Stories Told.' In S. Goodman and I. Trowler (eds) *Social Work Reclaimed: Innovative Frameworks for Child and Family Social Work Practice.* London: Jessica Kingsley Publishers.

Ruch, G., Turney, D. and Ward, A. (2010) *Relationship-based Social Work: Getting to the Heart of Practice.* Londn: Jessica Kingsley Publishers.

Saint-Jacques, M.-C., Drapeau, S., Lessard, G. and Beaudoin, A. (2006) 'Parent involvement practices in child protection: a matter of know-how and attitude.' *Child and Adolescent Social Work Journal* 23, 2, 196–215.

Schore, A. N. (2001) 'Effects of a secure attachment relationship on right brain development, affect regulation and infant mental health.' *Journal of Infant Mental Health 22* ,7–66.

Shaver, P. R. and Mikulincer, M. (2002) 'Attachment-related psychodynamics.' *Attachment and Human Development* 4, 133–161.

Shemmings, D. and Ellingsen, I. (2012) 'Using Q Methodology in Qualitative Interviews.' In J. F. Gubrium, J. A. Holstein, A. B. Marvasti and K. D. McKinney (eds) *The Sage Handbook of Interview Research.* Thousand Oaks, CA: Sage Publications.

Shemmings, D. and Shemmings, Y. (2011) *Understanding Disorganized Attachment.* London: Jessica Kingsley Publishers.

Skinner, B. F. (1938) *The Behavior of Organisms: An Experimental Analysis.* New York, NY: Appleton-Century.

Slade, A. (2008) 'Working with Parents in Chil Psychotherpay: Engaging the Reflective Function.' In F.N. Busch (ed.) *Mentalisation: Theoretical Considerations, Research Findings and Clinical Implications* (pp.20–234). New York: Taylor & Francis.

Spangler, G. and Zimmermann, P. (2007) *Genetic contribution to attachment and temperament.* Paper presented at the biennial meeting og the Society for Research in Child Development. 29 March–1 April, Boston, MA.

Sweet, C. (2010) *Change Your Life with CBT: How Cognitive Behavioural Therapy Can Transform Your Life.* Harlow: Pearson Education Limited.

Tan, C.-M. (2012) *Search Inside Yourself.* London: Harper Collins.

Target, M., Fonagy P. and Schmueli-Goetz, Y. (2003)'Attachment representations in school-age children: the development of the Child Attachment Interview (CAI).' *Journal of Child Psychotherapy* 29, 2, 171–186.

Testa, M., Hoffman, J. and Livingston, J. (2011) 'Intergenerational transmission of sexual victimization vulnerability as medicated via parenting.' *Child Abuse and Neglect 35,* 363–371.

Turnell, A. (2009) *Of Houses, Wizards and Fairies: Involving Children in Child Protection Casework.* Perth: Resolutions Consultancy.

Turnell, A. and Essex, S. (2006) *Working with 'Denied' Child Abuse: The Resolutions Approach.* Maidenhead: OUP

Venton, D. (2012) 'Power Postures Can Make You Feel More Powerful.' www.wiredscience/2012/05/st–cuddy/, accessed on 3 December 2013.

Weld, N. (2008) 'The Three Houses Tool: Building Safety and Positive Change.' In M. Calder (ed.) *Contemporary Risk Assessment in Safeguarding Children.* Lyme Regis: Russell House Publishing.

Woolgar, M. and Scolt, S. (2013) 'The negative consequences of over-diagnosing attachment disorders in adopted children: the importance of comprehensive formulations.' *Clinical Child Psychology and Psychiatry.* Published online at http://ccp.sagepub.com/content/early/2013/04/08/1359104513478545, accessed on 23 June 2013.

Yatchmenoff, D. (2008) 'A Closer Look at Client Engagement: Understanding and Assessing Engagement from the Perspectives of Workers and Clients in Non-voluntary Child Protective Service Cases.' In M. C. Calder (ed.) *The Carrot or the Stick: Towards Effective Practice with Involuntary Clients in Safeguarding Children Work* (pp. 59–77). Lyme Regis: Russell House Publishing.

Yeo, S. (2003) 'Bonding and attachment of Australian Aboriginal children.' *Child Abuse Review* 12, 292–304.

Zeanah, C.H. (1996) 'Beyond insecurity: a reconceptualization of attachment disorders in infancy.' *Journal of Consulting and Clinical Psychology* 64, 42–52.

Further Resources

Being Seen and Heard: The Needs of Children of Parents with Mental Illness. DVD and training pack by Dr Alan Cooklin.

The Nurturing Game. Available at www.familylinks.org.uk/onlineshop/nurturing-game.htm

Index